A CONNACHT JOURNEY

DESMOND FENNELL

A Connacht Journey

ECKHART HOUSE
19 CLYDE ROAD
DUBLIN 4

GILL AND MACMILLAN

Published in Ireland by
Gill and Macmillan Ltd
Goldenbridge
Dublin 8
with associated companies in
Auckland, Dallas, Delhi, Hong Kong,
Johannesburg, Lagos, London, Manzini,
Melbourne, Nairobi, New York, Singapore,
Tokyo, Washington
© Desmond Fennell 1987
0 7171 1521 6
Print origination in Ireland by
Wellset Limited
Printed in Great Britain by
Richard Clay Ltd (The Chaucer Press)
Bungay, Suffolk

British Library of Congress Cataloguing in Publication Data

Fennell, Desmond, *1929* -
A Connacht journey.
1. Connacht (Ireland) — Description and
travel
I. Title
914.17'104824   DA990.C6

ISBN 0-7171-1521-6

CONTENTS

Map

Introduction   1

1. From the Airport to Swinford   9

2. Swinford to Belderrig   32

3. Belderrig to Ballina   61

4. Sligo via Dromahair to Boyle   78

5. Boyle to Leenane   117

6. Kylemore via Aran to Kinvara   125

7. Kinvara via Galway and Tuam to Athlone   159

MAP

The journey narrated in this book started at Connaught Airport, which is therefore indicated by a large black dot. It proceeded through Charlestown and Swinford and into the west and north of Mayo. The main route is indicated by the heavily dotted line: after Mayo, it goes through counties Sligo, Leitrim and Roscommon and then into West Galway. From there, it crosses to the Aran Islands, the Burren and thus back to Galway. The journey finished at Athlone. Short tributary journeys off the main route are marked by the lighter dotted line.

INTRODUCTION

IN AN OLD Irish tale, set in Tara in the sixth century, a supernatural personage, Trefuilgnid, defines the attributes of the *cúigí* or 'fifths' of Ireland, which were later called in English 'provinces'. Learning was in the west, war in the north, wealth in the east, music or art in the south, and kingship in the centre (Meath). The Rees brothers, in their book, *The Celtic Heritage*, say that this corresponds to the old Indian caste hierarchy of priest, warrior, farmer and serf — minstrels and craftworkers belonged to the serf castes — and that in India, too, there was a tradition of relating these social divisions to the cardinal points. At all events, Trefuilgnid went on to spell out each province's characteristics in more detail. Connacht, the druids' domain, was distinguished by 'knowledge, foundations, teaching, judgment, chronicles, counsels, stories, histories, science'. That, so far as we know, was the first myth of Connacht. Doubtless, like all myths, it had a kernel of factual truth.

Around the middle of the nineteenth century, Connacht — or 'the West of Ireland' — again became the subject of myth. It was depicted as the essential, real, and historical Ireland: different from the human norm, rural/agricultural, poor, traditional and wild. Or rather, it was depicted as the former because it was seen and depicted as the latter. It had all begun with Ireland's being seen — by comparison with 'normal, urban/manufacturing, rich, modern, civilised' England — as different, rural/agricultural, poor, traditional and wild. Then, because the latter description seemed to apply more to the West of Ireland than to the East, the West was depicted as Ireland *par excellence*. The 'West' was a flexible term. Some western coastal areas to the north and south of Connacht had the 'typically Irish' qualifications; consequently, West Cork, Kerry, Clare and Donegal participated occasionally and marginally in the myth. But Connacht — thought of as the West proper, as the land and life 'west of the Shannon' — was its central focus. Within Connacht again, it focused particularly on the most westerly parts, but especially on Connemara and the Aran Islands.

Developed and projected in the East of Ireland, and principally in Dublin, this mythic view became the standard Dublin view of Connacht. Diffused from there throughout Ireland and, via London, throughout the world — and adopted by and large by Connacht as its self-image — it became a permanent resident of the Irish consciousness into the present century and into our own day.

Like all myths, its primary purpose was to satisfy a psychological need of its creators, not to present literal truth. In the manner of myths, it transformed relative and time-bound truths into an image of absolute, essential and timeless truth. The first of those relative and time-bound truths was that, in the mid-nineteenth century, Ireland was much less urbanised and economically developed than England, and was consequently much poorer, in some notable respects more traditional, and, by metropolitan standards, less civilised. Furthermore, Ireland had more wild landscape, particularly by comparison with the South of England (which was what people usually had in mind). Secondly, in that same period, much the same things were true of Connacht by comparison with the East of Ireland. Out of these truths was created an image of Connacht as a place intrinsically and immemorially different from the rest of Ireland: rural/agricultural, poor, traditional and wild — the real Ireland preserved in amber. An implicit corollary was that the rest of Ireland, and particularly the East, was *not* characteristically rural or poor, not wild or traditional, and consequently not authentically Irish, only factually so.

As this myth took shape, several factors helped to establish and solidify it. The fact that the West had more land of bad quality than the East or South, and that the great majority of Connacht people depended exclusively on agriculture, suggested that poverty was, indeed, an intrinsic condition of the province. The high death-rate in the West during the Famine, and the high rate of emigration in the decades after it, seemed to supply further proof of this. Then again, Cromwell's dealings

2

with Connacht, or rather, deductions drawn from these and from his reputed character, fortified the myth in two ways. His cruelty and hatred of Catholics were notorious, and he had ordered the Catholics of Ireland 'To Hell or to Connacht' — obviously, it was assumed, because, then as now, Connacht was a miserable place to live, a sort of Siberia. True to his character, he was offering them a choice of hells. But Cromwell was also seen as a major cause of the poverty of Connacht, for, by driving all those people onto that bad land, he had made the province overpopulated. Towards the end of the last century, when the population had fallen from 1,500,000 in the 1840s to less than half of that, the Congested Districts Board was established to tackle this perceived problem.

Once the myth's basic image of Connacht had acquired the status of literal truth, it underwent an imaginative development which has continued into our own day. It divided into two versions, one 'dark', the other 'bright', according to the differing values which people attached to the notions *different from the contemporary norm, rural/agricultural, poor, traditional, wild,* and *the real Ireland*. Those who regarded these as negative values saw Connacht as a dark, benighted and threatening place, or, more benevolently, as a distressful place. Those who regarded them as positive values saw the West of Ireland as a bright and precious life, the consolation and the hope of Ireland and even of mankind. At the same time, the association of ideas was working, in thesaurus fashion, on the basic concepts, developing them far beyond their original import. Out of 'rural/agricultural, poor, traditional' sprouted, on the one hand, 'backward, conservative, dim-witted, inferior'; on the other hand, 'uncorrupted, deeply-rooted, morally sound, truly human'. 'Wild', for its part, became 'primitive, boggy, desolate, isolated', or 'romantic, natural, unadulterated, unconstrained'. 'Traditional', which had originally referred principally to Connacht's language, house styles and dress styles, came in the latter part of the present century to refer primarily to its supposed religiosity, seen as mindless or meritorious. Encased in these extending and conflicting webs of concepts, Connacht, for over a century past, has been evoking strong feelings and passionate attitudes, particularly in Dublin, but also in the rest of Ireland and the wider world.

Obviously, when a place and its people are so 'known' about by hearsay — and so strongly felt about on the basis of that hearsay — a travel book about that place and people must take account of this. Its readers will naturally expect the writer, among other things, to report on how true or untrue the hearsay is. For my own part, however, I simply want to tell, as well as I can, what I encountered and discovered during a long month's journey through Connacht in the late summer of 1986. I want to portray, without grand theory, what life is like today in the West of Ireland. I have no wish to keep turning aside from my traveller's tale to comment on 'widely held opinions' which I imagine might be in some readers' minds. Much less do I want to do this when I am aware that most of those 'widely held opinions' about Connacht are derived from one version or other of the myth I have been describing, and are therefore illusions. So I am taking the bull by the horns at the outset, saying what I have just said, and asking the reader to suspend belief in all widely held opinions about the West of Ireland.

For one thing, I promise that the reality is much more interesting than the myth, either version. This is true not only of the present in Connacht, but also of the past; and it is particularly true of present-day Connacht perceived in the light of its past. One of the great disservices which the myth has done to Connacht is, by giving a false account and impression of its past, to deprive both its modern history and its present life of much of their intrinsic interest. It is useful, I think, to illustrate this.

In *Gaelic and Gaelicised Ireland in the Middle Ages* (1972) Kenneth Nicholls writes: 'There is perhaps a tendency, based on the experience of the eighteenth and nineteenth centuries, to regard Connacht as a backwater remote from the affairs of Ireland as a whole. As far as the medieval period is concerned, such an impression would be wildly misleading; the province was far from being (by Irish standards) either economically backward or politically remote and played a wholly disproportionate part in literary and religious activity. It has been remarked that the majority of surviving medieval Irish codices [manuscript volumes] are of Connacht origin.'

For centuries Galway was the second Irish port — initially, after Waterford, later, after Dublin — and during those centuries it was the country's principal port for trade with northern and southern Europe. Even in its decline it remained, until Cork replaced it in the eighteenth century, the second port.

The Cromwellian 'Settlement of Connacht', as the scheme was called, did not increase the population of the province significantly. The intention was not to transfer all Catholics into Connacht (and Clare), but only Catholic landowners and their families; and the great majority of Catholics owned no land. Some families made the move and stayed in Connacht. Others managed to avoid moving, while others again, after staying for a time in the West, were restored to their original lands or found their way back to somewhere near them.

What Kenneth Nicholls said above about Connacht in the medieval period still held true, substantially, in Cromwell's time: the province was not regarded as a place of hardship or a sort of Siberia. A part of the settlement scheme which is seldom mentioned is that it provided for Cromwellian veterans to be settled along the coast of Connacht and Clare to a depth of one mile — so as to prevent contact between the natives and the Spanish. Other soldier colonies were established in various places throughout the province.

Connacht has not been, immemorially, a rural society engaged in agriculture and fishing. For most of its history, until the early part of the nineteenth century, it was a largely rural society engaged in agriculture, manufacture, trading, and fishing. In the eighteenth century, besides the vast amount of manufacture carried on in cottages or in workshops adjacent to them, Connacht had many grain mills, breweries and distilleries. Professor Louis Cullen, in his *Economic History of Ireland since 1600* mentions that the first, partial Irish Census of 1821 shows Mayo as one of the six counties in which more people were engaged in 'manufacture, trade and handcraft' than in agriculture, and that the proportion so occupied in Mayo was higher than in any other Irish county except Louth. The same census gave the following occupational statistics for the Aran Islands: 114 linen-spinners, 91 wool-spinners, 21 wool-carders, 24 weavers, 32 stocking-knitters, 22 sewing-women, three shoe-makers, two coopers, six boat-builders, 35 net-makers, one rope-maker, three carpenters. To put it another way, the IDA and Údarás na Gaeltachta, in setting up factories in Connacht in recent decades, have not — not even on the western seaboard — been introducing manufacturing into a society that has no previous experience of it, but merely bringing it back in factory form.

The notion that 'rural equals agricultural' — applied to Connacht and, indeed, to the rest of Ireland — is derived from the situation that obtained increasingly from the mid-nineteenth century onwards, when rural manufacture, and trade in rurally-produced manufactured goods, had been largely destroyed by competition from English factory-made products delivered by the new railways. It is a remarkable comment on the general manner of writing and teaching Irish history that most Irish people are unaware of this revolution in the rural economy, though it was at least as significant as the abolition of the landlord system at the end of the century.

The extreme poverty of Connacht in the nineteenth century was not caused by the fact that a large rural population was living on land of poor quality. Only a small amount of Connacht land is useless for all farming purposes (the biggest Irish bogs, as it happens, are in Leinster). The province has larger areas of arable and good land than most European regions of the same size; and potatoes can be grown in almost every part of it. Leaving aside the matter of landlords' rents, the extreme rural poverty was caused mainly by the fact that the population — growing rapidly until the Famine, declining after that — had been deprived of markets for its manufactures and forced to depend almost exclusively on agriculture. In other words, the principal cause of the extreme rural poverty, and of Connacht becoming a peasant society, was the impact on Connacht of the English industrial revolution, or more precisely, of the trading advantage which that conferred on English as against Connacht manufactured goods.

What happened Connacht was, in an extreme form, what happened Ireland, apart from the industrialised north east, as a colony of English capitalism during the industrial revolution. Just as Ireland, in the matter of production, was made almost exclusively agricultural, so was Connacht even more. But these again were only local instances of what was occurring through-out the colonised world. In his book, *Ireland in Crisis: a study in capitalist colonial undevelopment*, Raymond Crotty describes the process as follows:

6

Free, unfettered trade between a capitalist colony and the metropolitan power could have only one outcome. Starting in the age of factory capitalism, as all such trade did, from the position where the metropolitan power had already established a comparative advantage in manufactured production, free trade emphasised the colony's dependence on primary production. Products made in factories located in metropolitan countries replaced those made by traditional craft and cottage industry in the colonies. Under nineteenth century free trade conditions, and according to the principle of comparative advantage, the colonies concentrated on primary production, which was subject to decreasing returns; and the metropolises concentrated on manufacturing, which was subject to increasing returns. This was the 'so-called *pacte colonial*, the exchange of colonial primary produce for metropolitan manufactures and services'. South and South East Asia ended the nineteenth century with smaller proportions of their workforces engaged in manufacturing and larger proportions in agriculture than at the beginning of the century. 'The proportion of the Indian population engaged in agriculture rose and that engaged in industry and commerce fell.' The same was true of Latin America where, at this time, 'exports were developed at the expense of subsistence economic activities'.

The English industrial revolution, by largely destroying Irish manufactures, made Irish economic activity, apart from agricultural production, predominantly commercial in character; and the commerce consisted essentially in exporting Irish agricultural produce to England and importing and distributing English manufactured goods. In this economy, Dublin and the East acquired a position of dominance *vis-à-vis* the West, thereby reproducing within Ireland something like the relationship between England and Ireland. In view of that, it is hardly surprising that Dublin developed a myth of Connacht that was virtually identical in form and content with the English myth of Ireland.

Finally, some factual data about Connacht today. In area (17,100 sq. kilometres) it is conisderably larger than Northern

Ireland and more than half the size of Belgium. Its population, at 424,000 (1981), is less than half Greater Dublin's, twice that of Iceland, and larger than Luxembourg's. A quarter of the population live in officially designated 'town areas'; the province has no large city. Apart from a few small Gaelic-speaking communities, comprising about 15,000 people or 3.5 per cent of the population, Connacht is English-speaking.

For many Irish people 'crossing the Shannon' has an emotional significance. This greatest of Irish rivers is felt to be nature's own dividing line between the everyday or normal world and that 'other land' out there. This feeling, which is pleasantly dramatic, is an effect of the modern Connacht myth which made 'west of the Shannon' a synonym for Connacht. In fact, however, it is only for the past few centuries that the river has been the province's eastern boundary for most of the way — it isn't, even today, in Leitrim, where half the county is east of the Shannon. Ancient and medieval Connacht included, under other names, Cavan and Longford, which together with Leitrim formed the *Garbhthrian Chonnacht* or 'Rough Third of Connacht'. However, in the journey I relate in this book I respected the Shannon's mythic significance. Once I crossed it in the plane taking me to Connacht Airport I did not re-cross it, even in Leitrim, until the journey ended.

1.
FROM THE AIRPORT
TO SWINFORD

SINCE Anglesey we had seen no land, only a fleecy plain of sunlit clouds under a pale blue dome. We knew we had passed Dublin twenty minutes before only because the captain had told us when we were over it. I had my eye out for the Shannon, but was losing hope of seeing it. We began to fall into the fleece; mounds of it rose above us and then it was a dense mist around us. I could see fields but not clearly enough to make out whether they had stone walls. Was it Roscommon? The fields vanished. The hostess told us to put on our seat belts. The steam outside the windows became a darker colour like rain. Then we saw fields again and they clearly had stone walls. The wheels extended. There was a piece of dark forest and bogland with puddles. I could see a straight main road, presumably the Galway-Sligo road, and then, as we passed over it, the small terminal building attached to the control tower, and the long runway. There were conifers behind the perimeter fence. We touched down, turned, and taxied towards the terminal building. Under a large D there was a glass door and people standing behind it had their faces pressed to it. 'Isn't it a lovely feeling? I'd never have believed I'd live to see it', a woman said beside me. It reminded me of arriving once at a small airport in Yugoslavia.

The building of Connacht Airport, as my ticket called it, or Knock airport, as it is popularly called, gave rise to a flare-up of that latent antagonism between Dublin and the West which is one side of their charged relationship. It need not have occurred, and indeed would not have occurred, if the Fianna Fáil government which gave its support to the scheme at the beginning of the '80s had remained in office. But it fell twice and was replaced both times by a government which contained, in both its Labour and its Fine Gael wings, a strong element of that anti-Western antagonism which coexists in Dublin with pro-Western romantic sentiment. And this government, after its second coming, endured. So on the one side there was Monsignor James Horan, backed by the people of Mayo, speaking up for the needs of Knock as a place of pilgrimage, and for the needs of Connacht as an economically disadvantaged province; and on the other side there was the government, backed by bureaucrats, technocrats, and the Dublin liberal bourgeoisie, decrying the airport as 'an unfortunate escapade in Irish political opportunism', and deriding it as a 'daft' scheme sited on a 'foggy, boggy hill, far from any town of any size'. Not only, these Dublin voices seemed to say, was it typical Western peasant stupidity, but it was also a typical emanation of that superstitious nonsense which, in typical Western fashion, went on at the Marian shrine of Knock. Thirteen million pounds would be needed to complete the airport; the government called a halt at £9 million. For Mayo, roused to anger, that was typical of how Dublin treated the West: it could spend over £100 million on electrifying a commuter railway around Dublin Bay, and £20 million on restoring the Royal Hospital at Kilmainham — and all this in a city which already had an international airport and everything else — and yet refuse £4 million to complete an international airport in a province that had no airport worth talking about, most of its railway system closed down, and its once-busy ports either idle or almost so. Monsignor Horan and his cohorts raised £3 million in donations throughout Ireland and abroad. That sufficed to have the airport more or less completed, and it had been officially opened a couple of months before I arrived.

I had seen it five years before, in its early, heroic period. Mayomen, grown skilled and rich in the construction industry in Britain, had rallied round: now they would do on their own soil the kind of work at which they had become past masters elsewhere. Giant diggers were scooping out an artificial valley, and loading the earth and stones on forty trucks which moved in a continuous line to the top of a hill where the flat area was being extended at the rate — I timed it on my watch — of four truckloads a minute. Each of the nine stages of the project was finished on time and at less than the cost budgeted for.

Now, in the terminal building, I looked around. There were a few baggage and ticket desks, a desk for Knock shrine and one for a car-hire firm. Boys and girls were officiating in airport uniforms. Until a few months before, they had been living country lives in a raw slice of Mayo countryside. A small restaurant in the corner of the building was serving customers, but had evidently just been completed. Two women, one on either side of its glass partition, were removing specks of paint.

I took delivery of my bicycle and pannier bag, which I had brought with me on the plane, and walked out into the car park. Bog cotton was waving through the perimeter fence. When I had got some distance from the building and looked back, I saw, with dismay, over the entrance, 'CONNAUGHT AIRPORT'. 'Connaught', even in small print, is a very ugly word both in appearance and in the suggestiveness of the 'naught' part — a spelling, moreover, which leads ignorant people to pronounce the word 'Connawt' — but in letters several feet high it is awful; it is menacing, like a black cloud. All the Dublin papers spelt the word the normal way when they were referring to the airport. My ticket, issued in Manchester, had 'Connacht'. I decided I must investigate.

I went back into the terminal building and approached a man who had been pointed out to me as the airport manager: Maurice Buckby, an Englishman. Introducing myself, I asked him why that spelling of the province's name had been used outside there, and was it official. 'I'm afraid it is', he said. 'In the beginning we spelt it "a-c-h-t" and I prefer that myself. We had it on all our paper, on trucks and so on. But the two representatives of the Department of Communications who are on the airport board said it must be "n-a-u-g-h-t" and the others accepted it. I suppose they thought it better in the circumstances not to make a fuss about it. We had to change all the paper.' I told him I believed him, but that it was still incredible.

I am, of course, well aware that the spelling 'Connaught' has a history. It was invented by English officials in Ireland — it was their practice here, different from that in Wales or Scotland, to 'anglicise' the spelling of Celtic words — and this particular anglicisation had a wide currency for a few centuries. I accept it, as an archaism, in, say, the name of the Castlebar newspaper, *The Connaught Telegraph,* which is in existence a hundred years or more, or in the name of a laundry or some such of similar antiquity. What I deplored that afternoon in Mayo was that, when the correct spelling had once again been stabilised in general use, this aberration had been *revived,* and given world-wide currency, by the diktat of Dublin bureaucrats; particularly when those same bureaucrats, in their Census volumes, Dáil reports, and everything else official except Ordnance Survey maps, used the spelling 'Connacht'.*

I cycled through the car park onto the new airport road and turned east towards the Galway-Sligo road. It was soon clear to me that I was on a hill. To the north towards Charlestown, and despite the hazy weather, there was a magnificent view of a broad plain extending to the Ox Mountains in Sligo. I began to ruminate again about that word 'Barnacooga'. The promoters of the airport had put it around that the hill on which the airport was built was called Barnacooga, or in proper Gaelic, *Barr na Cúige,* meaning 'the top of the province' — and wasn't that, they implied, a proper and providential place to build the Connacht Regional Airport? The media had taken this up, and journalist after journalist, both in the newspapers and on radio and tele-vision, had referred to the airport site by that name. But already back in Dublin I had had doubts about the story. 'Top of the Pro-vince' seemed a strange name for a relatively small hill that was much lower than many hills, let alone mountains, in Connacht. Besides I had always understood *cúige,* the Gaelic for province, to be a masculine word; in which case it should be *Barr an Chúige.* I checked in dictionaries and found that it was occasionally feminine. Very well, but I knew that *barr* in hilly country could also mean 'height' or 'ridge', and Monsignor Horan had streng-thened my hunch that it might mean that in this case by saying in one television programme which showed him standing on the airport site: 'Here at Barnalira . . .', which I had 'read' as *Barr na Laidhre.* Leave aside that his saying of that indicated some uncer-tainty about where the airport was: *barr* in that instance clearly didn't mean 'top', but 'ridge'; 'the ridge of the *ladhar*', of the space between two fingers. The V-shaped ridge. If, similarly, the *barr* in *Barr na Cúige* meant 'ridge', then the bottom fell out of the whole 'top of the province' story, for 'ridge of the province' didn't make sense. *Cúige* would have to mean something else, or

*The matter was resolved a few months later by the airport changing its name to Horan International Airport.

would turn out to be a corruption of some other word. And on the plane, what had I seen in my brand-new Michelin map of Ireland, so new that it showed Connacht Airport? No mention of Barnacooga, but on the road to Swinford, about two miles west of where the airport was marked, a village called Barnacahoge. *Cathóg* is an Ulster word, but there have been several Ulster migrations into Mayo. It means the cross-piece on the handle of a spade or large shovel, which makes a T-shape with the handle. 'The ridge of the *cathóg*', 'the T-shaped ridge'. Was Barnacahoge what they were talking about? A name that did not mean 'top of the province', a village two miles from the airport?

With my mind full of these suspicions, I stopped at a house when I reached the main road and asked the girl who came to the door what they called the hill where the airport was built. 'Kilgarriff', she said. 'You can see five counties from it.' 'And where is Barnacooga?' 'That's a village back in behind it', she said, pointing back in the direction from which I had come. 'Is that what they call Barnacahoge on maps?' I asked her. 'I don't know', she said, 'we call it Barr na Cúige' (that was how she pronounced it). I thanked her and cycled back towards the airport. Of course, I was thinking, Barnacahoge is bad grammar, a crude anglicisation. Correctly, 'ridge of the *cathóg*' would be *Barr na Cathóige*; which brought it a bit nearer to what she had said. But Kilgarriff, that was a discovery. Back in the terminal building, I asked the girl at the Knock shrine desk what was the name of this place where we were now. 'You're in Kilgarriff now', she said. 'And where's *Barr na Laidhre*?' 'It begins back there on the hill', she said, pointing west in the direction the runway ran. 'And *Barr na Cúige*?' 'That's a village further back, but when they were building the airport they said it was on Barr na Cúige because of what that means.' 'But this isn't *Barr na Cúige*?' 'Well, I suppose you could say it is really', she said. 'The top of the province.' The make-believe was becoming fact! But I saw the point now clearly: they would hardly say they were building the airport on Kilgarriff, which means 'rugged' something — 'wood' or 'churchyard' — when all their enemies were deriding them for building it in a wilderness. *Barr na Cúige* seemed a godsend.

I cycled off in search of it and had many encounters; but I will make a long story short. In a small cottage beyond the end of the runway a dignified old gentleman confirmed that the airport

13

was built on Kilgarriff land, and said that the hill had been called Kilgarriff Mountain. You could see five baronies from it. They used to cut turf on it in a bog called the Bonkeydoo, which I took to be *bancaí dú'*, black banks. In a two-storey house beyond that, near Mulligan's auction yard, an old man sitting at table with his two grandsons told me that the people had sold their land cheap for the airport because work was promised, but that Monsignor Horan had given most of the jobs to his own people from Knock. That girl I had been talking to, she was the only local one out of eight women working there, and only one local lad had been employed. 'This young fellow here', pointing to one of his grandsons, 'couldn't get work there.' The same lad explained to me that *Barr na Laidhre* was called that because it had five hills like the five fingers on a hand; and he held up a hand with the fingers splayed in illustration. It was a distant, garbled echo of someone, once, who had similarly held up opened fingers to explain what a *ladhar* was. I cycled down the road towards what everyone called *Barr na Cúige*, exploring a couple of by-paths on the way. It was a primeval landscape of hillocks and ridges cast in strange, tortured shapes. I talked to an old woman who said 'wasn't Monsignor Horan the great man now, if ever there was a great man? To build the airport and get the money for it.' I came to a national school near a cluster of houses in a valley. On a plaque in Irish on the school wall I read that the name of the place was *Barr na Cathóige*. It was the end of my quest. I glanced around at the humps and hillocks within sight in the hope of seeing something shaped like a cross-piece, but I was aware that it could be anywhere within the townland. When I asked a wild-eyed lad was there anyone in the village who knew about the old names of places, he pointed to the house nearest us, and said, with a passion that made me nervous, that all the land around had once belonged to one family, but that it had got divided among four, and that one of the portions would be coming to him. He and others I spoke to called the place *Barr na Cúige*, but none of them could say what it meant. I supposed that, as often happens with placenames, but especially when there is a language change, *na Cathóige* had been slurred with time into *na C'óige*, and had later become *na Cúige*.

There is no better way to encounter a new place, and to get immersed in it, than to pursue an enquiry to the end by questioning people. I *was* now, I felt, in Connacht, in Mayo. I had travelled narrow roads, trodden the grass, crossed stone walls, smelt the smells, been in houses, conversed with people, seen their eyes, experienced their address. Their accent and speech rhythm were in my mind. I had encountered and felt — more than I have described — their dislocation in a broken and tangled web of language, place and meaning. And I had encountered, twice in three hours, a very modern thing which made me feel I was in a very modern place: that deliberate *caprice with words* which Confucius warned against, as the fundamental social sin, in China two and a half thousand years ago.

Cycling back past Mulligan's auction yard and the end of the runway, and taking the back road to Charlestown, I passed the excavated valley from which the earth for the airport had come. A short distance on, in front of a cottage, a man with tousled hair, his swarthy face blackened by smoke, was working at a blackened concrete-mixer which had strange tin-can attachments. There was a small boy beside him. I stopped, and he came over to me smiling shyly. We chatted a bit. He said the place was Carn and yes, it was Carn earth was underneath the runway; I ought to see the full extent of the hole, it was enormous. As I left he went back to the mixer, and the boy went over and stood beside him, looking up at him full of wonder as he worked and chatted to him. I passed a ball-alley with BRITS OUT painted on it in large white letters. From a side road a tractor came towards me pulling a load of logs. A dirty-faced boy was driving it, and a little girl was sitting beside him on it looking happy and proud. It was the same look, or very like it.

Charlestown, a town of 600 inhabitants five miles from the airport, is the bustling traffic crossroads of northern Connacht. Most of the brightly-painted houses seemed to be offering food or drink or accommodation. In the middle of the small, irregular square, a tattered YES poster from the recent referendum on divorce hung from a telegraph pole. A wooden booth offered information on the Western Rose Festival due to open in the town on 1 August. I asked in a newsagent's for the *Western People*, but it had not yet arrived from Ballina. I bought a *Connaught Telegraph,* and read the start of the editorial, 'Joining the Jet Set' on the front page:

It was yet another glorious triumph for Knock Airport yesterday when the first jet from the United States touched down on Mayo soil to the applause of thousands. The people of the West, who have supported in word and deed the building of the dream, were out in force to witness the shaping of history. They lined the approach routes to enjoy the spectacle and to extend a warm *céad míle fáilte* to the visitors.

The tone of the reception took veteran airline personnel by surprise. They had never witnessed anything like it. But then they were unaware of the special regard which the ordinary people of the province hold for the airport, Monsignor James Horan and the men who made it all possible. The flight heralds the opening of a brand new chapter in the history of the facility, further evidence, if such were needed, of the asset it is proving to be.

Inserting the paper in my pannier bag, I set out for Swinford, seven miles away. The sky was still clouded and there was occasional drizzling rain. The stone walls between fields had been replaced by hedges. I noticed the scarcity of wild flowers. Apart from cow parsnip and ragwort, which didn't count, there was only meadow-sweet; lush patches of its tall, creamy flowers. I came to a roadside shrine and stopped. In a concrete box with a glass front there was a big statue of the Sacred Heart, smaller ones of Mary and St Joseph, and artificial flowers. In brownish letters, crudely written by a finger, I read: 'Erected by the citizens of Culmore 1929 to commemorate the Centenary of Catholic Emancipation.' And beneath that: 'Culmore village shrine. Consecrated to the Sacred Heart 1929.' Entering Swinford I passed a huge yard full of tractors and other farm machinery. Posters announced 'Siamsa Sráide. Busking competition extrordinaire [*sic*]! £500 in prizes. Followed by open-air céilí in the square.' O'Connor's Hotel looked sad, and O'Connor's Guesthouse across the street from it even sadder: it seemed to be closed. I entered a pub and made a phone call to Dublin in a room where Ulster Television was delivering a soap opera. In the Errigal bed-and-breakfast, a short distance away, I found lodgings. The woman of the house, Mrs Quinn, was from Crossmolina. The Errigal sign must have been her husband's idea; he was a guard from Donegal. In the yard, as I struggled to unfasten the straps of my pannier, he offered me a golf-tee, which was a help. Talking of his golfing on the local course, he said, 'It's so much easier here than up in Dublin. You can go in and play a round any time of the day.'

I crossed the street to a fast-food shop, Mr Chips. A board standing on the pavement said 'American Style Hamburgers'. In the large windows there were plants hanging and standing, and inside, girls in red, blue and white uniforms moved among the tables. I ordered shepherd's pie and onion rings and sat at a table opposite a red-faced man with tousled hair wearing a navy suit and open-necked shirt. Beside him sat a small fat boy with a Lancashire accent. Pop music from RTE Radio 2 was playing. There were three large paintings on the wall done in an att-ractive children's-book style: in a fairy-story landscape, teacups were walking, saucers chatting, and cartons of chips sat on swings hung from trees. The paintings were signed 'Rosemary Sweeney '86'. The man across from me said he was a farmer from Killasser. He had a farm of about thirty-five acres with eighteen cattle and he grew barley, oats and hay. The wet summer, following on the wet summer of the previous year, was giving him a bad time. Stocks of fodder were running low, the hay and corn lay soaked in the fields. His sister, the boy's mother, who was over from Lancashire, had told him they hadn't had rain there for eight weeks. 'But wouldn't you be com-plaining', I asked him, 'if that were the weather here?' 'Indeed, I suppose I would', he said.

I walked to Mícheál Campbell's pub, the White House, on Church Street near the Courthouse. I had met him many years before with Caoimhghin Mac Cathmhaoil, the solicitor, who used to live across the street. He said there was a sort of depression in the town, largely because the farmers around hadn't much ready cash. Last year, because of the wet summer and the scarcity of good-quality fodder, many cattle had died from malnutrition. The farmers were hard put to it to maintain payments on loans.

Mícheál, with spectacles over bright eyes, blue pullover, open-necked shirt and sports jacket, blotched face, sharp, hawk-like nose, looked scholarly, professorial almost. 'During the EEC bonanza', he said, 'the banks encouraged them to buy more

17

cattle, to build milking parlours, and to extend their houses. First it was teak windows, then the everlasting plastic ones. The donkey and horse became obsolete. There was at least one tractor in every yard. Boatloads of second-hand tractors were brought over from England, and there were two or three agents pushing them in every small town. They all got cars, and now the car is a status symbol which they'll do anything to keep. It's like the horse in the old days. I used see people starve themselves to keep the horse in fodder.'

He mentioned Halal, the Pakistani meat processors in Ballyhaunis, about twenty miles away to the south. 'I see they have an ad in the *Independent*', he said, 'saying they'll take 10,000 cattle a week, any quality.' He showed me the ad and I noticed 'Remember, Halal pays the highest prices for beef in Ireland.' 'Well, shouldn't that solve everyone's problems?' I said. But Mícheál said they paid low prices and their attitude was take-it-or-leave-it. The best prices for high-quality cattle were to be got at the mart up the street from him. People would sell cattle to Halal only if they hadn't passed the TB test or were sick or old. A man at the bar said he had just delivered three beasts to Halal and, though he wasn't sure what he'd get for them, he thought it would be fair enough. 'They're uncertain about prices', he said, 'because the trade is uncertain. The big firms haven't got orders yet from the Middle East because of the fall in the price of oil — they haven't the money there. And if the EEC stops intervention, as it's talking of doing, it'll be like the '50s again when you couldn't give cattle away. A while back there, you could get £1.25 a kilo in the mart, now it's back down to a pound.' He said no one in Mayo grew potatoes commercially. Some used to be in pigs. He was in pigs himself when he came back from England in the early '70s — he had 600. but prices fell, feed rose.

Mícheál said another effect of the bad times was that the farmers and their families had become very dependent on welfare, and the 'Pensions Officer', as they called the welfare inspector, was a figure of terror in the land. He or she recommended who should get the dole and other benefits, and how much. 'I'll tell you a true story. A lady vet on her rounds stops her car and asks this old man where she could find, say, Michael McDonagh. He has never heard of a lady vet and he thinks she might be the Pensions Officer, so he points vaguely towards the

18

hills and says, "Oh he's about three miles from here". She says, "His son phoned me and told me they've a calf in a bad way". He looks her straight in the eye and says, "Now isn't it awful these days how a son won't even tell his father what he's doing".'

I saw a card on a shelf behind the bar: 'Marriage is the main cause of divorce'. No, he said, that had nothing to do with the divorce referendum. His wife, Angela, had brought it back with some others from a visit to America. 'But I'll tell you a late referendum joke. A man and woman had been happily married for forty years. One day the priest sees the woman sitting looking very disconsolate at the back of the church, and he asks her what's wrong. "My husband", she says, "told me that if I don't vote No he'll leave me." Well, actually I got that story from my daughter who works in the *Financial Times* in London. It was in a cartoon she sent me, so I've had to adapt it a bit.' He said there had been very little campaigning in the town. 'It used to be a Fine Gael town, and I'm of that persuasion myself, but now it's nearly fifty-fifty [he meant with Fianna Fáil]. But the Fine Gaelers, even though the party was supporting divorce, didn't take much interest in it. They thought the government should be attending to more important things.' The local vote had been about 70 per cent against.

On the counter there were collection boxes for the mentally handicapped and the Third World. The walls were largely given over to sport: many pictures of GAA teams, a list of Swinford GAA Club fixtures, a Bank of Ireland poster of the GAA All-Stars, a big Smithwicks Beer picture of the boxer, Barry McGuigan. There was a technicolour picture of President Kennedy, a plaque about the Guinness/*Sunday World* All-Ireland Pub Quiz 1981, a signed football, and a notice saying that a group called 'Irish Mist' played Irish music there every Sunday night. When I visited the lavatory I was confronted with a notice: 'WARNING: Due to industrial action this toilet will be closed tomorrow, SO DO AS MUCH AS YOU CAN TODAY.'

A handsome young man sitting beside me at the bar turned out to be a traveller for a Dublin firm that supplied parts and machines to industries. He said he spent much of his time in the Gaeltacht areas in Donegal and Connemara. He spoke Irish and liked working there. He had just been visiting the industries

19

of South Connemara, and we talked about places and people I knew when I was living there in the '70s. He pricked up his ears when Mícheál starting talking about the industries of Swinford: an American pharmaceutical firm, a couple of joineries, furniture- and blouse-makers, two mechanical workshops. I took my leave and went off to bed, saturated with Mayo.

———————

I had taken with me in my luggage the volume of the 1981 Census which gives the population of towns, and before I went down to breakfast next morning I looked up Swinford. It had a population of 1,300. I noticed that a 'town' was defined officially as 'a Town under the Town Improvements (Ireland) Act 1854'. Within those terms, some places with very small populations, even less than 200 — places that are usually called villages — rank as towns. So in practice there is some confusion about what a town is, and in this book I will say 'town' or 'village' simply as it seems appropriate.

Mrs Quinn would hear nothing of Swinford's being 'depressed'. It had become a great business town, she said, and she did all her grocery shopping there. 'You might get things cheaper in Ballina, but sure when you go into Mellett's there with the kids, you'd find between having a cup of coffee and buying something for them that you'd end up spending more than you'd saved. I think Swinford's a coming place. There's 220 employed at the Travenol factory [the American pharmaceutical firm], and the District Hospital employs sixty-one. You should visit the day-centre there, it's really great what they do for the old people. They bring them in every day by minibus. They can have meals there and be bathed. They sit together and have great crack.'

She said the hospital dealt mainly with geriatric cases and convalescents. Younger people when they were sick, and maternity cases, went to Castlebar. (Castlebar is the county capital; Ballina, by a small margin, the largest town.) Swinford, she said, was the headquarters of a Garda district, so there were twenty-two guards, many of them married, living in it. It had four doctors, three priests and three solicitors. Like a couple of other guard's wives, she had got into the B and B business 'because if you're to give your children anything, you can't rear

20

a family on one salary today, especially when you've teenagers. My husband and I don't drink or smoke. In the summer we have four bedrooms for guests and three for the family. Of course, Swinford isn't a tourist town, it's a pass-through town. I used get a lot of Americans, but lately it has mostly been French and Germans. With the summer we're having it's been a bad season. But then I did well when they were building the Handicapped Centre — it was a Clare contractor, and I had several of the men staying with me.'

I went walking in the town. Essentially it was two streets. One very long one, which under a variety of names stretched from the tractor depot on the Charlestown side to the mart; the other, Main Street, joining it to form a T-junction. There was a secondary school, taught by priests, nuns and lay-teachers, and a vocational school, and two national schools for boys and girls respectively. Besides the District Hospital, there was a small fever hospital. Every Tuesday a street market took place, and on the first Wednesday of the month a fair; the mart was held every Friday. The town had no swimming-pool or public library; there had been a library until the lease ran out on the building which the County Council had rented for that purpose. There was no bookshop as such, but the biggest newsagent's had a selection of British and American paperback novels, some Irish books, including five on the GAA, some large-format hard-backs, most of them cookery books, and a selection of children's books. There was also a sizeable number of paperbacks on child care, parenthood, and sex. Neither in the magazine section nor among the books was there anything about religion. Posters around the town said 'Be a link in the Peace Chain up Croagh Patrick on the 16th August. Ring Castlebar Rehab'. Like most Irish towns, even proper towns, Swinford has no mayor, town council, or representative civic body of any kind. Administered by Mayo County Council with regard to housing and environ-mental matters, and by Dublin government departments for most other matters, it is in civic terms just a collection of buildings and people without any corporate existence.

I called into The Hagen, a pub which I gathered was the headquarters for the Siamsa Sráide I had seen advertised. Taped accordion music was playing. The owner, Kitty O'Hagan, told me it was P.J. Hernon of Cárna in Connemara,

21

whom I knew well. He had been playing in the pub the previous Wednesday. Every Saturday and Sunday night, she said, they had a band playing Irish and country and western music. The Siamsa was being organised by a student; they expected up to a hundred entries in the busking competition. It had been a great success the previous year. Mrs O'Hagan told me that the house in which we were had been a hotel originally and that General Humbert had spent a night there when his army of French regulars and Irish auxiliaries was marching from Killala to Castlebar in 1798. That was about as far back as the history of the town went, for it was founded by the local landlords, the Brabazons, in the late eighteenth century. They had come origi-nally from Leicestershire, and had named the town, it was generally believed, after the village of Swinford in that shire.

A large part of the Brabazon lands — it was called the Brabazon Park — had passed to the town in the early part of the century and was managed by a board of trustees, of whom Mícheál Campbell was one. That afternoon he took me walking there. Part of the land had been sold for housing. On another, more extensive part, I saw the golf course, the tennis courts, and the big, rather ugly community centre, which contained, besides a large hall, squash and badminton courts and a hand-ball alley. All of these were set against a background of forest and copses. Mícheál, passing near some of the old trees, said 'You've got to give it to them, everywhere the Brits were you find old trees.' He had said the Brabazons were good landlords, and I thought what a failure for them: two centuries of bene-volence and still foreigners.

Everything is a 'centre' nowadays. Our walk brought us to the centre for the mentally handicapped to which Mrs Quinn had referred. It was like a village: a group of single-storey buildings among young trees. Built by the Western Health Board at a cost of £14 million, it had not been opened yet, and the delay had become a *cause célèbre*. There was a dispute between the Western Health Board and Western Care, a voluntary association of parents and guardians of handicapped people, who wanted a say in the running of the centre; and it was believed that the Minister for Health, Barry Desmond, was using this as an excuse for not opening it — his real reason being lack of money. Mícheál knocked on a glass door of the main building, and the

22

caretaker, a young man, said we could look around. It was quite luxurious. I was struck especially by the lovely swimming-pool which had natural rocks standing on the edge at one end and coloured scenes depicted on the wall tiles. The original idea, Mícheál said, had been to make it an Olympic-sized pool which would be available to the townspeople at designated hours, but subsequently it had been scaled down. As we were leaving, the caretaker said to Mícheál — referring to a visit to the town by the Taoiseach, Dr FitzGerald — 'Did you tell your man the other day to get on with opening it?' And then, as Mícheál simply smiled the caretaker added: 'I'd have told *my* man!' It struck me that something was expressed there about the relationships to their followers of FitzGerald and Haughey respectively.

Back in Mícheál's pub his eighteen-year-old daughter, Siobhán, was behind the bar. She was one of nine children; apart from the sister in London, two other older sisters were working in Dublin and Westport respectively. I asked her where did the older teenagers in Swinford go out dancing. She said to the 'Path' — the Beaten Path — a disco in Claremorris, eighteen miles away. There was a special CIE bus every Sunday night. Or else to Kiltimagh, seven miles away, or to Charlestown. She said that for shopping, people used go to Ballina, but now it was mostly Castlebar. Several shops in Ballina had closed down, and Castlebar had better style in its clothes shops. I discovered that Irish Mist, the group advertised as playing in the pub, was a family affair: it had been made up of three of her sisters, but since one of them had gone to London there were only two in it now.

I had heard that the vet, Eddie Ruane, was a great Irish speaker and knew a lot about placenames, so I went to visit him to discuss my findings at the airport. People said the vets had become rich out of the TB eradication scheme, and Eddie's house on the edge of the town, with its fine garden, certainly suggested affluence. I found that his enthusiasm for placenames matched my own, and we soon had the dictionaries out. With a sad shaking of the head he agreed with me about *Barr na Cúige* — that nonsense about 'top of the province', and about its being on the site of the airport! But he was doubtful that the name of the place meant cross-piece ridge. Did the people who gave the name to the place centuries ago have spades or shovels with cross-pieces? I asked him if his veterinary travels on the following day would take him to Bohola, a few miles away, because I would like to go there after attending the mart. He said that would suit him and to come back in the morning after the mart.

I went to the Maple Leaf restaurant for a meal. It was situated, strategically, at the exit from the town in the direction of the airport, seven miles away. A bar called Bar-na-Cogae [*sic*] was being fitted out under the same roof. I had heard that the owner, Lorcan Cribbin — an Offaly man married to a Foxford woman — had returned from Canada a few months before. Shortly after I had begun my meal he returned from a run, dressed in shorts and singlet, and changed into his chef's dress. He had worked as a chef most of his life, he said, but had spent his last three years in Canada in the Toronto police. When his wife was back in Foxford on a visit, she had looked around for a site for a restaurant, and when she recommended this house in Swinford he bought it straight away. People travelling from Castlebar to the airport passed the door. The place had been packed on the day of the first transatlantic flight. But for his bread and butter he depended on local custom and he had carried on a vigorous campaign to win it, especially for lunches. I had heard already in the town about his advertising. He had distributed leaflets saying 'We need your bellies to run our business', and 'Lunch in eight minutes or you get it free'. If you ate your lunch there your name was written on the receipt for a weekly draw — unless you said you didn't want to enter — and the winner got a free lunch. I asked him what did Bar-na-Cogae mean. He said, 'That's the name of the hill the airport's built on. It's called that because you can see *cúig* counties from it.' He said that a local guard had taken a splendid photo of the transatlantic jet landing and he was going to display a blown-up version of it in the bar.

In Mrs Quinn's that night I finally found time to read the *Connaught Telegraph* I had bought in Charlestown. Three hundred people had attended the official opening in Dublin of the campaign to entice Mayomen to invest in their home county.... The ACOT agricultural advisory service was now being provided on a district basis. Mayo had four districts, with Terry Gallagher, CAO, the manager in Castlebar, Kevin Walsh in Ballina, Donal Murphy in Claremorris and Dan Fox in

Westport. . . . Pure Fresh Dairies, Ballina, were the first and only dairy in Mayo to win the quality mark for their products. This brought the number of companies having it up to ninety-one. . . . Vandals had run amuck [*sic*] in the former residence on Achill Island of Captain Boycott. They smashed 182 panes of glass in sixty-four windows, damaged the roof, pulled out light fittings and left the entire area littered with broken bottles, glass and dishes. . . . Eight countries were to be represented at the grand finals of the Castlebar International Song Contest which would be celebrating its coming of age this October. . . . In golf, ladies' honorary secretary Mary Horkan had taken the Swinford course apart when winning the captain's prize. Her class, power and concentration were all put to good effect to shatter the opposition with a 62 nett. . . . The Orena Hotel, Knock, was the venue on Friday night for a presentation to Mons. James Horan by the people of Knock parish in recognition of his airport development work. This was his first appearance since his recent illness and he was in fine voice, 'giving us a "blast" of some of his well-known songs . . .'

GAA news, especially Gaelic football, dominated the sports pages. There were scores of large advertisements for festivals, sports days, and entertainments. The Western Rose Festival in Charlestown, which was to last a week, was so-called because it selected a comely, personable girl on the lines of the Rose of Tralee Festival. But the Aughagower Round Tower Festival, spread over fifteen days, would also have its Rose of Aughagower. The one-day Killawalla Annual Sports offered 'Events for all the family'. A feature of the festivals which made them noticeably different from those of any other Catholic country was that they all had secular titles or themes: no mention of saints, or of Virgins of this or that. I was struck by the abundant comings and goings between America and Mayo, England and Mayo; not only private visits, but organised events. 'Mayo Football Clubs Jet into Chicago', 'Basketball Players on New York Trip', 'First Ballyvary/Birmingham Cultural Exchange Visit'. Twelve Pakistani children from Birmingham were to 'jet into Knock airport' for a week of cultural events, and a tree-planting ceremony marking the International Year of Peace, organised by Ballyvary village near Castlebar. There was also a constant coming and going of missionaries between Mayo and the Third World. The headings of the local Knock notes for the week illustrated both movements. After an introductory paragraph about a fund-raising social for Sister Maud Murphy, home on holiday from Nigeria, the headings included 'From Boston', 'In London', 'American Visitor', and 'From the Philippines'. In addition, of course, there was an 'Off to Lourdes'.

Comparing spellings of placenames in the newspaper with spellings of the same places in the maps and travel literature I had brought with me, I noticed that not only the name of the province, but the names of many towns and villages had two, or even three versions. There was Ballyvary/Bellavary, Ballin-tubber/Ballintober, Geesala/Gweesala/Gweesalia, and so on. In other words, the 'anglicisation' of a Gaelic placename had led, in many cases, not only to a second name alongside the first, but to a variety of versions of that second name. It was as if in Dublin we wrote Clontarf/Cloontarf, Rathmines/Rathmaines, or Merrion/Merian/Mwirrion, as the fancy took us. In Connacht the confusion seemed to have arisen from a combination of local caprice with the intruded caprice of Dublin bureaucrats. Consulting my Census volume, I noticed on page 40, in two adjacent columns under the respective headings 'Town' and 'District Electoral Division': Swinford, Swineford; Kiltimagh, Kiltamagh. It struck me that this officially sanctioned ortho-graphic mess — startling where one would expect clarity and order — might well be due to the reverent repetition, in govern-ment offices, either of spelling mistakes made by nineteenth-century clerks, or of misreadings of those clerks' handwriting.

On television that night there was a programme in the series 'A Home in the Green Land', about the noble houses of Ireland, and, as it happened, this one showed John Fitzmaurice Mills discoursing on Clonalis House in Co. Roscommon, the chief seat of the O'Conor family since the mid-nineteenth century. The O'Conors, Mr Mills said, were the oldest noble house in Europe: they had a known genealogy reaching back to 90 B.C. They had provided eight kings of Connacht, and two high-kings of Ireland — including, of course, Rory O'Conor, who was king of Ireland when the Normans came and who is generally reckoned as the last high-king. It was interesting to see the conventional Victorian portraits of O'Conors and their ladies in the last century, when some of them were MPs and others were serving in distant places as administrators of the British Empire. The film showed a secret chapel in the house from the Penal times, and, among the many relics preserved there, a Communion chalice which could be dismantled for purposes of concealment, and O'Carolan's harp.

From early morning there was a hum of traffic, mainly cattle-boxes and trailers pulled by cars and tractors, heading for the mart. When I arrived there at ten o'clock the auctioning was well under way in the two halls called 'rings'. In the pens, by my reckoning, there were more than two hundred cattle, the heifers and bullocks divided. I went into the heifer ring. Tiers of semi-circular seating faced a half-ring walled with tiles; and a gate of corrugated iron led from it to the pens. Most of those bidding, both dealers and farmers, stood at the railing enclosing the ring. They signalled their bids by raising a stick or an arm ever so slightly. The auctioneer's box was perched above the ring, and a small, two-sided blackboard beside him displayed the number of the lot, and the weight of the beast, being auctioned. As each beast stood there, and the bidding proceeded, a large dial above the corrugated gate showed the weight of the next beast standing on scales behind the gate. The auctioneer's assistant chalked this, and the lot number, on the side of the blackboard next him, and then, as the auctioned beast left, turned that towards the public. Beside the two men a couple of girls sat writing, or moved in and out with messages. Like all auction scenes with which one is not familiar, it was difficult for me to follow, but my impression was that most of the heifers weighed between 280 and 430 kilograms, and fetched between £310 and £480. 'This time of year they get a good price', a young farmer beside me remarked.

In the bullock ring, which was much larger and contained more people, the auctioneer and his assistant wore white coats. The heavier beasts were selling for £600 and £700. The men around me were talking in hundredweights, and I noticed, when I questioned them, that they were not at home with kilograms. The farmers, of all ages, wore short jackets of various kinds, sports jackets, and pullovers; a few had hats or caps and some

27

wore ties. Small boys, carrying droving-sticks, moved about self-importantly. A woman with curly red hair and strong cheek-bones, wearing eye-shadow, entered accompanied by her three sons. Smiling with inner contentment she took her seat beside a man. Most of the men sat watching, listening, chatting quietly, waiting for their lot to come up, adding to their long education in the cattle trade. Here, I felt, looking at them, are the People of the Land. For the sellers, here is the culmination of all the caring for, and careful feeding of, the beasts. Now their harvest is reaped. Occasionally, as a lot was sold, people left. 'This is a small mart', a man told me. 'Often there are more than 800 cattle and the selling goes on through the night until Saturday morning. You can't get through the streets.'

Éamonn Ruane — he preferred 'Éamonn' to 'Eddie' — was driving into his gateway as I arrived. With him was a young German vet who was working with him. We went into the house and were met by Mrs Ruane saying, 'Did you hear the news? Monsignor Horan is dead. He died in Lourdes of a heart attack. It was on the radio.' We were stunned. 'He'd had trouble with his heart', she said, 'and hadn't properly recovered from it. He shouldn't have gone there.' We all agreed that he had been pushing himself very hard. What was there to say? I felt the blow physically hitting people all over Mayo and the West.

Shortly afterwards I left with Éamonn for Bohola. I wanted to see the place because it was famous for the millionaires it had produced abroad — and because it was where Paul O'Dwyer came from. Éamonn wanted to take me first to see Peadar O'Donnell's grave in Swinford, but it was raining too heavily for a visit to a graveyard. I told him about visiting the Handicapped Centre. He said, 'It's modelled on the kind of homes for the handicapped they had in Holland twenty years ago. Now they think it's better to have them in smaller units, so it's really out of date. But Enda Kenny [a Fine Gael Minister of State for East Mayo] was trying to look after his interests by giving the people something, after his own crowd had let him down so badly by reneguing on the airport. One thing is sure, it will be opened before the election. Money will be found. Everyone knows that.'

We called into the O'Dwyer Cheshire Home built on the land where Paul O'Dwyer had grown up. He and his friends, acting through the Mayo Association for the Handicapped in New

28

York, had gathered the funds to get it started. Then more money had come from Ireland and England. It was a splendid home set in a beautifully-kept garden. In the main hall, as we entered, were pictures and documents about famous Americans who had come from Bohola. Pat Woods, who described himself as 'Chairman', but who seemed to be the animating soul of the place, showed us around. We met most of the twenty-six residents (not 'patients') and the staff. There was much talk of Monsignor Horan, who had often visited the home. At Christmas he would come with musicians in his train and give them a 'blast' of a few songs. Pat Woods said, 'Several of the residents cried this morning when they heard of his death'. One of the nurses said, 'We should have had Bob Geldof as President and Monsignor Horan as Taoiseach'. Pat Woods was very proud and grateful that the Home was not a penny in debt; even the extension had been fully paid for. A fund-raising committee in Dublin had worked wonders. We had seen a room named after a Bohola millionaire in England.

'But still it couldn't have been done', said Pat Woods, 'without the generosity of the people here. Do you know, Mr Fennell, that since this place opened ten years ago, we haven't had to pay for bread or confectionery. They have been delivered every day without a word said, by local bakers. Imagine that, bread for forty people for ten years. And a local nursery looks after the garden, and an electrician gives his services free. This home is £120 a week cheaper to keep than the Cheshire Home in Dublin.' He was also connected with the *Bohola Post* and showed me several copies of it: a twenty-eight-page tabloid. It went out once a year to the far-flung Boholan empire.

It was difficult to drag ourselves away from such enthusiasm. We drove to the village. There were three pubs and a couple of shops, looking as spruce as if they had been built only a few years ago, and behind them was one of the 'rural villages' which Fr Harry Bohan and his organisation have been building around the country. There were twenty-two neat houses built in semi-detached pairs. The thinking behind these schemes, which combine high quality with low cost, is to provide living accommodation for young rural people to marry into. We went into Mickey Clarke's pub where his daughter, Susan served us. She said that emigration had started again: a lot of young people had

29

gone to the USA last year. I got men at the bar to recite the list of eight millionaires, most of them in England — in plant hire, room brokerage, hotels, building — but the Durkan brothers were builders and racehorse-owners in Dublin. 'Why did so many from here do so well?' I asked. 'They started from such a poor place, they left home early, they held together as a *meitheal*', a man said. 'When is someone here going to do his money-making at home and give employment?' 'If you want to make money, you go where the wealth is.' 'When is one of your millionaires going to set up a business here?' 'The trade unions would break him, the taxation would break him.' But since he meant the unions and taxation 'in Ireland', that didn't account for, say, the Durkans.

We returned to Swinford in the early afternoon. We had been talking Gaelic all the time, and, intermittently, from the time we had left Swinford, we had been discussing the Gaelic versions of placenames which we saw on signposts and at entrances to villages. Just as many places had more than one spelling of their anglicised names, some places had two versions of their Gaelic name — arising mostly from different notions of its origin or meaning. On top of that there were occasional misspellings, such as one notices so frequently throughout Ireland, owing to the sign-painter's illiteracy in Gaelic and the lack of efficient inspection.

Often during that day people recalled that Monsignor Horan had said, 'I'm an old man in a hurry'. They took that to mean that he knew death was coming and that therefore he had to work fast. About ten that night I called into the White House for a farewell drink. A tall, gaunt, red-haired farmer was sitting beside me at the bar. 'I've thirty acres in Kilmaine', he said, 'with fifty cattle on them. Excuse me, I'm drunk.' 'That's down near the Galway border,' said Mícheál to me. 'It's prime land.'

'Would you like to buy it?' asked the Kilmaine man. 'How much would you give me for it?'

I thought a bit and for some reason £200,000 passed through my mind. 'How much would you want?'

'I'd need £200,000 anyhow,' he said.

'I was going to say that.'

'Watch yourself now, or maybe you'll have a farm bought before you leave the pub. It happened me once. My old devil of a

30

father promised me the forty acres we had and then, when I was away in England, he gave it to a brother of mine. So I stayed on in England, working in the tunnels and the plant-hire — that's where you make the money. I like Englishmen, they're straight, honest. I'm burnt out listening to my neighbours. Irishmen depress me. Always thinking something else than they say. Anyhow I came back and I was sitting in this pub in Balla one evening and I told this man beside me I was looking for a farm. And he said do you want mine, and do you know before I left the pub I had agreed to buy it if I liked the look of it, and that's the farm I have now with some acres added to it.'

I said to Mícheál, 'You called Kilmaine prime land. Where's the best land in Mayo?' 'A man told me', he said, 'if you start at Turlough and go on through Breaffy, south of Castlebar, and down past Ballinrobe to Kilmaine, that's the best land in Mayo and you'd get no better.' 'That's right', said the Kilmaine man. 'It's the best land in the country and you'd finish cattle there better than you would in the Midlands.' 'Isn't that', I asked, 'what they call the Plains of Mayo?' 'Yes', said the Kilmaine man, 'where Mayo Abbey is and Mayo town. That's what the county's called from.'

2.
SWINFORD
TO BELDERRIG

'O MÁILLE, O Méille maybe, that's what the people used call
that name, but the priest reading out names from the altar said
O'Malley, and so the people say that now. The priests and the
police, that's who decide what the people call things.' It was
Éamonn who said that as we set out next morning for Pontoon at
the southern end of Lough Conn. My bicycle was in the boot.
Since before landing in Mayo I had been dreaming of climbing
Slieve Nephin — a romantic place for me since I first read
Synge's *Playboy* — and then, the next day, cycling on to Ceathrú
Thaidhg, Mayo's only genuine bit of Gaeltacht, at the extreme
north-western tip of the county. Éamonn had agreed to take me
the first thirteen miles to Pontoon.

The entrance to Foxford was along an old-fashioned, poor-
looking village street. The Moy in flood raced under a bridge.
With our eyes out for the Foxford rugs which had made the
place famous, we drove to the craft shop near the Sisters of
Mercy convent, just above the factory which the sisters started.
The window displayed only china, and when I asked the girl
inside why no rugs, she said she didn't know, she worked there
only in the summer. But the rugs were inside all right, classical as
ever, unchallengeable rugs. The shop had many other lovely
things, from cards and book-markers to pottery, all of Irish
manufacture. Anyone who hasn't been in a tourist 'souvenir'
shop in recent years has no idea how these things have
improved. You find some exquisite, Irish-made objects there
which you never encounter in your everyday shopping environment. We went down a lane to the Moy to look at the factory,
which was closed since it was Saturday. One would never
imagine, looking at the dreary, dilapidated building — perhaps
the same one that was built a hundred years ago? — that such

fine things came out of it. Swallows were darting over the river stealing flies from the fish.

A short distance beyond Foxford we saw Lough Cullin on the left, then, on the right, the great expanse of Lough Conn. Passing between them we reached the little place that is called Pontoon and went into Healy's old fishing hotel for coffee. Seated near the window of the dining-room we could see a stretch of Lough Cullin dead still in the lee of a hill. The sunlight, falling from an unsettled sky, showed the water luminous and leaden, and a patch of hillside very green. Then the light moved over the hillside and a touch of blue appeared in the lake. It was like a shot being set up for some celestial camera. With that surprise which Irish people sometimes experience when they travel in Ireland, I understood why an Englishman or a German, coming here to fish, would think this paradise.

Outside again, I removed the bike from the boot, said goodbye to Éamonn, and took the road for Lahardaun, under Nephin, about halfway up the western side of Lough Conn. In front of a piece of woodland a notice of the Forest and Wildlife Service declared 'Bird and Wildfowl Sanctuary. Hunting Prohibited'. It was raining sporadically. This was the road the French had taken in '98 when they marched on Castlebar. The vegetation was lush. There were rhododendrons, alders, elders, bracken, flowering briars, and many sorts of wildflower: besides the meadow-sweet, which I had seen everywhere, foxgloves, honeysuckle, purple loosestrife, wild roses — all the usual crew of late summer. A sign pointing in the direction of the lake, said 'Terrybaun Pottery', but I couldn't dally. A mountain reared up in front, the southern bulwark of Glen Nephin. As I passed it, and the wide mouth of the glen opened out, there was Nephin herself, sunlit in all her majesty, her summit veiled in white cloud; 'and quite properly', I thought, 'until I climb her'. I had been passing many fine, newly-built bungalows and spruced-up older cottages. All were roofed with tiles or slates, and some had white wooden fencing enclosing a lawn or garden. I recalled that the Foras Forbartha report on Irish housing in 1980 had found that the houses of the West Region — Galway and Mayo — were bigger, and in many respects of better quality, than those of any other region. At some point, I suddenly realised, stone walls had reappeared. The land did not look good, and I could see no cattle, only goats occasionally.

I had friends in Lahardaun whom I had not seen for a long time, and I hoped that one of them, or someone they would find, would provide a companion for the climb. With the ground so wet, the occasional showers, and the cloud on the mountain, I wanted a guide. But with these conditions of ground and weather, would they think me mad? The matter was soon settled because, when I arrived in the long village street of Lahardaun and went to my friends' house, I found it deserted, and a neighbour said they had gone to a wedding in Galway and would be away for the weekend. In the newspaper shop, I picked up a giveaway paper from Castlebar, the *Post and Advertiser*. On the front page, under the heading 'Death of Airport Priest', the face of Monsignor Horan was framed in heavy black.

In Lahardaun I was over a mile from the lake. Now as I cycled through Castlehill onto the high ground north of Nephin, I was moving farther away from it. At first, as I climbed, there was a new profusion of wild flowers: I noticed lady's bedstraw, tufted vetch and moon daisies, and there were luscious clumps of bird's foot. The *seileastram* or wild iris was abundant but not in flower. I passed giant ferns and saw my first fuchsia; and soon afterwards, at a farm gate, the first milk-can of the journey. Then, as I turned due west, and a strong, soft wind came against me, I was on a plateau of bog and there were occasional clumps of heather. It was the beginning of the bog of Erris, that wide western territory that stretched away to the Atlantic and to my goal. I entered a plantation of thirty-foot pines, and half-way through it the rain came down heavily and soaked me. I could have put on my rain-cape, but I decided to let the wind dry me. I was wearing a beret, a light khaki jacket, and linen trousers of the same colour.

Shortly after the trees ended, the contours began to fall, and I saw the immense, green plain of Erris reaching to the low Nephin Beg hills, and, northwards, where I must go, to the cooling-tower of Bellacorick power station. Turning right at Keenagh Cross, I headed for it, the cycling easier now because I was no longer facing into the wind. On the flat landscape, large rectangles, shaved to a brown bog colour, suggested machines. In the distance I saw a caravan and machines beside it. Under a clump of trees, the wind eased wonderfully, and a man was gathering a flock of sheep into his farmyard. Rain came and went and I was alternately soaked and dried again. At a shop where I shopped, I mentioned the sheep, and the woman asked 'do you watch Irish television?' She said the farmer who owned them had been on it in a programme on sheep-farming. 'Are you a local?' she asked. I asked how could I be. 'Some of the girls bring their husbands home and you never know.' She said I must listen to the musical bridge at Bellacorick. Just draw a stone along the top of it and it would make music.

On the straight road through this flat immensity, cars streaked past and I thought of films of the American West. On arable patches there were houses and cattle. Beside a river away to the left a lone angler plied the flood. A house protected by a shelter belt, with bright red and white outhouses, was selling shrubs. Then the cooling-tower, which I had been seeing occasionally ahead of me, wraith-like in mist against the horizon, came into view directly ahead, and I thought now at last. But I descended into a hollow, the rain came on hard, and when the road rose again, there was no tower to be seen; only, as I peered, the ghost of its upper part. Then, after another turn in the road, it was there again clearly, this time with the generating station at its base. I reached the Crossmolina-Belmullet road a short distance from it, saw a bridge, found a stone, and drew it along the top of the bridge. No music. I tried again. Cars passed and I wondered what their occupants thought as they saw me. Deciding that I just didn't know the trick, I cycled to the power station which had a fine plantation of trees, rhododendrons, and other shrubs in front of it; civilisation in the wilderness. The station runs on milled peat. Behind it a little train was standing, and a covered conveyor bridge extended upwards from the wagons to the power-house. Far out on the bog stood lines of wagons and the big machines that scrape the surface.

Just beyond the plant was a group of four or five houses and a shop cum bar. In the shop an old man, a big strong man, and an engineer from the station in his boiler-suit, were drinking. A fourteen-year old girl, whom they affectionately called Teresa, was behind the counter.

'Monsignor Horan will do something about the weather now', said the old man.

'Well, he's in the power station that controls it now', said the engineer.

35

'He was a great man', said the big strong man. 'If we had more like him in the Dáil, we'd do well.'

'I'd say there won't be much work done today around Knock and Swinford and Charlestown', said the old man. 'Well, isn't it well for him, he's being brought home to his own airport.'

'I saw that picture of him on the television,' said the engineer, 'walking off across the runway of the airport, and I thought he looked like any tinker, he could have been a tramp. He was a man of the people. They'll never find as good a man to replace him.'

Teresa said she went to school at the tech in Castlebar, twenty-seven miles away, though there were two secondary schools nearer, in Crossmolina and Belmullet. The engineer said the bog had been too wet to work, and last summer had been bad too, so they were very low on fuel and the power station wasn't operating. But they would be switching on one of the two generators again soon. When they were going full blast, the station produced enough electricity for Mayo and more. Asahi used to be one of their big customers, and when there were factories in Belmullet they had to put in an extra line for them. 'Are the factories gone?' I asked. 'Well, Travenol is — that was an American firm — and it employed three hundred. There's a couple of small ones still.' I asked them about the musical bridge, and they said I had been trying the wrong one — the musical one was just outside, I had crossed it coming from the power station. I would find a stone ready waiting. I went out, found the stone, trailed it along the top of the bridge — and it worked, there was music! It was a succession of hollow notes making a sort of wild tune. It was particularly good when it bumped over the splits between the stones and hit the next one.

I headed west on the Belmullet road, the broad Owenmore river running parallel on the left. The rain had stopped. There were sheep everywhere. Soon I was in a long winding pass between low hills. Emerging from it into another plain with more low hills beyond it, I entered Bangor Erris. I had always thought of it as something like a Wild West town à l'américaine, but clearly some 'development' had hit it. There were two newly-equipped petrol stations at the entrance, and a group of bright, new, white council houses, some with dormer windows, and some more new houses up a side-street. I noticed a take-

36

away cum restaurant called Sizzlers, offering fish, chips and burgers. It was no longer the desolate 'end of the world' I remembered. The street was packed with cars. There was a wedding in The Talk of the Town. When I entered a band was playing in a large room at the back, and a square of floor among the tables was full of couples dancing. A young man with the band was singing 'The Galtee Mountain Boy'. Two large murals showed an Atlantic bay and beach, and a mountain road with a lone donkey among dark hills. Most of the men were wearing dark suits and white shirts, and some had their jackets off. The women, many of them in white blouses, wore mostly pink, red or blue. Many men and women were wearing a white carnation. Vigorous céilí music came on. After some hesitation, and pairs of women dancing with each other, two groups formed for the Walls of Limerick, with more women dancers than men. In the front bar, where I sat down, a lad was chatting up two girls on holiday from Wicklow and Westmeath. 'What do you call a man who does all the housework?' One girl said 'hen-pecked', the other 'an eejit'. A poster in the porch said: 'Redz Night Club, Crossmolina. Every Thursday. Nostalgia from the 60s and 70s plus the very best of the 80s. Cliff Richard. Elvis Presley. Rolling Stones. Beatles/Supremes — and much more.'

I decided I could not make Ceathrú Thaidhg, still nearly twenty miles away to the north west, so I turned south west for Geesala and the comforts of Ostán Synge. I knew that with Denis Friel there as manager, and his wife Éadaoin visiting from Dublin, I would be in good hands. The flat road brought me past a Bord na Móna station with machines standing around. As I proceeded I saw it was a major enterprise with tracks running cross-country, warnings about 'machines crossing road', and even a regular level-crossing with a gate. Nephin, and the Nephin Beg range, were now off to the east. I had an edge-of-the-world feeling. Rhododendrons, fuchsia and meadow-sweet accompanied me. Light broke through a sky of heavy clouds; a sea inlet spread on my left; and on low hills and flat country appeared that rural density of houses which characterises and proclaims the western seaboard. As I approached the village of Geesala, the modern building with its two storeys of balconied rooms was unmistakably Ostán Synge.

Denis Friel attended personally to my dinner and I still relish

37

its succulent memory. I had been acquainted with avocado pears, but my encounter with them that night, drowned in prawns and a luscious sauce, began a love affair. The main course was a juicy steak of fresh salmon. Denis said the tourists were few because of the bad weather, but the local custom was booming. Later in the bar, where I met Éadaoin, I saw evidence of that. The music, provided by a trio, was country and western and ballads. The hotel had a Dónal Foley lounge in memory of the well-known Dublin journalist. Denis told me Foley had been a friend of the owner, Seán Gunning, a local man, who had built the hotel on the site of his family home. He had done so with the help of a Gaeltacht grant obtained for him by another local man and friend of his, Pat Lindsay, the politician who had given his name to the 'Lindsay Gaeltacht'. Gunning, an ESB engineer, was now in Vietnam reorganising the electricity system. Éadaoin pointed out a man to me who was a millionaire in England and who, according to local hearsay, had given his wife a Mercedes for her birthday. As I passed out into the foyer, a girl said, 'Excuse me, sir, this girl here' — indicating another girl — 'has been looking at you all night, she likes older men.' The girl referred to covered her face in her hands and ran. 'That was cruel', I said, 'you never know what might have come of it.'

Before going to bed I took a stroll outside. Just beside the hotel was the newish-looking Ionad Pobal [sic]. So it said over the door, and meant Community Centre, but I had heard people referring to it as 'the Complex'. It consisted of a hall which was sometimes used for indoor soccer, and a handball alley which was used for squash. A plaque in the porch said: 'This AnCO Community Training Project has been funded jointly by the Local Community, Youth Employment Levy, and European Social Fund. 1984'. A poster in the porch advertised the Geesala-Doohooma Community Festival. It offered, on successive nights, Doc Carroll and the Royal Blues, Liam Ivory Céilí Band, Rock Stewart and the Plattermen, Fast Lane, Let's Go Disco with B. Redmond, and Old Time Dancing with Breezy. Across the road from the Community Centre was a bar called The High Chaparral.

38

Sometime in the small hours I was awakened by the light going on in my room. Squeezing my eyes open, I saw a young man in underpants moving towards me. 'Who's that?' I groaned. 'The boss', the young man replied, smiling. But as he came to within a couple of feet, the smile vanished, he uttered a horrified exclamation and bounded away into the entrance passage. I heard him muttering to himself and making rustling noises, which I supposed came from putting on his clothes. 'Put the light out', I bellowed. He did and I heard him leaving. Considerably later, at a late breakfast, when I described him to Denis, I discovered that he was staying in the hotel with his wife.

The sun was shining splendidly when I accompanied Éadaoin and her three children by car to the beach at Trawmore Bay near Srah; not the main beach in the bay, but the one you reach through the sand dunes, facing south towards Achill. To the west across Blacksod Bay I could see the flat, narrow Mullet peninsula ending in a hill above Fallmore. But the spectacle was the blue mountains of Achill under great banks of white cloud. Recalling the view of Lough Cullin from Healy's Hotel, I thought, yes, indeed, Ireland is paradise. But after a cold swim, not being a beach person, I took my bike from Éadaoin's boot and cycled back to Geesala.

I should explain about the Lindsay Gaeltacht, which Denis had referred to when telling the story of the hotel. In 1956, when the Gaeltacht was being officially demarcated for the first time, Patrick Lindsay from Geesala was Minister for the Gaeltacht. For decades previously, governments in Dublin, in an effort to end the dire poverty of many Gaelic-speaking communities, had accorded them certain financial and economic benefits. They got £10 per year for every Gaelic-speaking child, larger grants than elsewhere for private house-building, special development schemes and so on. It was therefore a matter of some moment for people in and around Gaelic-speaking areas whether or not they were included within the new, official Gaeltacht boundaries. Pat Lindsay was reputed to have seen to it that considerable areas of western and northwestern Mayo which contained some Gaelic-speaking pockets, but which were mostly English-speaking, were included. Thus the term 'Lindsay Gaeltacht', meaning in effect 'pseudo-Mayo Gaeltacht', came into being.

When I surveyed the Gaeltacht generally in 1976, and published an up-to-date map of the real, as distinct from the official Gaeltacht, I found some small, disintegrating pockets of Gaelic speech in three places in Mayo, and a solid, though small, Gaelic-speaking community (including all generations) only around Ceathrú Thaidhg. Not only in Mayo, but generally, I found that, whether measured by territory or by population, most of the official Gaeltacht was English-speaking, and that the Gaelic-speaking communities comprised 29,000 people — as opposed to the 72,000 which was then the population of the official Gaeltacht. In recent years, some care has been taken to confine the financial benefits for persons living in the Gaeltacht to members of households which actually speak Gaelic — the commonest criterion being whether the children of a family have passed the oral test for the £10 grant. However, the Gaeltacht benefits tend to be exaggerated to mythical proportions by the inhabitants of neighbouring, non-Gaeltacht areas. Apart from the now largely symbolic £10 per child, the financial benefits today consist, essentially, of larger grants for the building of a new house (£3,000 as opposed to £2,000) or the improvement of an old one, and, in the case of a native Gaelic-speaker or a Gaeltacht co-operative, the payment of 66.6 rather than 60 per cent of the capital investment in a new industry. The only advantage accruing to an outsider setting up an enterprise in the Gaeltacht is a better back-up service from Údarás na Gaeltachta than is given by the IDA. An unfortunate result of the linguistic make-believe in the Lindsay Gaeltacht — and indeed, in other similarly circumstanced areas — are the frequently misspelt or ungrammatical Gaelic signs on public buildings, shops, workshops and so forth, which have been put up as appeasements to officialdom or to communal guilt by people who do not know Gaelic.

The landscape around me as I cycled back to Geesala was flat, gentle, and except when a car or tractor passed, infinitely quiet under the great dome of blue. The white or yellow houses, grouped in village clusters, or strewn around, were comfortable and well-kept. Cattle were grazing on what looked like good grass, and sheep cropped a low hillside. I asked a woman standing at her gate had the houses a water scheme. 'It's always being talked about, but it hasn't come yet. Every house makes its own arrangements.' But the Belmullet phone exchange — I noticed she had a phone — had been automatic for a year, and the Geesala one had gone automatic a few days previously. I passed a large state forest of conifers. This being Sunday, business or official vehicles of various kinds stood outside the houses of their owners or drivers: an ESB van, a school bus, a big lorry licensed as a carrier, an Isuzu car and van bought from a dealer in Sligo. Behind the hotel, in a Telecom Éireann depot, stood three vans with ladders on their roofs. Recalling the big Bord na Móna operation which I had seen the evening before, and putting it together with the state forest and all these signs of state and semi-state employment, I thought how similar it all was to a place like Geesala in an East European socialist country. Observing, moreover, the general air of material well-being, I felt a throb of admiration for the Irish state. Not so very long ago there had been dire poverty here.

Back in the crowded hotel bar I looked around me. They were not 'country' people as those around Swinford and the airport definitely were. They reminded me of Connemara people, and of Gaoth Dobhair people in Donegal: this western seaboard thing. They had an 'un-country' lightness; many of them, men and women, had a degree of physical and sartorial 'style'. They were urban people in the country, or rather rural people who had been touched by big cities and who moved easily around them. They were not, of course, and this underlay it all, farmers in any serious sense; nor, indeed, so far as I had been able to see, fishermen. I sat down beside three young men in attractive pull-overs and grey slacks, two of them with wavy, styled hair — one black, the other red. Wavy-black-hair, who was handsome in an Italian way, was expostulating about extra money he was being asked to pay for a flight to New York and Chicago. The third man (with straight black hair) was consoling him. 'But sure when you think of it, you'd spend the difference on a night out here.'

'Excuse me', I said, 'I have lived in Connemara and there's a question I'd like to ask you?'

'Why we're not speaking Gaelic?' wavy-black came back like a shot.

'No,' I said, 'it's that I see no quays or boats. Is fishing done here?'

'Up in Porturlin, a little in Belmullet. Go to Belmullet if you

41

want brought out.' Porturlin was over twenty-five miles away, near Ceathrú Thaidhg; Belmullet was eleven. They added, nodding to each other, that some salmon fishing was also done nearby from Doohooma and Tullaghan.

'What do people here live from?' I asked.

'Farming', said one. 'The dole', another.

'Don't you write for the *Sunday Independent*?' said straight-black-hair.

'I used write for the *Sunday Press*,' I said.

Across from me, red-hair smiled slyly, with satisfaction — another prying spy unmasked! — and they resumed talking about wavy-black's American trip. Straight-black wrote him down a (312) American telephone number.

Most of the cars outside the hotel were Cortinas and Toyotas, but there were also Volkswagen Turbos, Vauxhalls, big Renaults, and a few Mercedes and BMWs. I cycled to a cemetery on a hill looking down on Tullaghan Bay. There were black and white marble headstones, made mostly in Ballina, and some religious statues and Celtic crosses. Munnelly, Sweeney, Coyle, Collins, Monaghan and O'Toole, seemed to be the most common local names. In three of them I noticed the intrusion of Ulster which gets stronger as you near the North Mayo coast. Cycling farther along the road I saw an inlet some distance ahead with five currachs lying on the shore and a motor-boat anchored.

I returned to the village. Raucous pop music from Radio Two was blaring from the Community Centre. The local curate, who was reputedly a live wire in community matters, was just entering the building. By contrast with Dublin, where in work places and public places you usually hear some pirate station, RTE's second radio channel is often heard in Mayo. I entered the High Chaparral. In the porch I was greeted by a poster inviting me to get my shoes repaired by a cobbler on American Street, Belmullet. There were also posters for a '15k road race' and the Miami Showband. Inside, above the bar, three pennants were affixed; they bore the names, Harvard, Boston College, and some other Boston college or team. Behind the bar, alongside the usual GAA pictures and cuttings, were a picture of Manchester United, and one of Sraigh (see Srah above) United 1979. The red-haired chap who served me said that Sraigh United had broken up. 'They had to keep changing for every

42

match — some of the fellows worked in Dublin. Now there's an Erris team with many fellows from around here.' An old man sitting on a bench — he may have been the owner — said that the Manchester United picture was of the team who were killed in the Munich air crash. He had been in Manchester then and had known them all. On the counter there were collection boxes for St Anthony's Bread and two missionary orders. A large Glasgow Celtic flag was pinned to a wall.

The hotel bar was crowded again that night. I met an Irish businessman from Manchester with his English wife. She said she saw many more signs in Gaelic now than when she was last here. 'It seems the language is really reviving. I like that, I think it's good for people to have their language.' Local people, when I told them I was going on to Ceathrú Thaidhg, said 'That's where you'll hear the Irish' or words to that effect. They knew the score. Éadaoin said she had met Mícheál Ó Seighin from there in the hotel a fortnight previously, and that he sang very sweetly. I knew he did, music and song are his life; I hoped to stay with him.

I met P.J. Carey from Bangor Erris and discovered, when I mentioned Sizzlers — the fast-food shop I had noticed there — that he owned it, and had opened another Sizzlers in Killala. He was a stocky, corpulent man of about forty, with faraway eyes. He spoke about his efforts to get only the best potatoes for his chips — no frozen chips for him — and about how he made a point of having both shops open from twelve noon to one-thirty in the morning, with food available at all times, both in the take-away and the attached restaurant. He had been disgusted going into places in Dublin and elsewhere to be told that 'you'll have to wait till six o'clock' or that 'lunch is over'. 'I've got a factory in Belmullet making boxty,' he said. 'It's my latest venture. Packaged boxty. You must come and see it.' He said he would collect me next morning, bike and all.

P.J. Carey collected me in the morning and we took the Belmullet road. I told him I thought that boxty was a Scottish dish, perhaps an Ulster one: was it traditional here too? 'In the old days they made it here too,' he said. 'It's important to me that it's made from potatoes. There's nothing so basically Mayo, so basically Irish, as the potato. I thought it was important to do something with it, and with this traditional way we had of

43

cooking it. To give it a chance with the best modern equipment and good packaging. Already it's selling in Dublin and Belfast. I'm negotiating with outlets in England — at the Irish Food Fair in London people from many countries snapped it up. I'm playing on nostalgia.' I listened with fascination. They were unusual sentiments in the West, where the old and the traditional, because they are associated with poverty and lack of status, are generally held in less regard than in other parts of Ireland — and the potential of what lies to hand is usually ignored in favour of the imported product or the distant place.

He said that while the other three children of the family had emigrated to America, he had gone to England when he was seventeen. 'In England I had a greed for work, like all the others from here who went there. We knew what we were there for.' He took courses and got into civil engineering. When he had some money, he bought the Talk of the Town in Bangor for £6,000 and gave it to the manager to run. He was the first in the West with pool-tables, and later the first with gaming-machines; not only in his own pub, he put them in others too. As we drove past some low hills to the right, there was a sign pointing to Mínfhéir Teo. 'That was a semi-state company,' he said. 'They reclaimed tracts of land, grew grass on it, and made grass-meal nuggets for calves. Gave a lot of employment. Then we read in the newspapers it would be closing, just like that. Now Myles Staunton from Westport is moving in machinery to make peat briquettes. He's letting the land go back to bog.'

We turned west onto the Bangor-Belmullet road. 'There's a very good doctor in the hospital in Belmullet,' P.J. said. 'Dr. Kelly. He diagnoses better than many a specialist. People will often go to him, if it's something serious, rather than to their local doctor.' I said I had heard the richest GP in Ireland was in Erris. Could that be he? 'Maybe', he said. 'All the people around here have blue cards, of course, but when they go to a doctor they always like to give him something.' Belmullet, though it has only about a thousand people, looked a substantial town with a lot of new housing. P.J.'s factory, Beeseas Iorrais Teoranta, was in the industrial estate, in what had formerly been the canteen of the Travenol factory. It employed eight people. When we entered, the chef was ejecting blobs of boxty mixture — grated potatoes with flour, salt and water — from a tubular device onto two hot baking-trays. They could produce five thousand cakes a day. The chef gave me a bit of a finished cake to taste, and like all cooks, eyed me as I tasted it and pronounced it good. In an adjoining room women were packing the cakes into transparent packages which bore the legend '4 Genuine Irish Boxty. Staple Diet for a Nation' in a circle of Celtic design. The cakes were blast-frozen, as soon as they had cooled, then packed in fifteen minutes and put into a 20 minus zero store. P.J. gave me a publicity leaflet which contained a history of the potato and of boxty in Ireland, and assorted potato lore.

Back on the Bangor road, he said, 'Don't ask me what village or townland we're passing through, I never know. I have my eyes always on the road, thinking of how I could be using this time to make money. I have a dream of a turf machine that would slice into a bank, press the sodden turf into a drying chamber, and emit it as dried briquettes.' When he heard I had been in Japan, he asked me what he could learn from a visit there. I said the Japanese advantage in business came from their whole way of life and of working together. A person going there on his own couldn't transfer that to Ireland. To do that, you'd need at least a team visit. He said that reminded him of the Mannions of Belmullet and England who had a totally integrated business operation. 'There's about six of them, working tribally, applying resources where the need arises, helping each other out, accounting for every penny. In Belmullet, apartments, a dancehall, shops, in England, building filling stations and dealing in property.'

P.J. left me at the turn for Glenamoy. I could see the bare mountains around Ceathrú Thaidhg directly to the north, but knew I would have to detour inland around deep sea inlets to get to them. As I descended into Glenamoy, a great forest of conifers, flanked along the road by rhododendron hedges, gathered around me. I came to the deserted brown wooden buildings of the Glenamoy agricultural experimental station which in its time made quite a name for itself in the land. At the central building, with its pagoda-like roof, I could see through the glass door a sign 'Enquiries →', and scientific literature on display in a glass case. Somewhere near there I saw the second thatched cottage of the journey — the first had been near Swinford. At the end of the glen, where signposts pointed north to Porturlin, Rossport and Belderrig, I turned onto the first bad road I had encountered, and reflected, ironically, that it led to Mayo's only Gaelic-speaking community. Stones were showing through the tarmacadam and I bumped over ridge after ridge after ridge, just managing to avoid large potholes. The road climbed into wide spaces of mountain moor, with the bare mountains once more ahead. I stopped to ask a man at a turf-stack was there a pub near, where I might get something to eat, and he replied in a Lancashire accent that there was a pub ahead just below the church. Looking past him towards the coast I saw a long, narrow inlet. A short distance on I remarked to a woman walking her dog that the road had improved, and she told me in an American accent that she had been living there only since January. In Doherty's pub, below the church, there was accordion music, and a man drumming two coins on a table was giving an effective imitation of spoons. When I ordered a pint and a sandwich from the girl in pullover and jeans behind the counter, she said they didn't do sandwiches but she'd see what they had in the kitchen. Noticing her accent, I asked her where she was from and she said Chicago. She went into the kitchen and a short time later a man, whom I learned was her husband, emerged from there with a plateful of thick ham sandwiches which he offered to me and the other customers. Then I saw her out on the floor near the accordionist, standing still and smiling. He struck up a jig and she danced, flinging out her be-jeaned legs precisely. A man beside me asked me where I was from, and when I returned the question he said, 'Rossport — Ros Dumhach'. I understood the signal but remained silent. 'I suppose you don't know any Gaelic,' he said. 'Labhraim go leor Gaeilge,' I answered, and we continued in that language. I asked him what might seem a strange question in other parts, but which I knew was not strange in that enclave of mythological memories. 'Isn't there a sea inlet around here where the Children of Lir spent 300 years — what's it called? Is it that one down below us?' He said it was and that it was called Rossport Ferry. 'But in Gaelic?' He asked a man beside him who said, 'Sruth Mhada Con'. 'Gaelic is going in Ros Dumhach', said the first man, 'but I've never spoken a word of English to my own children'. I left, and as I was moving off with my bike a man who had followed me from the pub said, 'We were looking at you in there and wondering who you are. Where are you going?' I looked at him, shuddered at the mixture of suspicion and fear in his eyes, and walked past him.

At a signpost pointing right to Porturlin, I turned left through more open moor that rose on one side to a glimpse of cliff. If, I reflected, one didn't know what lay ahead here, one couldn't guess it, nothing suggested it. And then, after a couple of miles, where a signpost said Port a' Chlóidhe ahead, there it was on a hill to the left, Ceathrú Thaidhg, climbing into the sky. Children on bicycles whizzed down the hill past me, calling out 'Dia dhuit'. I recognised a Dublin accent and knew they were from a summer college.

I climbed into the sky, my eye fixed on a new-looking, square building which might be a church. As I came among the first houses, I saw two men, whom I took to be builder and house-owner, standing in front of a house on which work was being done, and they were discussing the job in Gaelic, the builder gesturing this way and that. On the brow of the hill I came to a wide, unkempt grass triangle. An old tyre and empty plastic sacks lay beside a casual pond of rain. There was a trampled pile of sand, and, over to the right, near what looked like an old school, a broken wall and a heap of stones. The door of a telephone kiosk hung open. To the left, away from the green, was P.J. Garavan's house. It had seen better days when it was a guesthouse, the Síghaoth, known for the young Germans and French who stayed there, working for their keep. Getting no reply to my knock, and seeing no sign of his shop, I examined a square, white, flat-roofed building which I had walked past. With its narrow closed doors, and small windows high up, it looked Middle Eastern and reminded me of P.J.'s sojourn in Bahrain. Gaining entry to it by a narrow side-passage, I found myself in a shop, and P.J. was standing at the counter talking to a customer. Tall, lean, fair-skinned and blue-eyed, he looked youthful despite his years. He said the shop had been burned down and it wasn't insured. This had been a dancehall. He invited me to have supper with him at seven-thirty.

I walked across the green to Mícheál Ó Seighin's house. He had come to Ros Dumhach from Co. Limerick as a teacher in

47

1962, married a Ceathrú Thaidhg woman, and been there since. Small, dark, intense as ever, he was in front of his house, busy, as on my last visit, with construction work. He brought me inside and I met his wife Caitlín again. Yes, I said, I would like to stay with them. When Mícheál heard I had been in Swinford, he said he had just been in East Mayo, looking for a fiddle, and had been talking to a lot of people. 'Fear ruled the countryside,' he said, 'fear of the pensions officer. One man told me he was only twenty years in that place, so he didn't know anyone of the name I mentioned, didn't know anyone around.' It appeared that Mícheál had taken to teaching traditional music in the surrounding country five nights a week in term time — fiddle, whistle, accordion, flute. He went as far as Bangor Erris. Getting to the point about Ceathrú Thaidhg, he said, 'It is dying as a Gaelic-speaking community — this is the last generation. I don't like that because I don't like belonging to a dying place, and it is not fair to my children. All they'll have to build on soon is bad English. I like English, but good English, not some picturesque *Playboy of the Western World* patois.'

I went for a walk up the road beyond the village towards the cliffs, smelling the turf-smoke with satisfaction. Besides Ceathrú Thaidhg, and Ceathrú na gCloch which is attached to it, there are two other villages in this Gaelic-speaking community: Port a' Chlóidhe and one called Cill Ghallagáin, whose whereabouts I had forgotten. Suddenly, now, I saw it on a hill beyond a deep dip in the road, its roofs and windows glinting in the evening sunlight. Their glinting drew my eyes to the golden disc itself, two-thirds of the way down the sky, a sheaf of its rays striking gold into the ocean. Gallagán is the name of the local saint, and if I am to believe Mícheál, it is one of the many traces in these parts of the ancient fame and influence of Balor of the Evil Eye. Behind the village there were cliffs, and, to the left beneath it, the pier of Rinn Rua. Out to sea the Mullet peninsula presented its broad, northern end. Inland, I could see up the length of Sruth Mhada Con, where the Children of Lir, changed into swans, spent a third of their 900-year sentence. I thought of Ferdia, Connacht's champion against Cúchulainn, who was from hereabouts, one of the ancient Fir Domhnann. Erris, in Gaelic *Iorras*, means a promontory, and I was sceptical of people's strained attempts to show that the territory which is called by this name is a promontory. I was convinced, looking across at the Mullet, that it was the original Iorras, and that the name had later extended inland to cover a wider area, much as 'Connemara' extended, in the nineteenth century, far beyond its original confines.

I had supper a couple of evenings with P.J. Garavan, and one stormy, wet night, contrary to his wont, he went out with me to the pub, where I talked to some of the men and enjoyed their Gaelic. A blend of Ulster and Connacht Irish, it is less adulterated with English words than the language of more accessible Gaeltacht districts, and has a somewhat archaic or classical quality. When P.J. gave me a taste of the local *poitín,* it struck me that it was the first *local* drink I had drunk on my journey. In Ireland today, local drink, like local radio, is illegal. We are ruled by an antagonism to the local which is also an antagonism to diversity and a zeal to impose monotonous uniformity.

P.J. talked to me about the old days when his father started the shop. He used get his goods in by boat from Sligo. When he ran short he would go with horse and cart to Belmullet for supplies. He was the first in those parts to buy a ton-truck. P.J. left home at seventeen and worked in Bristol and London. He spent four years with Standard Oil in Bahrain, and another year working in the States, before settling, finally, in Ceathrú Thaidhg and taking up where his father had left off. 'There was no public lighting then, no electricity, no bathroom or tele-phones — it was like Siberia,' he said, 'like an open prison.' There were no bedrooms for visitors, so he started the guest-house. He got a drink licence in the early '60s, but lost it in 1975 when the authorities found he shouldn't have one. He was the first to get a twin-engined motor-boat, but couldn't get anyone local to operate it, so he employed an Englishman for a time, and then had to sell it. With Harry Corduff he agitated about the state of the roads, refused to pay road-tax, spent three days in prison. He tried once to get elected to the County Council. 'Things *have* improved,' he said, 'but that's mainly thanks to BIM. All the new houses are built out of fish money. There was a time here when there was a premium on dirt — if you had a dunghill in front of your house you got most, if you put in a window the rates went up. Now everyone's trying to build a

49

house bigger than his neighbour's. People are becoming house-proud, they want shrubberies and flowers. Many of them have central heating. Still, it's unfair that running a car costs as much in a place like this — where you must have one — as in a city where it's a luxury.' As he spoke, I thought of the desolate 'village green', and the phrase 'private splendour, public squalor' came into my mind. I was not surprised, when I asked him was there a community council, that he said there wasn't. Most people, P.J. said, would support Fianna Fáil, but they were fed up with politics. Many were Republican. Back in the early '70s, 'when everyone was for the IRA', 300 IRA men had been trained in batches of twelve on his land. I asked him had he any regrets. 'I can't understand Ireland,' he said. 'To get anything done is such a struggle. Looking back now I regret I didn't stay away — I could have made more money and come back and built myself a fine house.'

Across the green, P.J.'s brother had opened a shop four years before. Beside it, in the old lace-making school, there was a woollen goods factory which employed twenty women, and which was being run successfully by a Dubliner. Down a road descending steeply from the green towards the sea was a factory called Potiasc, making lobster-pots out of iron rods covered with plastic. It had been started, Mícheál said, by a 'Ballina gangster' who, after a couple of years, 'went on the run to Spain', and it was then taken over by a young Longford man.

'The Irish', Mícheál said, 'are like North American ghetto Indians. They were beaten and they've never recovered from it. But at least the Indians are great at bingo. They've become multi-millionaires from bingo. American laws don't apply in the reservations, so they set up bingo games just inside the border. The Irish, if they were any good, would have made bingo a major industry. Of course, I'm being unfair. I know we're limited by belonging to the capitalist system — while we do we must accept its standards and do things its way.' That brought us to discuss capitalism and its opposite, whatever that is. I told Mícheál I thought he was too harsh on 'gombeenmen' and that he had a puritanical aversion to money-making itself. It seemed to me that for a life of any quality to exist — morality, art, culture — there had first of all to be *life* — crude energy, ambitious barons of a money-making or political kind, and that the immorality inherent in this was mysteriously necessary if you were to *have* those higher things, which were in fact refinements of that living raw material. Out of apathy, non-life, death, nothing came. He took the point and said he was not against money-making if it benefited others besides the money-maker. 'Of course the quality of life is all that matters, and for that you need life. Ideology produces nothing of itself, or rather, what it produces depends on the intellectual and cultural quality of the life. That shapes the ideology, not the other way around. I know that.'

Caitlín Uí Sheighin took me on a drive to Porturlin. The harbour was in an opening in the cliffs at the end of a bleak valley. Eastwards along the cliffs towards Belderrig was desolate country with no road. Houses, some of them unfinished, were strewn out along the valley's sides. I had an impression of people attached, crab-like, to the hillsides and scuttling down to the gap in the cliffs to wrench a living from the sea. There were about sixteen motor-boats of various colours. Caitlín said they fished salmon, cod, lobster, crabs and mackerel, and sold to dealers from Donegal, Geesala and Dublin. Most of the people in the valley were on the dole. 'But isn't it obvious that they fish?' I asked. 'That has to be proved in each individual's case', she said. 'Oh I know', she added after a pause, 'that people go on about the dole being abused. But whatever about that, I wouldn't see it go — I remember too well the grinding poverty of meagre subsistence living.' (I heard later from a social welfare official in Ballina that sometimes two or three boats are registered in one man's name, and he has about four men of a crew in each boat.) Talking about Mícheál's work with the fishermen's co-operative and on other fronts, Caitlín said with conviction, 'He has made people here stand up for themselves.' On the way back out of the valley, she pointed out Sranataggle, a huddle of houses with smoking chimneys off to the left on the open moor. 'A lot of people there', she said, 'came home from England and are making a good living out of sheep. There's a lot of commonage.' I looked and thought to myself: what do those people know or care about Dublin, or Irish politics?

A word about the dole in rural parts. For obvious reasons its administration in rural circumstances is more complicated than in towns and cities. Until recently, moreover, besides the two standard forms — unemployment assistance and benefit, both based on means tests — there was a 'farmer's dole' paid to owners of farms with low valuations. This no longer exists. In the summer of 1986, benefit and assistance were being paid, in the country as in the towns, to unemployed persons who were 'available for work, fit for work, and actively seeking it'. Benefit was for men and women, previously employed, who had paid PRSI contributions for specified periods. For obvious reasons, many seasonally-employed small farmers and fishermen could not qualify for this, but might be eligible for 'assistance' — paid to single persons and married men. Apart from pay-related benefit which lasted for fifteen months after cessation of employment, the maximum benefit for a single person was £41.10 per week, for a married person £67.70. The maximum long-term assistance for a single person was £35.50 per week, for a married man £61.30. Clearly, under these and other heads, various social welfare payments could be coming into the same house. The maximum old-age pension for a single person ranged from £45.75 to £53.45. There were also benefits arising out of injury at work, and disability benefits paid when one was disabled for some other reason. In the less prosperous areas it was common enough for a family with three 'adult' children to be getting £80-£100 a week in social welfare; but the income to one house could, occasionally, be as high as £200.

Porturlin, Caitlín said, had 'never' been Gaelic-speaking, but she remembered when Gaelic extended almost to Glenamoy, and she had seen it retreat from there. 'One bad effect of the Lindsay Gaeltacht was that it made people around Ceathrú Thaidhg cynical about the Gaeltacht thing, when they saw people who did not speak Gaelic getting benefits as if they did — sometimes more than themselves.' Driving up the hill into Ceathrú Thaidhg, she named the *bailte* as we passed them on both sides of the road: Féachán, An Cnocán Mór, An Cnocán Rua, Pollán, An Baile Thall, An Pháirc Bhán. I asked her to stop at the new church, so that I could take a look at it. It was a white square building with a window running around the top of the wall. A wider block of black roof extended above that. The entrance and the sacristy were in a white rectangular block protruding in front. A plaque on the wall said in Latin that the first stone had been laid by Thomas McDonnell, Bishop of Killala in 1974. Remembering what Mícheál had told me about the unwillingness of the Church to provide services in Gaelic, as it did in other Gaeltacht areas — he told me of a priest who had stated to the people 'I can speak Irish but I don't like saying my prayers in Irish and can't be forced to' — this odd use of Latin, in the post-Vatican Two era, seemed to be the Church's way of evading the language issue. Inside the porch there were notices on a board in English, and a little plaque asking prayers 'for the souls of Patrick and Bridget Naughton, Carrowteigue'. The interior was very handsome. Altar table, separate tabernacle pillar, and lectern, were all in white marble, and were set off against a red back-wall. The other walls were white. On the front of the lectern hung a red cloth showing a stylised dove and the words 'Come Holy Spirit'. At the back of the church, with entry from outside, were two lavatory cubicles.

We drove on through the village, through Cill Ghallagáin on its hill-top, down past the harbour at Rinn Rua, and were returning through Ceathrú na gCloch, when I saw a stone shine a short distance from the shore. The inscription on it read: 'This shrine was erected at the request of the late Sgt. Michael Henry, US Forces and formerly of Stonefield. Go ndéanaidh Dia trócaire air.' A short distance on, we stopped again at the summer house of Séamas Ó Catháin, a folklorist from UCD. Like half the male population of the district, he was doing something to the house, but he took us into the kitchen where I met his Swedish wife. Through the window they pointed out to me the house of David Goldberg, a painter son of Gerald Goldberg, the Cork solicitor. A neighbour, Jimmy Bournes, who was visiting them, told me that his ancestors had owned much of the land thereabouts, and he went home and brought back a book to prove it. When I remarked to Séamas that the people of Ceathrú Thaidhg seemed to have little sense of their language rights as Gaelic-speakers, and did not use their language for public writing, he showed me a poster, in a sort of English, advertising 'Rinroe, Carrowteigue Sports'. It included under 'track events' a 'Married Mother's and Father's Race'. We fell to talking about the relationship between the West and Dublin. With a shrug of his shoulders that said 'Sure what's the use of bothering?' Séamas told a story of successful mental coloni-sation. He had occasion when in Dublin to telephone Geesala and asked the operator to get him a number there. 'Would you repeat the name?' she said. When he spelt it for her, she said, 'Oh *Gee*sala!', using the emphasis on the first syllable that is typical of placenames in England. 'The people there call it Gees*ala*,' he said. 'Well, we call it *Gee*sala,' she said. Then, when she got through to Geesala exchange, he heard the girl there answering '*Gee*sala'.

That night the *Western People* arrived from Ballina. Under 'Outsells the combined totals of all other Mayo papers' and 'The Leading Journal of the Irish Provinces', a heavy black headline said 'West Mourns a Giant among Men'. The Monsignor's body had been brought back to the airport on the Aer Lingus plane St Jarlath, and was greeted by six thousand people. The *cortège* bringing it the nine miles to Knock had taken an hour. It was to be buried 'today' after mass concelebrated by fifteen bishops and 250 priests. RTE did not broadcast the burial service, and since Connacht has no radio or television service of its own, it was not broadcast. That night the nine o'clock RTE television news opened with a report on the burial of an RUC man and went on to tell us what Mrs Thatcher had said about sanctions against South Africa. When it did get, in fourth place, to Monsignor's Horan's burial, we heard that the Cardinal had presided at the mass, and that 500 priests had concelebrated. The emphasis in the report was on 'the man who succeeded in having an airport built on a boggy hillside'. Who, we wondered sarcastically, was the unsung hero who 'succeeded in having Shannon Airport built on a marsh'?

When I told Mícheál I was going on to Belderrig to visit an archaeologist, Seamas Caulfield, Mícheál described him as 'a mate' and said that since he had discovered those ancient field patterns near Belderrig, he had found that they existed all over northwest Mayo. Next morning, Caitlín, who was taking a child to a dentist in Belmullet, gave me a lift as far as the crossroads at Glenamoy.

In a pub in Belderrig I was put through by phone to Seamas Caulfield's father, a retired schoolmaster, who told me that Seamas was in his house down by the sea giving a talk to some people and would be leaving with them shortly. His house, I discovered, was literally beside the sea. Rectangular, and of cut stone, it stood at the head of the shingle almost within reach of the spray from breaking waves. I hadn't met Seamas previously: Michael Gibbons, a young archaeologist from Clifden whom I met in Dublin, had advised me to visit him on my tour. I had heard of the ancient fields discovered in North Mayo, but hadn't been aware until then that the UCD archaeologist who discovered them actually hailed from there. I found him showing slides of his excavations to two women and two men, one of them a priest. He put me sitting with them and continued. I gathered that the priest and the two women belonged to the cultural-exchange party from Birmingham that was visiting Ballyvary. The other man was one of their hosts.

When he had finished showing the slides, Seamas took us in his van, in teeming rain, to see the first site he excavated in Belderg [*sic*] Beg, near the village. Under the cutaway bog, we saw pre-bog walls standing on the original surface, and the stump of an old pine tree whose roots were resting on the original soil but not penetrating into it. This suggested, Seamas said, that the tree had drawn its nutriment from a thin layer of bog which began to grow when the site was for some reason abandoned. The tree had been dated by the radiocarbon method to around 2900 BC, so, allowing a hundred years for the thin growth of bog, the walls must belong to a farm laid out before 3000 BC, over five thousand years ago, in the New Stone Age. Nearby we saw how, when the site had been abandoned, the bog grew up almost to the tops of the old walls. The forest returned. Then, about fifteen centuries later, Bronze Age farmers reclaimed the land and built new enclosures, partly with stone, partly with oak posts. Perhaps they were copper-miners — there is a seam nearby. We saw one of their enclosures where the oak posts had been dated to 1500 BC. The tillage plots, with the original ridges, were still visible. But the *pièce de résistance* was a circular house with its base wall of earth and stone still intact. Remains of internal posts were found, suggesting that the house had been roofed with rafters standing on the base of earth and stone. We saw the central flagstone; probably a fire had burned there with a hole in the roof above it for the smoke. Since no domestic material was discovered in the house, Seamas surmised that it had been used as a granary. A number of saddle querns, together with the rubbing stones used for grinding, had been found in it.

We drove back to Seamas' house and he gave us coffee. Then, with some zest, as if he were really enjoying himself, he did something he must have done with groups of students he brought to Belderrig. He showed us around the house, insisting that we look into every room. There were four bedrooms, kitchen, bathroom, and sitting-room. Then he asked us, and fastened on me, which of the rooms I would imagine was about the same size as the ancient house in the bog. I opted for the largest bedroom, then switched to the sitting-room which was the largest room of all. Laughing triumphantly from having pulled it off again, Seamas told us both houses were virtually the same size — 710, 720 square feet. All right, I said, feeling properly fooled, but the arched roof in the bog house would take considerably from the standing room. Seamas's house had been a fish-processing factory. It was set up as a result of Maud Gonne's visit to poverty-stricken Erris when she was in Mayo rallying the people to celebrate the centenary of 1798.

Seamas' father came in while we were talking, a powerfully-built man of eighty-three. Son of a schoolmaster himself, he had married the daughter of a Cornish coastguard and had many relatives in Cornwall. Seamas told us how his father had written to the National Museum in the 1930s, telling them about stone walls that were being uncovered under the cutaway bog. When Seamas in turn became a schoolteacher, he had got a post in Kildare near Dublin so that he could attend night classes in archaeology in UCD. Later, a trained archaeologist, lecturing in UCD, he went back and excavated the site his father had written away about. The enclosed fields he discovered were a thousand years earlier than any that had previously been found in Europe.

His father and the priest from Birmingham got to talking about spirits. Master Caulfield told of an eerie experience he had had during the war when, as a Local Defence Force man, he was out walking the coast at night. All of a sudden he had felt himself, unmistakably, in the presence of evil. Gripped by deep fear, he continued walking. Then he passed through a gate and the fear left him. There was an old *piseog*, he said, about a spirit not being able to follow you through a gate or over a stile. 'What does your theology tell you, Father, about that sort of thing?' 'Not my theology', said the priest, 'but my experience, tells me that there are wandering spirits — people prevented from getting to heaven, stuck between earth and heaven, because of a grip that the Devil had on them in life.' 'Do you mean something like purgatory?' I asked. 'No', said the priest, 'it's not the same thing at all. Sometimes the Devil forces them to lodge in a living person.' Should I say that we sat for a moment silent, listening to the waves breaking and the water rattling through the shingle?

We did; then the visitors from Ballyvary left us, and the Master took his leave. Seamas had intended leaving immediately for a wedding in Dublin, but he very kindly delayed his departure to show me some other things. We drove five miles east along a coast of very high cliffs. Sheep pursuing choice grass often get stuck some distance down them, and the men who look after them have to be skilful operators on the cliff face. At one point the road took us around a deep cleft in the land, which was the break, Seamas said, between the hard, Pre-Cambrian rock and the softer carboniferous shales. Beyond it the cliffs weren't compact and gnarled, but layered, and sloping inwards at the bottom. Dr Bob Collis used have a house there where he brought Seán O'Faolain and Frank O'Connor to stay; later they stayed with Master Caulfield in Belderrig.

At Céide, where Seamas had his other main site, the road touched the cliff-edge and an iron barrier guarded the spot. In a U-shaped chasm of whitish rock-wall, falling sheer to the distant water, seagulls wheeled at middle-distance. We clambered into the sodden, boggy fields on the landward side of the road. Here, for the most part, the bog — I was going to say Erris bog, but by now we had passed into another ancient district called Tirawley — still covered the ancient field-patterns. Tops of the old stone walls showed through here and there, but most of the archaeological exploration had had to proceed by driving long rods at intervals into the ground and plotting the course of the walls by the length of penetration. The pattern that had emerged was of immensely long, parallel walls extending inland roughly at right-angles to the coast — following the contours of a hillside — and cross-walls connecting these at intervals so as to form large fields. The people who had farmed there, Seamas said, had cleared the forest first. We looked at an oval stone enclosure where he had excavated and found the postholes of a small circular hut. There had been some pottery, flints, and a stone axe; and charcoal from a hearth had been dated to around 3200 BC. Seamas was willing to show me a court tomb, but I said I thought we had been mad enough: not only was the ground sodden, but the rain was falling continuously.

'The people in those days', said Seamas when we had got into the van again, 'used live on hill-tops. So they had a wider view, in every sense, than the communities which came after them and lived mostly in valleys — because the heights had reverted to bog. It takes an effort of imagination to see this countryside as it was before the bog took over most of it — probably it was much like ordinary farming country today. Before we did this work here it was supposed that Newgrange was built in a forest clearing, that the area around it was "wild". Now that's questionable. But they can never explore the old field-patterns in Meath. Here, because of the bog, there's a fossilised ancient landscape, five hundred square miles of it. There was a different approach to capital investment in Meath and here. There they built large tombs and didn't have walls — they had hedges. Here it was stone walls plus tombs, so the tombs are smaller. There was a vast expenditure of labour on walls. Indeed this wall-system gives you a new view of the "archaeological artefact" — a whole landscape. Or were the tombs smaller here because they were more "down-to-earth", less religious, than the people in Meath? In both cases we know nothing of their religious beliefs except that they believed in an afterlife. But the boundary between religion and politics is so tenuous. A larger tomb might mean more importance given to the afterlife, or it might mean a display of political power and prestige. Large tombs are "concretised labour" — what a man can command.' He had a vivid way of describing ancient economics and technology. At the house, talking to the group, he had spoken of the wall networks as 'herding by automation' and a means of 'reducing current expenditure'.

Seamas dreams of an interpretative centre somewhere on this coast — something like in Kilfenora in County Clare — that would bring archaeology, folklore and geology together. 'You saw that iron barrier there at Céide', he said, 'where you get the view of the cliffs. Everyone stops there to take a photograph and drives on. They've no idea what they're missing.'

We stopped to look at a standing stone, probably pagan, on

which Christian crosses had been carved, and again, to look from the van at Ballyglass tomb behind a farmhouse. At a restaurant called Doonfeeney House, run by a Mr Busby, an Englishman, who had been chef for a while in the Asahi canteen at Killala, Seamas ordered a meal for later. Then we skirted Ballycastle to drive out to Downpatrick Head.

That name is one of several pointers to a connection between St Patrick's mission and North Mayo. That he should have come here is not surprising when one takes into account Bishop Tírechán's testimony in the seventh century — he was a native of the region — that the wood of Foclut was in these parts. Patrick tells us in his *Confession* that he worked as a slave near that wood. Downpatrick Head is a massive headland sloping upwards towards cliffs. About half-way up the slope, in wind and rain, we came to a large square hole with a fence around it, and looked down to the toiling sea far beneath. It was evil and frightening. There is a legend that the pagan god, Crom Cruach, had his fire on this spot, and that when St Patrick threw his cross into it, the fire burned this hole. Crom Cruach then retreated to Dún Briste, a three-hundred-foot pillar of rock with grass growing on top, which rears up out of the sea a short distance from the headland. In the aftermath of '98, when the redcoats were sweeping the countryside, local men hid on a ledge at the bottom of the hole, linked by ropes to the surface. But the redcoats stayed longer than expected and a stormy sea drowned the men. Some years ago a woman and her three children fell in. That was when it was fenced. We moved higher and stood near the cliff-edge, looking across at Dún Briste. Seamas said that the annals recorded the collapse of a fort on it in the fourteenth century and the rescue of thirteen people. He told me of his exciting descent onto it, with two others, from a helicopter — each time one of them jumped, the helicopter, being less burdened, rose higher! They spent a night there, and in the morning, when the helicopter returned and landed, a large woman emerged from it declaring, 'I wish to point out that you are trespassing on my land.' It was all fascinating, even thrilling, but I was terribly conscious, as he spoke, of the vast drop a couple of feet away, of the wind and rain beating me . . . and of swaying.

It was very good, then, a short time later, to be sitting in

Doonfeeney House, eating avocado with cooked ham and pineapple, and beef deliciously filled with oysters, and drinking beer. We had already greeted T.K. Whitaker who was sitting with family and friends at a neighbouring table. He used occasionally summer in Cárna in my time there, but had deserted it for a house somewhere near Bangor Erris. I brought Seamas back to Newgrange and probed him on what I knew was a hot matter in Irish archaeology: the theory put around by Swedes, who had excavated and carbon-dated the great collection of neolithic tombs, and the shell midden, at Carrowmore near Sligo. The Swedes held that these tombs, far from being an outcrop, so to speak, of the Boyne Valley culture that had spread across the Central Plain, represented the earlier stages of a culture that had spread from Sligo and culminated on the Boyne. They had their Irish supporters, in Sligo and in UCC, but UCD, I had heard, was solidly against; so I wasn't surprised when Seamas answered sceptically. He said they had started from a dating theory based on tombs in southern Sweden, and had pushed too hard, on shaky evidence, to uphold it. 'But I don't really want to get involved,' he said. 'I'm not a tomb man, I'm an agricultural archaeologist.'

He gave me the keys to his house by the sea. He had arranged by phone with his father to pick me up at the restaurant and drive me there. It must have been around ten when he finally set off for Dublin.

3.

BELDERRIG
TO BALLINA

EXCEPT for the deep defile, where the Pre-Cambrian rock
was separated from the carboniferous shales, the road to Ballycastle was easy enough on a bike; and it was downhill into
the town itself, which is a bit inland. Then the main street rose
steeply to the top of a hill. I noticed that the Ulster surnames had
disappeared, that there was a Protestant church, and that Bible
quotations were posted on lamp-posts. Not having seen the *Irish
Times* for some days, I asked for one in a shop where other
Dublin papers were displayed, and was told 'Maybe in Polke's
down the street, though I think they might only keep a few for
certain people. But try'. Of seven vans from Ballina and Sligo
that were parked along the street — including a mobile Ulster
Bank — five were Japanese and two Fiats. A poster in a window
advertised the Ballina Agricultural and Industrial Show. 'Class
competitions include horses, ponies, cattle, sheep, goats, dog-
show, farm-produce, horticulture, cookery, crafts, flower-show.'
The sponsors included Martell Cognac, Ulster Bank, two insurance companies, the *Western People*, Odlum's Flour, and Brother
Sewing Machines. The street did not have a real *town* look
because the houses were not 'of every colour', as is typical in
Connacht and Irish towns today. They were restricted to grey,
white, cream and yellow — the colours of farmhouses — as if
Ballycastle did not want to separate itself, town-like, from the
surrounding countryside, but to show its kinship with it. Did this
make it a 'country town'? It was more a village really, but still
town-like because of the absence, for miles around, of anything
near it in size or stateliness. On the outskirts there was a group of
new County Council houses, strikingly attractive, as much of the
new local authority housing is.

I took the inland road towards Killala Bay and after some

61

miles turned into side-roads looking for the Breastagh ogham stone. I came on a farmer loading bales of hay onto a cart, and in the field beside him was a group of large stones protected by an official notice. 'What's that?' I asked him. 'Some class of a monument, that's all I know', he said. No, he said, there was no name for it. Occasionally, now, I could see Killala Bay, and in the distance, on the other side of Sligo Bay, Benbulben in mist. I found the Breastagh stone in a field a short distance from the road. It stood, it seemed to me, about eight feet high. A notice on it said it was probably a Bronze Age standing stone that had been inscribed between 300 and 600 AD, centuries after it was erected. One side was indecipherable. On the other side it read 'Mac Corrbri Mac Amloitt'. Seamas had told me that last name, Amlott, was the known historical person from whom Tirawley (Amlott's Country) had taken its name. The chipped strokes on the edge of the stone were clearly visible. It was the first ogham stone I had seen *in situ*, and those cut strokes brought me very near to the man who had stood there making them over fifteen hundred years ago. They were the Irish voice beginning to speak in writing.

Cycling on in the direction of Killala, I thought I might look at another antiquity marked on my Ireland West map, and I asked a man coming out of a lane where it was. 'I've no idea', he said, 'never heard of it. I just know there's old things around here but I know nothing about them.' Killala appeared ahead, clustered around its fine round tower that had a church beside it. Having heard so much in recent years of the big Asahi factory at Killala, I expected to find the town transformed and booming. But it looked stunted and unhappy with itself, a mixture of delapidation and tawdry newness. One of the first sights that met my eyes was two electricity poles, complete with fittings, lying in nettles near a gaunt, ruined store with rows of gaping windows. The poles with fittings amazed me until I remembered hearing that the town had had all its poles and wires removed from the streets for the filming of *The Year of the French* some years back. It is the only town in Ireland with all its wiring concealed. Not far away I came on a freshly-painted pub called The Village Inn, with a bright-red cartwheel standing on one side of the door and a palm-tree on the other. Inside, a bellows and a horse-shoe, which looked as if they had never been used, hung on a panel on the wall, and a saddle and some harnessing were displayed. I supposed all of this was meant to give a 'country atmosphere'. But the coffee was only 25p and the Corkwoman behind the counter was most obliging with information. Attached to the Inn was a premises called The Fiddler's Green. It advertised a Monster Disco for Saturday night 'with Top DJs'. On the footpath beside the Inn were two rusted petrol pumps that had long ceased functioning. The houses and shops of the town maintained the 'country colours' I had noticed in Ballycastle.

I walked around to have a look at the round tower. The small church beside it turned out to be the old Church of Ireland cathedral. Two German tourists were trying to get into the round tower which was about twenty yards away behind a locked gate. 'To gain admittance to Round Tower, contact caretaker next door', said a notice. The next door was the red sliding door of a workshop; it had 'Ireland Needs Fascism' chalked on it. In response to my knock an old man emerged and explained that you could only walk around the tower. 'You can't get in. There used to be wooden floors and stairs but they've fallen.' The Germans still wanted through the gate. 'Well,' he said, 'the second thing is you have to pay 20p.' 'Why?' I asked. 'Isn't it a national monument?' He began to tell a long story about how the key used to be in the Garda station because they couldn't get anyone to look after it, and then he had taken it. 'What need is there of a key?' I asked. He said there was a right of way to the tower which he claimed.

Leaving the Germans to do as they pleased, I walked across the street to an old Georgian house with a view of the harbour, which I took to be the house where Bishop Stock had been made a house prisoner by the French in 1798, and where he had kept a diary of those events. I could see eight fishing boats at the pier, and nearer, just below the house's well-kept garden, eight attractive holiday cottages. I climbed the steps to the open door, and a woman who appeared in the hall told me the house no longer belonged to the Church, and was not the house where Bishop Stock had lived, but the old deanery. Killala had long since ceased to be a Church of Ireland diocese, it had been incorporated into Tuam; and since the last dean died five years ago, it was no longer a deanery either, but was looked after by Dean

63

Graham in Crossmolina. But the house had a connection with '98: it was being built when the French ships arrived, and workmen on the roof who saw them thought they were English.

Before leaving Killala I called into P. J. Carey's second Sizzler's in the hope of tasting some of those chips made from his own potatoes which he was so proud of. But the girl said only the Bangor Erris shop had them; they used frozen ones. I had some cod which I'd say had been frozen too. But with its small restaurant next door it was a stylish premises. On the way out of the town I was amazed, as so often in the West, by the sheer size of some of the new houses I passed.

The Asahi factory is up a new side-road about two miles south of Killala. Being a great Japanophile, I was excited at the thought of meeting this 'Little Japan' in Ireland. So my disappointment was great when I found the flower-beds in front of the office-building in a state of neglect and disarray. Don't they realise, I wondered, that everyone coming here knows how well they do that sort of thing in Japan, and expects to see something of it here? When I told the girl at the desk I would like to speak to one of the Japanese managers, she said the only one who was there was busy, and two others were away in Ballina. Then, as I stood there, one of these came back; but his English wasn't really up to a conversation and I felt I was frightening him by attempting one. Michael Honan, an Irish director, emerged and saved the situation. He explained that they changed the Japanese personnel fairly frequently so there were always Japanese there who didn't know much English. The one I had been talking at departed smiling, and Michael and I sat down for a chat.

Asahi, one of the leading Japanese producers of chemicals and synthetic fibres, has plants in twenty-five countries. They began production near Killala in 1977. If nearness to the EEC market, and the financial inducements of the IDA, were the principal reasons for the choice of Ireland, the practical reason for choosing this particular site was the availability of water to draw from, and of other water for the discharge of effluent. Between three and four million gallons of water are brought every day from Lough Conn, six miles away, and the effluent goes into the middle of Killala Bay. The factory makes an acrylic fibre called Cashmilon, exports 95 per cent of it in tow form, and spins the remainder into yarn suitable for knitting. Once a day a special train brings the finished products to the North Wall in Dublin, and returns with supplies of a liquid chemical called acrylonitrile, a derivative of crude oil, which is the principal raw material. There were difficulties initially because of the relatively high costs of oil, electricity, and transportation. 'The east coast', said Honan, 'is on the periphery of the Community, and we here are on the periphery of Ireland.' They found they were over-manned, and reduced the work force from 460 to 330, while at the same time increasing production. This brought a period of upset in labour relations. 'The management got depressed for a while, but they were extremely committed and they won through. In 1983 they drew up a survival plan, and since then, but especially during the past year, the business has become profitable.' It was at the survival-plan stage that Honan came to Asahi, from Clondalkin Paper Mills, as its first Irish executive director.

'I'm surprised', I said, 'that it doesn't really seem to have impinged on Killala. I thought the town would have been transformed.'

'It has grown a little,' he said, 'but the truth is it would have benefited more if it had been between the plant and Ballina. The Japanese live in Ballina, and most of the work force are from the Ballina area.'

'How did the Japanese take to Ireland?'

'They loved it from the start — the sense of openness and freedom, the wide open spaces, the ease with which they could fish or play golf. They were surprised at the lack of discipline. When their first general manager was leaving, and there was a party to mark it, he was asked, "What's your most important memory?" and he said, "How people who are so nice and lovely individually can be so disagreeable collectively."'

We took a walk through the immensely long building that housed the manufacturing plant. We passed great machines and piping systems, working with low noises, or silently, in empty or almost empty halls. I saw the acrylonitrile, which had been mixed with catalyser in reactors, emerging as a white, liquid acrylic polymer. Dryers extracted the moisture so that it became a white powder, which was then dissolved in acid so as to form a syrup. This, pumped through a plate containing many small holes, emerged as filaments of raw fibre from which the wool-like tow was made. In the spinning plant the tow was processed, reduced in thickness, and spun onto cones of single and two-ply yarn.

Michael Honan himself lived in Ballina. When I asked him about hotels, he recommended the Belleek Castle because it was on my way into the town, was furnished with exquisite care, and was pleasantly situated. He talked about shopping in Ballina, and once again, as in Swinford, I heard of how the supermarket chains — Quinnsworth and Dunne's, but even Tesco in Sligo, thirty-one miles from Ballina — were hitting the town's old-established businesses.

I returned to the main road and turned off it to join the old Killala-Ballina road nearer the bay. This is Bohernasup — *Bóthar na Sop*, the road of the straw-torches — so called because, when the French marched on Ballina by night, the countrypeople lit their way and the sight was remembered. Here, in the shelter of the bay, there was once again a 'normal' profusion and variety of wildflowers such as I hadn't seen since that sheltered stretch of road near Lough Conn, between Pontoon and Lahardaun. I was looking for Moyne Friary which the signposts would doubtless call 'Moyne "Abbey"', with inverted commas around 'Abbey', as I had already noticed on other signposts to ruined religious houses. The point is that such ruins are generally referred to in Ireland as abbeys, regardless of whether they in fact housed communities ruled by an abbot or abbess — I suppose the habit was acquired from England during the Romantic period — and the learned gentlemen who write the texts for signposts want to show they are fully aware that, in many cases, the appellation is wrong. Why don't they simply use the correct word — friary, priory, or whatever? No one would complain, and all would be in order.

A parked car from France alerted me and, sure enough, just beside it was the sign as I had expected it would be. It pointed towards a gate beyond which, as far as one could see, lay a muddy mess. Untying an adjoining gate, I walked up a dry boreen into a farmyard of utter squalor: trampled mud, ruined outhouses, empty plastic containers lying around a rusting wrecked car. A sad grey house, its back to me, looked deserted except for grey-white washing hanging on a line. Striking out valiantly through the mud, and over a broken wall, I entered a

66

field and saw the French party coming towards me. 'Allo', they said. 'Vous l'avez trouvé?' I asked, but they passed, smiling enigmatically. And then I came on it, in really fine condition, set within a fence that had a wooden stile for crossing it, and with black bars closing most of its doors and windows. Close at hand, on both sides of a rushing stream which issued from what seemed like the privy, a reconstruction in stone suggested a simple mill. I went around the building to the front entrance, crossed through the roofless nave, and in the cloister found a plan of the friary, indicating chapter-room, kitchen, refectory and so on. Built about 1450, and burned in 1590 by Sir Richard Bingham, governor of Connacht, it had the simple, austere beauty of the Observant Franciscans. Climbing the square tower to the top, I surveyed the bay with its sand-dunes, saw the white houses of Inniscrone across from me, and the bay narrowing southwards towards invisible Ballina.

I hoped to visit Rosserk Friary also — a foundation of the Mendicant Franciscans, built by the Joyces and burned by Bingham — for it was said to be the finest Franciscan building in Ireland. The map showed it on the water's edge, a couple of miles further on. But when I came to the turn I realised it would be quite a detour, and a glance at the declining sun made me decide, reluctantly, to head for Ballina.

It is the biggest town in Mayo, with a population more than six times that of Swinford. The Belleek Castle Hotel was situated in a wood beside the river opposite a suburb of the town that I later learned is called the Quay. Through the trees I could see small boats moored. An eighteenth-century manor house, gothicised in the nineteenth century, the hotel has been given its 'castle-style' interior by its present owner, Paul Doran, a rich hotelier and businessman who lives in the Channel Islands. The castle style has been done well, with fine old chests, tables, tapestries, four-poster beds with curtains, suits of armour and chandeliers. After booking in, I cycled down the long drive to the front gate — I had arrived by the side-entrance — and found myself in the town. It had the bustle, and the multi-coloured look, of a real town. But bunting strung across the streets took from their appearance. Put up for the Moy Festival three weeks previously, it had that wind-blown, tatty look that bunting left too long gets.

On Upper Garden Street, a small, working-class crowd was gathered in front of a house, waiting for a plaque to be unveiled to James Wallace Melvin, founder of the Stephenites, the oldest Gaelic football club in Ballina. There were speeches from a club official, Seán Healy, and from a member of the Urban District Council. Mrs Garroway, who lived in the house, was thanked for donating the wall, and Mrs Gillian for making the 'veil', in green and red, which was pulled back to reveal:

> This stone marks the residence of James Wallace Melvin, founder of Ballina Stephenites, Aug. 1886. Erected by the club, Aug. 8th, 1986, to mark the centenary.

In Mullins' newsagent's, not far away, when I mentioned I had seen the unveiling, the woman behind the counter said, 'All sorts of things have been happening in town'. When I asked her what else, she said 'Humbert's statue has been removed because it was a traffic hazard. It's to be re-erected in Bohernasup.' That's the part of the town where the road enters. A customer buying a paper said, 'A caving in to the motor-car'. She said the town had had two good weeks because the rain had driven all the caravaners from Inniscrone and Easky into Ballina. I saw the *Frankfurter Allgemeine, Le Monde*, and the *Herald Tribune* among the newspapers. 'Someone in the crowd told me there's a book about the Stephenites,' I said. She said it was sold out, but she had a thumbed copy which her son had been reading, and I could have a loan of it for a day or two to look through.

It was a fat book, called *The Goal of Victory*, written by Terry Reilly, managing editor of the *Western People*, and printed by the paper. In bed that night I read:

> A gentle summer breeze is blowing. It is the last Saturday evening in August of 1886 and James Wallace Melvin emerges with a sense of purpose from his house on Garden Street. 'Where are you going, Jemmie?' enquired P. G. Smyth, well-known author, editor and manager of the *Western People*, and County Board GAA President. 'I'm going out, Patsy, to start a club that will shake all Ireland' . . .
> Contrary to local public opinion, the Ballina Stephenites GAA Club was not the first to be established in

the town. That honour fell to Ballina Commercials, who formed probably late in 1885. Castlebar Mitchels were founded in December of that year and it is likely that movement was made in both towns around the same time, if only to provide opposition for each other.... For some reason the Commercials club decided to limit its membership to persons who were engaged in commercial pursuits, thus barring all those who lived by manual labour. Unwittingly, this limitation of membership was to prove the club's downfall.... It was then that a few got the idea of establishing a club to be composed of working men, yet open to any others who wished to join....

Melvin and his supporters held their first meeting at Barney's Boreen, at the top of Convent Hill. The Crown Forces were most active in the country at the time and 'illegal assembly of the disaffected', as the British termed it, was prohibited. That was why they chose not to hold their first meeting in a private house. It must be remembered that they were naming the club after the Fenian leader, James Stephens, for whose head, before that time, the British Government had offered £1,000 . . .

The original Ballina, and most of the modern town, are on the west side of the Moy. Ardnaree, on the east side, was incorporated at the end of the last century, and from Ardnaree the town extends down the river past St Muireadach's Cathedral towards the Quay and the grand houses beyond, looking down on the estuary. To the south, the green dome of Nephin dominates the skyline. The town has a telephone directory and a street-map, two signs, I always feel, of urban self-possession. Or at least you can get a street map on a card in Padraic's Restaurant on Tone Street. The central streets proclaim republicanism: besides Tone, Lord Edward, MacDermott, Teeling, Kevin Barry, Pearse, Connolly, O'Rahilly and Casement. There are three trains daily from Dublin via Claremorris. The biggest employer is Hollister, an American pharmaceutical firm.

Michael Keohane's bookshop on Arran Street had one of its windows given over to *Lucky*, 'Jackie Collins' raunchy new blockbuster now in paperback'. In the other window was a poster for the Sixteenth Annual Éigse Mhic Fhirbisigh, or MacFirbis Historical Week-end, in Inniscrone. It offered Ecumenical Prayer (at the opening), a talk on 'the Irish political system in crisis', Irish music by the Donagher Family and Friends, and a lecture on 'The Lecan Scribal School under Giolla Íosa Mac Fhirbishigh c. 1390-1418'. I bought a copy of *Lucky*, for purposes of research, of course. Michael Keohane, a cousin of a friend of mine in Galway, said that books on Royal Weddings, do-it-yourself books, and books about TV series, sold well. 'The best-sellers in the *Bookseller* are best-sellers here. It could be mid-town America. The only difference is you sell a lot of poetry.' There was a shelf of religious books — mostly prayer-books with a couple of Bibles and a book on Lourdes. We talked about the old shops in Ballina that had been closing. Like Sligo, but to a lesser extent, Ballina once had a strong Protestant business community. 'The big chain stores', said Michael, 'are destroying the whole fabric of commercial life in the West'. (I discovered later, and it struck me as symbolic, that Humbert's statue was moved because of the traffic generated in its immediate vicinity by Dunne's Stores). Emigration was under way again. *Getting into America* by Howard David Deutsch was another of Michael's bestsellers. A girl assistant in the shop said, 'Most of the crowd I grew up with are over there — ten out of fifteen. It makes you lonely.'

'Mayo Boardsailing School', said a poster on Tone Street. 'Join Ireland's fastest growing sport. Sites at Lough Conn and Westport'. Looking at the people, it occurred to me again that Mayomen use the pot belly and the drooping belt as proc-lamations of success or of male self-assertion. The shops had smart clothes, but it was difficult to spot a woman who looked well-dressed: was it their walk or their smallish stature? The woman serving me in a pub said she didn't know of any Irish music in the town except at the Riverboat on the Quay on Tuesday nights — the McAndrews Family. 'The town isn't much good for Irish music', said a man, 'though it isn't that there aren't people who want it. The McAndrews and the McNultys are fine, but they're young, they need to be older to have refinement.' In a music shop called Hot Stop, most of the music on display was country and western. Mick Leonard, the owner, said most of the pubs preferred three-pieces playing country and western or pop. There was no Irish music apart from the Riverboat. 'You might have an "Irish Night", but that would generally mean just ballads.' He was the DJ in the rugby club, where there was a 'big scene' on a Saturday night.

That evening I went out to James Stephens Park, the GAA grounds. It is a fine field, with a large stand, and advertisements around the field and on the stand. In the spacious, well-kept club-house, downstairs, there were changing-rooms for men and women, and courts for handball and racket-ball — an American game, I was told, which has been taken up in recent years. Doors had bilingual signs thus: *Cistin* (Kitchen), *Teach Ól* [*sic*] (Bar). Upstairs were the main drinking lounge and the Ballina Stephenites Squash Club with two courts. On the wall opposite one of the courts hung three framed sheets of rules, with illustrations, 'officially approved by the Squash Rackets Association'. The rule-sheets, I read in small print, could be had from an address in Hatfield, Hertfordshire.

In the lounge I found Seán Healy sitting with some older men. 'The book is splendid', I said, 'but I haven't time to read it all. Tell me the club's history in a few words.' In thirteen successive years, he said, 1904-16, they won the senior county championship. In those times the clubs in a county fought it out among themselves and the winning club represented the county. In 1908 the Stephenites won the Croke Cup for Mayo. Then from 1916 onwards special county teams were formed. In the '20s, the Stephenites won the county championship frequently, and later, occasionally. They opened James Stephens Park in 1933. In 1949 Ardnaree, across the river, hived off to form its own team. The clubhouse was opened in 1973, and extended in 1980 — the year they visited America. In 1984 they put up the stand and held a Welcome Home Week for teams from Australia, America, Scotland and England. Twice, in 1978 and 1985, they hosted the GAA Congress.

When I said I didn't see many young people around, one of the older men said, 'We don't really compete in the Saturday-night scene. Teenagers wouldn't come here because they know they wouldn't get drink. And we don't allow discos.' He said their dances, when they held them, were 'old-time and ballroom'. Seán explained: 'It's sport we're into, and our support in the town ebbs and flows according to how the team do. This year

71

we've had a bad year. Last year, when we were doing well, you'd see three to four thousand people attending a *practice* in the park. Many people are away in summer. In winter the squash courts are active all the time and the bar is crowded.'

Back in the Belleek Castle, I had a chat with the manager, Tommy Fitzherbert, who belongs to a well-known Navan family. He had started out in partnership with Henry Mount-charles in a restaurant in Slane Castle before coming as chef to the Belleek. He showed me the museum collections which his remarkable employer, Paul Doran, kept in the hotel vaults: European armour of all sorts, cross-bows and other weapons; toby-jugs and various kinds of drinking vessels; and an amazing collection of fossils that included huge snails from the bottom of the ocean, crabs, sponges, shark's teeth and a mammoth's tusk. In the small, candle-lit dining-room, with panelled and pale red walls, I had sliced avocado and smoked salmon with lemon and dill sauce, for starters. The four-course dinner menu was priced at £12.50 plus twelve and a half per cent. Passing the television room afterwards I heard that forty-seven men had been charged in Belfast as a result of disturbances on the anniversary of Internment. A car-bomb had exploded in Strabane, and Keady had been battered by a loyalist mob. In the drawing-room, which had very comfortable seating — despite, shall I say? for it isn't always so, the 'castle' effects — an American man and woman were playing lutes. After a selection of English Renaissance music they gave us Carolan pieces. Men and women of the local business and professional bourgeoisie, dressed casually or grandly, sat listening and applauding.

Later that night, besides the disco at the rugby club, there would be discos, I had gathered, at Tingles and Pearls, and the Basketball Club would be running one at Rasputin's in the Beltra House on Pearse Street. In Molly Maguires, on the riverside, a Dundalk rock group would be performing. We, in the Belleek Castle, were to have the best-known local musical talent, a rock group called Mother Hubbard.

It took place in the cellar. Big logs blazed in an enormous fireplace and several refectory tables stood at right-angles to it. Beyond them was an empty square of floor with a bar to one side, and, at the end of the room, the five-man band getting ready on the platform. Psychedelic lights flashed their changing patterns from the ceiling. The young people arriving were in their late teens and early twenties. Some sat at the tables, others stood near the bar. Two of the musicians wore black sleeveless vests; one of them, an American, baggy, clown's trousers. They began predictably, with much loud noise and raucous singing, emitting anger, frenzy, menace. A solitary be-jeaned girl lured a boy onto the floor and they disco-danced for long alone. Then the band changed to slower music and the floor filled with couples moving slowly, hanging on to each other, moving their hands. Then it was fast again, the menace was back, but a number of couples stayed, and others, arriving, joined them; and the floor became covered with gyrating and gesticulating bodies, in a variety of clothing from the stylish to the sordid, making no pattern, forming no semblance of sequential dance, but rather, of a witches' sabbath from some Wagnerian opera. But gradually, surreptitiously, the band grew in strength, and a strange eerie sweetness began to come into their music though it was as loud as ever — a sonorous organ-sweetness. And gradually they seemed to tame the floor, bringing a harmony into the movements, so that the crowd became like a swirling animal with the group on the platform as its head; and some of the dancers in front knelt to the band, raising and lowering their arms with the music. Then there was a flash and a puff of smoke on stage, and a pause as the American in the baggy trousers ran to one side holding his hand in pain, and one of the black vests turned his back to us. Then, slowly, the music started again, rising in waves to a sounding swell, and there was another flash, and smoke drifted into the hall, dimming the coloured lights, and the two American lute-players were out among the dancers, he in a long, loose-sleeved pullover, head down, swinging his limp arms like a rag doll, and she dancing daintily in front of him, her eyes down, or twirling away from him. And it was all sound and all dance, and the voices were part of the sound, and the bodies on stage and the bodies on the floor formed one physical chorus.

Coming from Dublin, I had been finding the Mayo culture strange. As it presented itself, kaleidoscopically, it seemed at first to be simply Irish-American culture extended into Ireland.

Certainly it is more American than Dublin culture is; the older English elements in it, which are common to all of Ireland, have been pushed into the background by its up-to-date American overlay. (Cycling through Ballina, and noticing no other cyclists except children or occasional Continental tourists, I recalled motorised America where only children ride bikes. When I did, finally, at the other end of a street, descry a man cycling, I actually took out my glasses, as on the sighting of a rare bird, to make sure that I was seeing right. Later, I'll admit, I did see some other adults cycling.) But the strong living connections with England, and the fact that Mayo people at home are involved in Irish, not American, politics, make the description 'Irish-American' unsatisfactory. What Mayo culture is, in fact, I think — and the same may be true of other parts of the West, but I am talking about Mayo — is an Irish/American/English amalgam which Mayo people have so shaped that it is both *their* culture, and one which they can have equally, and be at home in, in Chicago, Mayo or Lancashire. It is a culture, in other words, shaped to fit the facts of their life during the past hundred years. Catholicism, country and western music, 'old-time and ballroom' dancing, the *cúpla focal* in Gaelic, all these play bonding roles in it; but its central institution, in which all its elements meet, and which contributes to the common culture its most strongly and distinctively *Irish* mark, is the GAA. I even heard how the GAA is facilitating the new wave of emigration: young men getting a place on a team visiting the US, and then staying on as 'illegals'. Certainly it would be a foolish Irish politician who would undertake anything in Mayo that was disapproved of by the GAA.

St Muireadach's Cathedral, begun by Archbishop MacHale and finished in 1893, is a tall cruciform neo-gothic church, fronting onto the Moy between the two bridges. Coming up to eleven o'clock mass on Sunday morning there were about 250 cars parked outside it. In the porch I read that there was a vigil mass on Saturdays at 7.30 pm and four Sunday masses. The *Universe* and the *Irish Catholic* were on sale. Alongside notices about pilgrimages to Knock and Lourdes, and about centres in Ireland and Britain where emigrants could get assistance, there was a list of 'parish organisations': Parish Council, St Vincent de Paul Society, Legion of Mary, Catholic Boy Scouts, Catholic

Marriage Advisory Council and so on. Inside, the cream and red running up the great ribbed pillars continued across the ribbed roof. All the windows were of stained glass. One, beside me, showed, surprisingly, Saints William, Henry, Elizabeth, and Francisca Romana — in memory of Francis Devanny. But, of course, I said to myself, the family Christian names. The confessional in carved wood bore an intimidating notice: The Bishop. He was saying mass. There were some mass-leaflets lying around, but most people were not following the readings, and the reader was only intermittently intelligible. A girl sang the antiphonal verses, responses included, while the people either remained silent or answered with ragged murmurs. The Bishop, reading the Gospel, could be clearly heard. He preached on the virtue of faith and its difficulties. At the Communion a young woman in a 'diaconal' garment came and stood beside the Bishop's box, distributing the hosts. Meanwhile the girl sang hymns from the lectern, very sweetly, sometimes attaining the heart-rending quality of a boy tenor. 'That I may be the channel of your peace' — those words, sung in her voice, I took away from that mass with me. After the closing blessing and dismissal, spoken in Gaelic, we poured out towards the waiting collection-boxes of Fine Gael. Besides the Irish papers, most of the English Sunday papers were on sale, but especially *News of the World, Sunday Mirror* and *The People*.

The sun was shining as I cycled off along the Moy to get a good place at the jazz session in the Riverboat. Since my days in Galway, when Chris Dooley's All That Jazz played, first in the Great Southern, later in Twinks on the Salthill seafront, jazz on a Sunday morning is one of my delights. This too would be a waterfront. I passed the salmon-fishing stretch of river, a large children's playground, the municipal tennis courts 'presented by the Soroptimist Club, Ballina, 1968', and the sign pointing to the Golf Club. At the bridge across the Bunree, with the Downhill Hotel off to the right and the Boxing Club ahead, I turned left past the Anglers' Club and 'Boats for Hire' into the riverside village of Crocketstown that terminates in the Quay.

Jack Ruane and his boys were tuning up in the Riverboat. Who in Ireland, or in the Irish centres in England, in the '50s and '60s, hadn't heard of Jack Ruane's Orchestra? It was the first Irish dance-band to tour in the States. Jack is the father of

Judd Ruane, owner of the Riverboat. Judd's wife introduced me to him, a white-haired, fine-featured, blue-eyed old man. 'You've spent a life-time in music', I said. 'And loved every minute of it', he answered. 'Oh I was very despondent back in 1977 when the band broke up, but that only lasted till we started the jazz here.' One of his sons was with him in the jazz band. They played a mixture of Dixieland and Blues, with occasionally a bit of pop. The upstairs lounge filled, the usual Sunday-morning family parties. I should have said something before now about the children, all those little people, who had been giving me their smiling, confident 'hellos' along country roads, by riversides, on village streets, or who played pool with me in the back-room of the pub in Belderrig. From the age of three or four upwards they stared at the jazzmen with wonder, and led the clapping. I watched Jack Ruane playing the clarinet, after fifty years in music; swaying into the music as he played, his devotion like that of a monk at the Divine Office. The brother-hood of music: anyone putting that tube to his lips to play a piece made well known by other musicians is brother to them, and knows it; is playing to them, and for them, in his own mind.

I went out to the riverside wall to listen to the jazz with water. Up river, beyond the town, Nephin stood guard. Near at hand, on the quay, were old warehouses. A man standing at the wall told me the port, once a busy one, had been reopened the previous year for a man who imported coal from Germany; he brought in a load, then absconded. In the pub again, I got to talking with Judd Ruane's brother, Harry, who was on holiday from Galway where he worked with the American computer firm, Digital. When I told him I was sorry to have missed Rosserk Friary, on the way into Ballina, he said he'd take me to it by boat that afternoon — he had been thinking of going fishing.

I went to lunch in the Downhill Hotel, which was full of family parties, many of them from the North and Dublin. One of the attractions seemed to be facilities for sports and games; it had everything from sauna and jacuzzi to squash courts and table tennis. In the dining-room, which looked out through big windows onto the Bunree river, I liked the flurry and abundance of the service staff and their liveried hierarchy. There were two women in red blouse and black skirt, several girls in striped

76

blouse and mauve skirt, two in white blouse and black skirt, and a boy in striped shirt, violet waistcoat, bow-tie and short striped apron, carrying a folded cloth on his arm. According to their dress, they put down or took away plates, presented the bread basket, opened bottles and so on. I had avocado with ham and cheese. Coffee was served in the lounge by a boy in white shirt and black trousers, but I took my coffee in the new cool-coloured, split-level bar, looking out on the garden. This was Frogs Piano Bar, which I had heard about, and should have mentioned when I was talking about Ballina on a Saturday night.

Back at the Quay, Harry Ruane fixed an outboard engine on a boat and we set off baywards on the dead calm river, helped by a strong pull from the outgoing tide. Looking down on us were the mansions of Quay Road. After twenty minutes Rosserk showed up on the west shore, a square tower over peaked roofless walls. We tied up the boat at a seaweed jut of stones which may well have been the friars' pier, and reached the friary after a short walk. It was almost intact except for the roof. Once again there was a chart of the building in the cloister, which didn't have a covered walk as at Moyne. The chapel windows had graceful traceries and there was a small sculpture of a round tower — that of Killala? — to the right of the altar. On the way back to the Quay we had some trouble from large pieces of rubble that had been washed down the river, Harry told me, by the flood waters.

On the afternoon of the following day I took a bus to Sligo in a thunderstorm.

4.
SLIGO VIA DROMAHAIR TO BOYLE

SLIGO, with a population of 18,000, more than twice that of
Ballina, is the biggest town in North Connacht. If being distinct
from the country in atmosphere and manners is what makes a
town a town, then Ballina has that quality to a relative degree,
and Sligo absolutely. Whereas in Ballina, in the quieter streets
away from the centre, people bid you the time of day, in Sligo
this does not happen. You can see girls in Sligo with that
washed-out look which you find only in towns. The young man
in the newspaper shop has a defensive, aggressive edge to his
voice which implies that your custom is a purely formal matter,
of complete indifference to him, and that he could just as easily
be driving a Ferrari down the *autostrada* from Florence to Rome.
Many buildings are in cut stone or weathered red brick; there
are fine civic and ecclesiastical edifices, and banks that look like
temples of commerce. Some of the brightly-coloured streets
present a fine ascending perspective or capture a framed vista of
a tower or spire. When the river is in spate, as it was when I was
there, the foaming brown water, making a curve that is bridged
at both ends, binds the central streets together and gives them
brio. True, the lack of green spaces — though compensated for
somewhat by the riverside walks — takes from the town's
amenity; but it also intensifies its urban atmosphere. Sligo, in
short, insofar as the frontal aspect of its streets is concerned, is a
very handsome town. But I enter that reservation, 'frontal', for I
also saw the huge car-park off Wine Street, which has been
created to cater for a couple of supermarkets, and which adds to
its own intrinsic desolation ugly back-views of several of the
central streets. There is everything to be said for keeping supermarkets, with their consequence of hundreds of parked cars, at a
far remove from handsome town-centres.

Talking of cars, before leaving Dublin to catch the plane in Manchester, I had asked a friend to drive my own car to Sligo and to leave it there for me. I knew that, in the month to five weeks I had at my disposal, I would not be able to cover all of those great Western distances at bicycle pace. But for the present I left the car where it was and cycled to the docks.

Sligo, earlier in this century, was a busy port and the acres of dockland bore witness to it. I passed stores of timber, flour, whiskey, coal, and a few small industries, and came to the deserted quays. They are situated at the head of a deep inlet that is sheltered, towards the sea, by a bund-wall on the docks side and, on the far side, by the promontory leading to Rosses Point and Coney Island. Directly across from where I stood, the newer sections of the town extended towards Benbulben. On a sand-bank in the middle of the harbour seagulls were sunning themselves. A trawler from Dublin lay against the quay. Two mobile cranes stood idle. Piles of containers lay beside a railway siding. I walked towards a man who was moving bales with a forklift and asked him what was that fine white house standing on a promontory opposite us, and surrounded by a lawn and trees. 'It used be a Protestant girls' school', he said. 'Then it was a sanatorium. Now it's a health centre with dentists and people like that. That low building further over there is the Regional Technical College and that's the Tech and AnCO beside it.' I had already recognised the Technical College from its dreary ugliness, like the one in Galway which I knew. He remembered fifty years ago when Sligo was a busy port. He had even seen sailing ships coming in. 'There used be a weekly passenger-boat to Glasgow and Liverpool which called at Ballina and Westport. Cattle were exported, corn came in. Now you get the odd ship with coal or timber.' But they were building an oil terminal at the 'bundy-wall', and dredging up the silt; that would mean more traffic. Apart from the port, they'd had about twenty good years in Sligo until a few years previously. Since then work had become scarce. Five hundred jobs had gone with the closing of SNIA, the Italian firm that made nylon. Abbot Laboratories, an American firm, were the biggest employers; eight hundred worked there. 'But things will improve', he said, 'when they begin on the new four-lane bridge and the dual carriage-way to Ballysadare and Collooney. And there's to be a £37 million

79

extension to the General Hospital.' I stood in awe of his knowledge of his town, and I admired him, shifting crates around a quay that he had known for fifty years, for his self-possession and his buoyancy.

Signs in the docks pointed towards the Finisklen Industrial Estate, and there was something I wanted to find out. In the pub in Swinford the salesman for machines and parts had mentioned that Sligo was 'the centre of the Irish tool-making industry'. I had assumed for years, when I heard 'tool-making' referred to in an industrial context, that it meant making hammers, chisels, pliers and so on. But I had begun to doubt that, and I wanted to clarify the matter.

In the IDA office on the industrial estate, the manager, Éamonn Howley, clarified it rapidly. The 'tools' referred to in tool-making are, essentially, moulds and dies used in the mass-production of objects, such as door-handles, lamp-stands, telephones or car fittings, that are made from plastic or soft metal. But they are not merely that, for with the mould or die goes a support system allowing it to be fitted into a machine, fluid material to be injected into it, and so on. As for Sligo being the centre of Irish tool-making, yes, that was true, and it had happened for a historical reason. After the Second World War, James Gallagher and his brothers, from Tubbercurry, twenty-two miles south west of Sligo, established a successful building business in England, and wanted to do something for their home town. So they set up a factory there making door and window fittings. But this factory used 'tools', which needed to be maintained and repaired, and there was no tool-making factory in Ireland; so the Gallaghers set up one of their own in Tubbercurry called Tool and Gauge Company of Ireland Ltd. That was in the mid '50s. 'Tool and Gauge', as it is referred to, was the seminary from which the tool-making industry in the Sligo region developed. In Sligo town there are now three tool-making factories and one design firm for the industry. Besides Tool and Gauge, South Sligo has two other factories, and the industry has spread out to implant itself in Charlestown, Ballina, Roscommon and Carrick-on-Shannon. Sligo Regional Technical College is the national centre for tool-making apprentices, and the local AnCO centre specialises in tool-making.

Mr Howley made a couple of phone calls and arranged for me to visit Stet, a tool-making firm on the estate, and later, Techno Design, the design firm. He walked with me the short distance to Stet, introduced me to the managing director, Andrew Cullen, and left me with him. Mr Cullen said that Stet employed thirty and worked mostly for the motor industry; but they also made moulds for telephones — he showed me one for British Telecom. He was especially proud of a tool they had made for a firm in Louisiana to produce a gadget that blew leaves off lawns. They sold to Ireland, Germany, England, and had done well in the USA when the dollar was strong. Tool-makers, Mr Cullen said, used to be all-rounders, doing all the different jobs — milling, turning, sparking, fitting. But since computers came to be used a lot, and machines were invented to do the particular jobs, workers were becoming specialised either as machine-programmers, as operators supervising the programmed machines, or as fitters assembling all the machined parts. 'And the factories that use the tools are being automated too. The perfect arrangement — and it is coming — is a robot operating a tool to make telephones, door-handles, lampstands or what have you. The robot doesn't have a tea-break, go to the loo, or stop to give someone a light, thereby letting something heat a fraction too much. There's better work and more production.'

Pondering on this vision of the future, I walked over to Techno Design and met Pádraig Neary, who is joint owner with Oliver Cawley. Both of them 'graduated' from Tool and Gauge, where they had been designing. 'Each tool', Mr Neary said, 'requires a specific design, so there is a high design content in the industry. The theory requirements are principally maths, especially trigonometry, and an understanding of mechanical drawing, so you can read drawings. The design element in a tool has three aspects. Aesthetics, which is not our business. That it functions as it should — we're involved in that a little but it's not our speciality. That the "part" — the product the tool makes — can be manufactured economically: that's what we specialise in.'

After what I had heard at Stet, I was not surprised that he was soon talking computers. 'The Japanese are excelling in computer-aided tool-making, and Irish tool-makers must move further in this direction to keep up with them. But computers are also making big inroads into the design end of things, and we have had to take account of that. Three years ago we bought a computer for a quarter of a million, a big investment, and we're put to the pin of our collar to make it pay. We have now employed a chap who specialises in the programming. The quality of Irish tool-making is acceptable and the price OK, though without much profit, but we are behind in delivery times, partly because of management methods, but also through under-computerisation as compared, say, with the Japanese. And delivery time is all-important, for products today often have a short life on the market. So there's constant pressure to shorten the time it takes to get a product from initiation to sales. And tooling is a significant part of that process.'

He said the main Irish exports were to the States — especially in the previous year because of the dollar rate. US sales normally comprised 60 per cent of an Irish company's work, and it was much the same for English and German tool-makers. 'The Americans don't do much tool-making themselves, but import a lot from Europe, especially Portugal, and the Far East — Korea, Japan. Since the '60s, Portugal has developed tool-making into its third export. A tool-maker there gets about £250 a month, in Ireland about £200 a week.'

'But isn't it a disadvantage', I said, 'that the industry gives little employment — about 150, I've been told, in Sligo town and county?'

'Yes,' he said, 'but if you look at it from the social point of view it is a very important industry. It trains people in discipline. It's a trade in which you can't fool yourself or anyone. So a lot of the men who have worked in T and G have gone on to supply the technical management of successful industries, such as A. T. Cross of Ballinasloe, who make ball-points, and whose productivity so far exceeds what the American parent firm considered possible that they have become probably the main Cross factory. And others from T and G have set up their own industries on this estate or become technical managers in others. Indeed, the trouble with a good tool-maker is that as soon as you've trained him and he's good, he's in the market for a management job in many other industries.'

I could see, listening to him and looking at his swarthy face under its shock of black hair, what he meant by discipline, especially the mental kind. I was fascinated by how he combined broad vision with precise knowledge. 'It's an interesting business to be in,' he said, 'especially now when the competition is so keen. Within the next year it's make or break. Perhaps this whole industry that has grown up here over the past thirty years will go down, become obsolete, like the cooper, say. But then if we're to go down, it's better go down fighting. This year will tell us, it's make or break.'

As I cycled past the factories towards the gate of the estate, my head down, I looked up and saw grey Benbulben like a great wall directly ahead of me, the intervening country removed from sight. At the end of Quay Street a bus passed heading for Lough Derg, and I remembered the story I had heard in Mayo about the Sligoman who said he had been made rich by Hitler and Lough Derg — by cross-border smuggling during the Second World War and by provisioning and lodging pilgrims for Lough Derg. I came to Conway's Cellar Bar on O'Connell Street. Whereas republican street-names occupy the centre of Ballina, in Sligo it is O'Connell and Grattan along with John, Stephen, Wine, Bridge and Castle. Except for Teeling, the republican names are relegated to off-centre.

The Cellar Bar is a place I touch down when I visit Sligo, though I must say that part of its attraction is gone for me since they removed 'Wine' from the title. You enter it by a sloping, cool-tiled passage leading down into an 'inner alcove' — I am romanticising a bit — and on the hot day when I first visited it I felt it was the nearest thing to a *bodega* I had discovered in Ireland. It is a favourite haunt of the Yeats Summer School scholars, so I was not surprised, since it was in session again, to find quite a gathering of them there: Helen Vendler from Harvard; Norman Jeffares and his wife from Stirling; Michael Kenneally from Toronto; Declan Kiberd, the Director of the School; Denis Donoghue; and a folklorist, Angela Partridge, who had read her paper that afternoon. Donoghue and Kiberd were in disputation about the latter's paper which had opened the session, provocatively, by depicting Yeats as a propagator, and the Revival as an embodiment, of all the wrong, conservative ideas. 'There is no theory of literature', I heard Professor Donoghue saying, 'which states that a poet may express the prejudices of the centre or the left, but not those of the right.' Declan had just spent a term in Minnesota and was depressed. He had seen more energy there in three months than he had seen in Ireland in a lifetime. After a while we went for a meal in a really splendid little seafood restaurant, the ODW, which Frances O'Dowd had opened ten months previously. Later, flowing with the tide of this most civilised of summer schools, we walked to the Hawk's Well Theatre and, together with students from a dozen countries and Sligo people, heard John McGahern give a reading from his stories. Fresh from saving hay on his Leitrim farm, and looking the countryman, he added to that silk-smooth prose of his a soft, strong voice. Introducing a reading from a novella set in the Co. Roscommon of his childhood, he said: 'I am describing a society that was still in the nineteenth century. I think we were in the nineteenth century in Ireland until the 1960s. I don't know where we are now'.

I had intended seeking out Garreth Byrne, whom I knew to be working in Sligo and whom I hadn't seen for years, and chance presented him to me the following morning in the Quinnsworth Arcade. He was seated at a Gorta table, helping out a friend who was collecting money for 'Sligo's grain store in Tanzania'. I arranged to see him in his office that afternoon and to go home with him that night to Dromahair, just over the Leitrim border.

I got my car and drove out north of the town, beyond Benbulben, to Ballintrillick to visit Doris Manly, an American, whom I knew of as editor of the *Ballintrillick Review*. She lived in a valley in the shadow of Truskmore. A couple of miles from her house I passed a large, solitary, pointed rock, a few hundred feet high, which I recognised, from talk in the town, was the rock on the point of which a German wanted to build a restaurant con-nected to the ground by a funicular railway. At first, when I came to the grey, derelict-looking cottage beside a big empty barn, a tractor, and a load of turf, I thought I must be mistaken; the house seemed uninhabited. But as I knocked tentatively at the side-door, I saw through a window a large pile of the magazine on the floor of an empty room. Doris Manly was a tall, dark, bespectacled woman, wearing trousers, and she made me welcome in the kitchen. First things first, she gave me what remained from her lunch, with good brown bread and beer. Her husband, David, who besides being the local ESB meter-man is business manager of the magazine, was away in Dublin distributing the latest issue. She gave me a copy. Much of it dealt with the divorce referendum and the victory for her side. There were articles by such notables of the Catholic intelligentsia as Mary McAleese, Joe McCarroll and Brendan Purcell.

What had begun for the Manlys as a back-to-nature venture — they had come to Ballintrillick from Britain in 1978 — had turned into something quite different. 'We bought this ruined cottage, with sheep dung on the floor, rain coming through the roof, and cows sticking their heads in, and we hoped to transform it. But we found that two people couldn't and we got distracted into other things. I found, too, to my horror, though it took four years, that I was a consumer at heart — I'd thought if you read good books you couldn't be! But I also realised that it didn't really matter. Our new life, I mean the *Review* and all that, just grew and displaced the other. We had a cow and a calf, but they didn't pass the TB test and had to be slaughtered. We had a flourishing vegetable garden — those tomatoes you're eating are from the last of it, a few plants there in the conservatory. It was the abortion referendum was the real turning-point — when I saw that all the Dublin media were taking one side and suggesting that Catholics hadn't the right to think as Catholics and to express themselves as Catholics, and that there was no opposition press. I don't mean that the local papers here, or some of them, weren't taking the pro-life side, but that no one was criticising or answering the Dublin media which affect everyone in the country. I had already been writing a bit for a self-sufficiency magazine, the *Northwest Newsletter*, so I knew how a magazine was put together. And so, well, I started, and it's going nearly three years now. I type it all and do the lay-out and paste-up, and get headlines enlarged by a photocopier in Sligo, and print it in the *Donegal Democrat*. David used help me roll up the copies for subscribers, now we get two girls to do that. It changed our lives, it took over.'

What had she learned, I asked her. The first thing, and it was a shock, she said, was the existence of conspiracy theories. 'All sorts of literature began arriving in the post, and the people who sent it obviously assumed I would agree with them. And I came to realise that this was why the clergy and others, whom I was impatient with, didn't make strong statements countering the anti-Catholic propaganda, and naming the groups and bodies responsible for it. Out of fear of being identified with the conspiracy theorists, they were afraid to suggest that there was *anyone* around trying to promote ideologies at variance with Catholicism. Whereas I, who was no conspiracy theorist, simply knew that to be a fact. I find it quite normal that people have ideologies and pursue them. And specifically, where there's Catholicism, there's always anti-Catholicism. An American who visited us recently told us that exactly the same things that were being said about the Church here by the pro-divorce people had been said about it there in relation to abortion. Secondly there was the Granard affair, when that poor girl was found dead with her baby, and certain women journalists began praising certain health education programmes that were being used in the schools. I got curious about these, especially when I heard that one of them — indeed, the pioneering one, as it turned out — was being promoted by the North Western Health Board here. I asked them for a copy of the programme for review, and they refused but said to come and chat. I thought there must be something very odd afoot. So I published their refusal, and that triggered off a lot of things. I found that the Health Education Bureau in Dublin were giving training courses in these "life-skills programmes" as they called them, and ultimately I got copies of everything from moles, and found that they were about attitude formation, and choosing values, and that it was all based on moral relativism and subjectivism. And I said to myself, what's going on here, these are being used in Catholic schools; do the parents know what's in them? And how is it that this country, with all its Catholic education, has this sort of thing being promoted from its capital city?'

She said that in the early days of the magazine she had been worried that people would regard her as an interfering American, but when she found that in the anti-Catholic, feminist contingent in Dublin quite a number of them were in fact Americans, she stopped worrying on that score. 'Anyhow', she said, 'everyone around here has relations in America and they're back and forth all the time. Indeed I think that was the reason for the heavy anti-divorce vote here in the West. Divorce isn't just ideology for them, as it is for so many people in Dublin. They know it at first hand, through their own experience, often in their own families.' A couple of hours had passed and I had to meet Garreth Byrne. Just before I left she showed me a really shocking cartoon from the *Irish Independent* which she had re-printed in the latest issue of the *Review* beside the headline 'Horrible, Horrible Us'. Commenting on the overwhelming victory of the anti-divorce side in the referendum, the cartoon showed a large brutal man, with a club in his hand and standing in mud, smashing the head of a little woman in high-heeled shoes with a kick from his enormous boot. The caption underneath it read: 'Pluralism and compassion has been answered'.

Garreth's office was on High Street, which is true to its name. A note on his door on the second floor told me he would be back shortly, so I sat on the stairs and read the *Sligo Champion*, which 'outsells the combined sales of all newspapers circulating in the county', and which was celebrating its 150th anniversary. The paper confirmed something I had already noticed: in Sligo and its environs you can hear traditional music fairly easily. But this was only what I would have expected in view of the fame of the county, and particularly of South Sligo, in this respect. There was a page of pictures devoted to 'Garland Sunday in Tobernalt'. Tobernalt, a short distance from the town, has a holy well which, very unusually, is not dedicated to any saint. Doubtless it is a place of ancient ritual or assembly, and mass was said there during the penal times. But like many things in Ireland which are regarded as immemorially 'traditional', the pattern which takes place there each year is of quite recent origin. It sprang from a marriage of two initiatives at the beginning of this century: the Sisters of Mercy built an altar there in thanksgiving for the abatement of a fever in the town, and the Gaelic League organised the pattern as a religious occasion associated with Irish song and dance. It is one more in-stance illustrating how, from high to popular culture, the end of the last century and the beginning of this one was a culturally creative time such as we have not experienced since.

When Garreth arrived, I pointed to the notice on his door, 'World Education Project', and said, 'Some project!' 'Well, it's development education really,' he said. 'We had a much longer name and shortened it.' The 'we' was a Derry organisation that he had applied to six years before, when they were looking for an education officer in Sligo. On the wall inside his office a silk picture of Mao hung beside a large map of China and another map, of the Developing World, in French. When I had got to know him, years before, he was back and forth to Africa and had brought out two pamphlets on Afro-Irish connections. Now he said that taking a job in development education in the north west of Ireland seemed logical to him. 'Especially when I ended up living in the most undeveloped part of it — North Leitrim. It reminded me of Africa, it was a sort of Sahel with rain.' A man came in who wanted Garreth to lecture to Sligo Young Enterprises in the Enterprise Centre, and he said he would. When the man was gone Garreth explained that Young Enterprises was a scheme funded from the Youth Levy for young people between eighteen and twenty-three — 'early school-leavers and kids referred by social workers'. The girls cooked for a local restaurant, made soft toys and industrial clothes. The boys made and sold furniture. He had already given them a lecture on how scrap is re-cycled in India. 'I thought that might suggest the same sort of thing to them. I don't talk so much to people about the misery of the Third World as about its creativity. There are enough doing the misery and compassion bit. I don't want kids blinded by starving babies. I've just been to Inis Mór (one of the Aran islands) lecturing on "Teicneolaíocht Simplí sa Sahel". I think the Third World has a lot to teach us in present circumstances.'

But Garreth's real pride and joy, I discovered, were his exhibitions. He had organised four in Sligo — on India, Africa, world water problems, and South America — and was planning one on China. In each case he got help from embassies in Dublin and London, from local schools — who did projects — and from local people who lent all sorts of things. 'Especially for the African one, because so many people in and around Sligo had worked in Africa.' 'In a sense', he said, returning to his previous theme, 'I'm competing with the "misery industry". I use these exhibitions not so much to stir up compassion — which will be there anyhow while we're a Christian people — as envy — envy of what those people do in face of adversity. That's my hidden curriculum.'

I put my bicycle in the boot of the car and followed Garreth eastwards out of the town, through wooded hills, until the beauty of Lough Gill appeared on the right to shock me. The lake had a silver sheen from the sinking sun, and a full, strong rainbow, transecting the hills on the far shore, touched down in the water at the point of a rocky eminence. Just beyond Park's Castle, over the Leitrim border, Garreth, who still had something to do in the town, stopped and left me to cover the few remaining miles on my own. As the road curved around the end of the lake, I again had a full view of it, and the sun's silver light on the water reminded me of its gold on the ocean that other evening above Ceathrú Thaidhg. A few minutes later Dromahair announced itself as 'Seat of the O'Rourkes, Princes of Breffni'. Along the main street of the pretty village, signs above two or three premises continued the Breffni theme. The ancient territory of that name, embracing all of Cos Leitrim and Cavan, became divided in the late medieval period into Breffni O'Rourke (Leitrim) and Breffni O'Reilly (Cavan). Garreth's house was in a small housing estate built by Fr Bohan's organisation. When I had left my things there I went to Stanford's, the village inn on the main street, to meet the man of the house, Tom McGowan, at the fine old bar counter.

It was polished yew, he told me, from the eighteenth century. The interior of the pub was in handsome bare brick and wood. It had a restaurant at the back and bedrooms upstairs. Outside the restaurant, a terrace with rustic tables, and a garden beyond that, led down to the river Bonet. Tom, the son of a postman, grew up in the village in the days when, as he put it, 'it was run by Protestants'. 'Most people were poor but, by exchanging services, they had little need of money.' He grew and sold vegetables to pay for the train that took him to the tech in Manorhamilton. After training as a carpenter, he spent some years in the construction business, and married a daughter of the Stanfords. Now, in his mid-forties, he was a teacher of construction in the tech in Sligo. He told me of the old days when people travelled by boat across the lake from Sligo to connect with a coach the Stanfords ran to Carrick-on-Shannon. Listening to him and other local people until Garreth joined us, and after that, I began an immersion course in North Leitrim which lasted two days.

Garreth, with some anger, had dinned the statistics into me. Co. Leitrim in 1841 had a population of 155,000; today it was 27,500 — since 1926 it had been halved. In 1979 only 6 per cent lived in town areas against a national average of 56 per cent. Forty-seven per cent of today's population were in the dependent age-groups. Narrow the focus to North Leitrim, the less populated and urbanised half of the county, and you had a situation for crying. But was it all for crying, I asked myself.

It was tragic, certainly, for the old rural society that was dying inexorably, in frustration and anger, and for a town such as Manorhamilton whose human hinterland was evaporating while it was being hit by lower prices in the shops across the border. (It had also suffered in recent decades from changes in transport. First when its railway link went, later as cars became commonplace, much of North Leitrim turned towards Sligo.) Here, it seemed to me, was a people who, having been thrown out of home manufacture by the industrial revolution, and forced to depend for a livelihood on their wet, clayey, drumlin soil, had been defeated by the soil's marginal productivity in cattle when it was farmed by the old methods — I heard of a German who was raising cattle very successfully by new methods — and by their failure to move successfully into other areas of production. To put it another way, their society had fallen into a socio-economic crisis which required vigorous leadership to initiate counter-measures and change, and the only people who could have effectively given that leadership — their educated and comparatively well-to-do elite — had not given it; for the most part they had emigrated or, if they remained at home, sat tight. There are no two ways: by one means or another a society either overcomes the challenges to its existence, or fails to do so, and this one had failed.

The distant Dublin state, encountering a socially prostrate people, had provided mainly doles and other compassionate measures and afforestation — the climate and the clayey drumlin soils are pre-eminently suitable for trees. Old people were moved from isolated farms into Council housing in Dromahair. Finding themselves now with other people all the time, 'towny' people in their eyes, they felt they had to behave accordingly, and that was a strain. A man who before might have dressed up twice a week now felt obliged to do so every day.

Many of them, who might have lived on in their own way, in homely destitution, died. I heard of a social worker who found a man living somewhere out in the mountains, sleeping under an umbrella in a house held up by a forest of posts. They gave him a mobile home; he kept it for visitors and continued to sleep under his umbrella. Afforestation, for its part, has meant acquisition of land; first by the state, now increasingly by agents of distant financial institutions. Not only the acquisition of land, but its negation as land, its removal from availability; and often, therefore, as one man sees a neighbour selling out, the defeat of a long-cherished ambition for more land. Those who opt out benefit; those who remain see the trees as enemies, and neighbours as actual or potential traitors. As the draining and planting of new areas provides flows and ebbs of employment, sons work for trees cursed by their fathers and perhaps by themselves. At night, now in one place now in another, anger vents itself on machinery and saplings. Tom McGowan, caught up in his people's crisis and feeling it from the inside, said 'I'd like to think the old ways but I can't. You have to join the rat race, meet the targets.'

However, on the ruins of the old life a new life is emerging from two factors which partly overlap. The forests, as they come increasingly to characterise the environment and form a forest world, are giving rise to related activities. A motley immigration of English, Dubliners, Northern Irish, Germans, Dutch and Americans has been moving into vacated cottages and other abandoned buildings. Practitioners of the self-sufficient life, organic farmers, artists, hippies, individualists of many kinds escaping from the rat race, they have been settling not only in North Leitrim, but in adjoining parts of Sligo and Leitrim, in South Donegal and North Roscommon. The Manlys and Garreth Byrne (he comes originally from Co. Kildare) are part of this. The *North West Newsletter* is the immigrants' linking magazine. When I saw a copy of it some years ago, I was struck by its vaguely 'colonial' atmosphere, as of a bunch of expatriate Europeans communicating with each other from isolated homesteads in the African bush. There was much talk of jams, herb plants, scented shrubs, milking goats, wind generators, working visits to London to earn some cash, and homely get-togethers on 'Saturday the 15th at Jim and Sue's house' in some

91

obscure townland. I was not surprised, then, when Garreth lashed out at the 'types who come from Dublin, despising country bumpkins, and anti-Catholic, so that they fit in well with the Brits', meaning the English immigrants. True, they did try to educate the natives in new ways, 'but they've such contempt for their culture that they're not going to influence it'. Some of the Germans and Dutch had better attitudes, he said. Partly, I suppose, because Tom was an innkeeper, he spoke more kindly of the 'blow-ins'. 'If they contribute something useful, they're welcome.' He spoke to me with affectionate respect of an Englishman, Andy, whom I had met in his pub along with a wild-eyed local girl. Andy, who came from Oxford, eleven years ago, had invented a special machine for harvesting reeds at lakesides. It moved on balloons over swamps. He used it to harvest reeds — which are better for thatching than rushes — and sold them in Leitrim, Sligo and the Six Counties. But even Tom could speak harshly of Dutch people who fenced in their land and put up 'Keep Out' notices, when the local landlords had traditionally let people wander over their lands, and fish within reason. 'They don't know how savage they seem', he said. I heard of the German who grew cannabis and of the German hippies who bought up old cottages, renovated them, and sold them at a profit to their fellow countrymen. The fact is that the immigrants are a very mixed lot and that the more exotic or insensitive of them give rise, as one would expect, to chat, resentments, and generalisations. From what I saw of recent issues of the *Newsletter* — edited from Castlebaldwin in South Sligo — it seemed to have settled down more into its environment.

But the forests and the activities connected with them — immigrants figure in these too — are my most abiding memory of North Leitrim. Tom and his son Fergus had a workshop for making tables, benches and lettered signs, out of local wood. On Tom's advice, I visited Aedan and Frieda Rountree on their farm near Dromahair. Aedan, a rector's son, had inherited it from his grandmother seven years previously. Before that they had been to college in Dublin and travelled overland to India. As well as sheep, they had a hundred acres of woodland which yielded abundant thinnings, and most of their time was divided between a sawing business based on these, and organising motor-bike racing in Northern Ireland and Leitrim.

Behind the house, near a pile of thinnings and an assortment of planks, Frieda, a small woman with long dark-blond hair, wearing corduroy trousers, sleeveless pullover and check shirt, was feeding wood into a fiercely whirring circular saw. A short distance away, beside a white van with 'Rountree Racing' on the side, Aedan stood talking to two men. Frieda explained that he was organising a race for a Sligo club in Carrick-on-Shannon because Sligo County Council didn't permit motor-bike racing. She asked a young man to take over from her on the saw and brought me into the kitchen. Their thinnings, she said, were mostly Sitka spruce, and they made fencing posts, logs, and anything that people needed if they were going to build something. They had gone into wood because more money was to be made from it than from farming. She came from a farm in Co. Offaly, and had begun to learn about wood only since they came here. Forestry magazines lay around the kitchen. Her knowledge of wood lore impressed me. I learned that what I had taken to be mixed natural woods on the road out from Sligo were not that, but 'scrub', that is, trees, generally ash and hazel, growing wild, without thinning. Natural forest was characterised by 'final' trees, usually oak, but sometimes beech, which because of their height had overshadowed and killed all lesser trees. Scrub developed as hedges around small fields gradually grew together — blackthorn, bracken and briars leading the way, then ash and hazel taking root in that *mélange*. She told me of coppiced oaks nearby, that is, oak-stumps after felling which are let produce branches freely. The branches were often used for firewood, and the expression 'by hook or by crook' had come from the ancient custom by which tenants or villeins were allowed take all the firewood they could get from a coppice by either of those means. Aedan and she had three or four young people employed the previous year, but they had all emigrated — gone on visitor's visas to the USA. 'During the '70s', she said, 'people came back here from England. Now, in the last couple of years, word had got around about America, and it's all the thing. But really the two of us working together is sufficient. Maybe we don't turn out as much, or delivery takes longer, but you can be sure the work is done well. Here I am chatting to you, and I'm thinking I should go out and see how that chap is doing.' We went back to the saw and she took over, feeding planks deftly with her bare hands into the merciless steel cutting machine. The 'Rountree Racing' van had disappeared.

Brendan Lacey, a young assistant forestry inspector for the Sligo district — which includes North Leitrim — took me on a tour by car. Apart from trees, we talked about literature. He had been at the McGahern reading in the Hawk's Well, was active in drama at UCD, and had once organised a poetry reading on the shore of Lough Gill, during which a massed chorus shouted poems at Inishfree. He told me that the Irish drumlin belt, because of its clayey soil and moderate, damp climate, is the most productive land in Europe for trees. The soil's clay content makes it both retentive of water and easy to drain. Measured by 'yield class' — cubic metres of timber growth per hectare per annum — continental Western Europe averages 4-8, Ireland 14-18, the Leitrim drumlins 20-24; but some areas of Leitrim reach a yield class of 30. Sitka spruce is the commonest tree planted in Leitrim, with pine on poorer soil and blanket bog. When I mentioned the farmers' opposition, Brendan said a scheme was underway to meet their objections halfway. Land acquired for forestry would remain in the farmer's ownership and he would receive a share of the proceeds when the wood was sold.

In pelting rain we visited a plantation of three-year-old spruces on a slope. In the boggy soil at the bottom, where they had to struggle with reeds and overcome them, they reached about three feet; but as we mounted the slope their height increased to six feet. Brendan said that the two wet summers in succession, which had been bad for tourism and farming, had been excellent for trees. We went to a drained hillside, still free of trees. The draining had been done by a device which sank two rods, each with a small ball on the end, into the ground. As these were pulled through the soil, they bored parallel narrow drains two feet under, and cut corresponding marking lines on the surface. At right-angles to these drains, deep open drains had been dug, and looking into one we could see a series of small sub-terranean holes issuing into it. The ground around was noticeably dry by comparison with the mucky ground we had trudged through on our way up to it. We went on to visit a couple of the forest 'amenity areas' which the Forestry and Wild Life Service has created throughout the country in recent years. At Slish Wood on the south shore of Lough Gill there was a clearing beside the road with some rustic tables set out and running water. Brendan remarked that they always tried to include running water because people liked it. Unmarked forest paths departed in two directions. I learned that the magnificent rhododendron is regarded by the forestry people as a prime enemy of trees, and that one of the reasons which induced them to open forests to the public was the knowledge that visitors would prey on it — taking away roots and branches! At Dooney Rock amenity area, there were marked paths, one leading to a picnic site, the other to the Rock. Leaflets available from a box gave explanatory information. We walked to the Rock and had a fine view of the lake. Finally, leaving these tourist playgrounds for the really serious stuff, we headed off east beyond Killarga into the mature 'commercial forests', on high ground near the Cavan border. We passed a thinned forest of twenty-year-olds which was due for another thinning soon. Trees are first thinned when they are between fourteen and twenty years old, and then every five years after that. Fittingly, the end and culmination of our tour was forests of majestic forty-five-year-olds, broad of girth, soaring to fifty feet, and creating an awesome, whispering stillness. From start to finish it was a fascinating and moving expedition, but that was largely because I was so fortunate in my genial, omniscient and tree-struck companion.

The evening that I left Dromahair for Boyle I stopped at the top of the village, beside the ruins of Villiers Castle. It was built, Tom had told me, out of the principal O'Rourke castle. The countryside around was redolent with O'Rourke memories: Park's Castle which I had passed on the way from Sligo was built with O'Rourke stone, and there was a mountain nearby called O'Rourke's Table. Next to Villiers Castle stood a group of fine holiday apartments. Two French couples, leaving one, were getting into their cars. I crossed to an old house and yard on the opposite side of the street and, wandering through them, came on various rooms and workshops in which Germans, Irish and Americans were engaged in arts and crafts — weaving, furniture-making, painting. Returning to the car, I set off to visit McCartney's Nurseries at Tawnylea, intending after that to follow the shore of Lough Allen and to turn away from it, near Drumshanbo, for Keadew and Boyle — a distance altogether of about thirty-three miles.

Just beyond Killarga I had a puncture. Since the car was one I had bought recently, and this was its first puncture — and I am not a genius with cars — I went through quite a trauma, first searching for, and then trying to use, the unfamiliar tools. Fortunately a kind Englishman, his car filled with wife and children, stopped to ask me the way to Dowra and helped me with his much better tools. McCartney's tree nursery turned out to be less accessible than I had expected. When I reached it, a few miles from the main road and high up among spruce plantations, the sun was noticeably sinking. Looking down before I approached the house, I could see the full length of Lough Allen to Drumshanbo. The door was at the end of a long glass verandah along the side of the house. Marjorie McCartney had reddish blonde hair, was wearing green trousers, and spoke with a Northern accent. She was struggling to get the children to bed, so I said I would have a look around. Several fields in the immediate vicinity of the house were planted with young trees. Behind the house I counted fourteen long, broad polythene structures standing in a row.

Talking to Marjorie later in the house, I heard that she and her husband, Peter, had come there from Belfast nearly nine years before. Neither of them had felt happy about where their professions were leading them; she in domestic economy teaching, he in civil engineering. They started with a farm of thirteen acres and later got thirteen more from the Land Commission. 'We cringed then,' said Marjorie, ' — we cringe even more now — when people talked of self-sufficiency and back to nature. People supposed we were hippies, and hippies are dirty and have the reputation of taking drugs. We simply wanted to have a farm.' They tried cattle and poultry, and fattened sheep for the French market with advice from ACOT. But Halal wouldn't sell their sheep to the French market, preferring the Italian market, and that meant lower prices. For two years they were on the dole. They went into vegetable growing, made a living, and got off the dole. 'Then a very helpful ACOT adviser put us onto trees. We brought a batch from two years to four years and the County Council bought them all for shelter belts, and we were off. We started in seeds in a small way. It grew and grew. Now we sell a million trees a year — mostly Sitka Spruce and Norway Fir, but also Noble Fir, the in-tree now for Christmas trees, and Contorted Pine, and more or less everything else, beech, alder, maple. And I got into ornamental shrubs and rockery plants and that's going a bomb too.' She handed me their twelve-page printed catalogue. She had started the ornamental shrubs in the verandah and then, needing space, asked Peter to get her a polythene tunnel — such as I had seen outside. That started them on the tunnels, and now they were using them for all sorts of trees. But they were keeping their fingers crossed, for they had just made their first delivery of trees grown that way and hoped they would work out. That was in Connemara, where they had been asked to 'do the beating up' on a 500-acre new plantation — to replace the trees that had failed in it. It belonged to a company which was growing the trees for re-sale to an insurance company or bank.

Their own first child, Marjorie said, had been the first child born thereabouts for twenty-two years. Since then two others had been born to other couples. In the first years after the McCartneys' arrival, the numbers in the school built up as people returned from England; now they were falling again. The previous year fourteen people had left for America. We went out to the tunnels. Most of them contained endless trays of plants and seedlings. One contained a vegetable garden. 'Do you like cauliflowers?' she asked, and when I said it was my favourite vegetable, she lifted one, broke off the root and gave it to me: I broke off the surrounding leaves. 'I left them on to keep it fresh', she said, and I, who thought I knew something about vegetable gardening, felt a fool.

Back on the main road, in the dark now, I passed through Drumkeeran, kept company with Lough Allen for some miles, and then, about two miles from the turn for Keadew, had another puncture. Yes, I know, punctures come in series; this proved it. I pushed the car into the side of the road and, holding one of the punctured tyres, stopped a passing driver, a fat, moustached, friendly man, who drove me to Drumshanbo. He told me the garage I should go to in the morning to get the puncture mended early; but just in case they couldn't drive me to my car, he left me his telephone number so that I could phone him to come and fetch me.

I found a B and B above a pub. Leaving my tyre in the bar, I followed a fat, shapeless young woman, with an empty face, through a hall and up a stairs, passing on the way the Proclamation of 1916 and a reproduction of 'The Holy Face' from the Turin Shroud. The room had sinister green wallpaper and two double beds. 'That one's been slept in,' she said, 'but you can have this one.' I saw toiletries on the wash-hand basin. It was too late to be choosey. 'Is there a fast-food shop still open?' I asked. 'Would chicken and chips do you?' she asked. I said yes and she said to come down to the dining-room. When I did, some time later, passing pictures of the ten Long Kesh hunger-strikers who died, a plate with chips and a leg of chicken lay on a table in lonely solitude. Taking salt from another table, I began to eat with my fingers, finding the chicken tough and dried-up. When I had eaten most of the food, she came into the room from the bar and said 'Oh, I forgot to put out the other things. Do you want bread?' I said no, but that I'd take coffee. She disappeared into the bar again and did not return. After a while I went into the bar and had a whiskey. I sat at the counter looking around me at a festive party who were talking about a wedding next day. She passed by and, recognising me, asked 'Did you get the coffee?' 'No,' I said, 'I decided I'd prefer a whiskey.'

Sometime in the early hours I was abruptly wakened from sleep by voices and commotion in the corridor. I heard the door of the room bursting open and a loud thud beside me as a body fell to the floor. It seemed — the head of the bed was behind the door — that the fallen body was raised erect again by helping hands and conveyed elsewhere. The door closed. Meditating on these events, I sensed a rancid communication between my stomach and my mouth, and groaned remembering the chicken and chips. I became aware that I wanted to vomit. I reached the bathroom in time to do so. After that I slept deeply. When I arose in the morning and went downstairs to the dining-room, it was deserted. A look into the kitchen made my stomach turn again. The only difficulty about leaving, which was all I wanted to do, was that my tyre was in the bar and the bar was locked. Fortunately there was a loud knocking on the front door which brought the woman of the night before shuffling, in her dressing-gown, to open it and let a man in. After talking to him for a minute or so, she said she would get me breakfast. 'I don't want breakfast,' I said. 'I'm not feeling well. The oil in the chips last night was rancid. I'd just like my tyre out of the bar.' She said it was impossible the oil was rancid, she had got the chicken and chips from a fast-food place nearby — her brother's or some relation's — and it was fresh oil. I did not dissent. She got the tyre, I paid her, and left. The garage mended the tyre, and the lad who did the job drove me out to the car. While they were mending the other tyre, I had a walk around the town. Drumshanbo by day seemed quite a pleasant place.

It was a warm sunny day — it was a summer in which one noticed such days — when I drove through Keadew in Co. Roscommon, and north of Loughs Meelagh and Skean, and back into Co. Sligo through the hills east of Lough Arrow, to visit Des McDonagh in Heapstown at the head of the lough. When I had mentioned to Séamas Ó Catháin in Ceathrú Thaidhg that I would be going to Boyle, he said I must call on this friend of his whom he had encountered on the folklore trail. Heapstown is a place, a townland I suppose, rather than a village; it lies around an ancient heap of stones and was doubtless originally called simply Carn. Des McDonagh, I found, lived in a large house that branched out into shop, pub and guesthouse. His wife told me he was out on the farm making silage. I sat in the pub reading the *Roscommon Herald*, 'the leading provincial paper in the Northwest and Midlands', which had just arrived from Boyle.

The main story on its front page was about the newly-published County Development Plan which 'defines the county's future in tourism'. Analysing each of the county's main towns in turn, it found that those of the south, Castlerea and Roscommon, were suffering most from the recession. After a growth of population in the '70s, out-migration from these towns and from their spheres of influence was now occurring 'at an accelerated rate'. Boyle, on the other hand, in the north of the county, near the Sligo border, had increased its population slightly; and that of its environs had increased by over 100 per cent in the ten years under review. From another news item I learned that my visit to the town would coincide with its Arts Festival. The leading article dealt with the sufferings of some old people in the bad summer:

It may come as somewhat of a shock to learn as we have, in recent days, that elderly people are dying from cold or hypothermia, as the condition is termed medically, in the month of July, and apart altogether from what it says about our Irish summer, it says much about the type of society in which we live.

An advertisement from the county's ACOT Advisory Service began:

> The weather this season has made it impossible to save good quality hay. Any grass to be cut now or later should be made into silage. Even at this stage every effort should be made to use any extra fields possible for a cut of silage later in the season.

From a Dublin paper which Mrs McDonagh lent me I learned with sorrow of the death of Madeleine Stuart, wife of Francis Stuart, the writer. I was very fond of both of them. From the interior of the house I heard a radio news bulletin, and it struck me, half-listening to the Western voices in the bar: these people never hear their own accents reading the news in English on the national broadcasting service — Northern and English accents yes, but Western ones never.

Growing impatient, I went outside and a few minutes later saw the cavalcade returning from the fields: Des McDonagh in a car with two neighbours who were helping him, a contractor and his assistant on a grass pick-up truck. Des was a tall, grey-haired man with strong facial features. While the others ate, he took me into the pub, asked about Séamas Ó Catháin, and started telling me about his farming. Two Americans came in, a father and son, who had travelled on the Transamerica flight to Connacht Airport, and who were doing some fishing on Lough Arrow. They asked Des about a boat, and he told them they could have his, with oars but without the outboard, because they didn't know the lake. He took me into the house for dinner.

At the beginning of the '70s he had fifteen cows on his land. Then prices went up, and, as he put it, 'the smart fellows in white coats came telling me what to do'. 'Foolishly, I listened to them. They told me how to improve my land so that it could take more cattle, and I did the things they said, and soon I had fifty cows. But that was too many — they poached, they starved, and I strained myself buying nuts and meal and things to supplement the grass. But it wasn't only me. The smart fellows from the Department encouraged many people to go into milk, and instead of keeping to the traditional Western cow, a shorthorn crossed with an Aberdeen Angus bull, they brought in Frisians. Over the past couple of years I've reduced my cattle to a viable number.'

The bitterness with which he spoke of 'the smart fellows in white coats' had a deep root. He remembered a lost paradise. It had existed back in the hills to the east when he had a shop and a pub there, in Loughbo. 'In the hills around were a community of decent, self-respecting, hard-working people who needed no dole and had none. They lived by a system of exchanges that had almost no need of money. In our shop forty pass-books hung on nails on the wall, and a woman would bring her eggs, and buy her groceries with the proceeds, and if there was anything over, it would go into her pass-book. Some of them kept pass-books themselves. A woman would bring her butter, and I'd examine it on the table for hairs or other impurities, and if it was right I'd buy it. If young fellows wanted cigarettes, I'd say bring me rabbits. A man would ask for credit till his oats were cut or his pigs slaughtered, and then come and pay back on the nail. I took in horsehair, feathers, there was use for everything. I stored it all in a big shed and a van would come every week from Carrick and buy it. There was a mill in Ballymote, and a butcher in Riverstown who'd come and do the slaughtering. Everyone had his turf to burn and thatched his roof with rushes. If I ask myself when did the rot set in, I'd say when the first tractors came, sometime in the '60s. The Department started grading the eggs and it ruined the egg business for the women. Then they started grading pigs. Some people got rich and had new houses and a tarmacadamed drive. Neighbours looked at them, knew they could never equal them, sold out, and emigrated. Oh, people still live there, and they have more land, but the community is dead, and that way of life which was there between Riverstown and Carrick is gone forever.'

But beyond that again, further back in time, another lost estate inhabited Des McDonagh's consciousness. The MacDonaghs had been lords of South Sligo; they had four chief

101

castles there, the main one in Ballymote. They had emerged from the MacDermots, lords of Lough Key and North Roscommon, just as these had sprung earlier from the royal O'Conors, whose ancient heartland lay farther south. (It appeared that this sort of thing happened when the offspring of a certain Dermot or a certain Donagh decided to derive their surname thenceforth from their father's name.) 'But foolishly,' said Des, 'we went to war with the Cromwellians, who had better equipment and tactics, and we lost and had to go into the hills and reclaim land there.' It occurred to me that, in his eyes, the bureaucrats of agricultural development, from the '60s on, were neo-Cromwellians. It was Eoin O'Mahony, the genealogist, who made him interested in his clan; they used meet in Sligo, when Des had a business there. With the help of some others he researched where the MacDonaghs had gone throughout the world — there were even some of them in Argentina — and they held a clan gathering in Ballymote. But after that, people from all sorts of places never stopped annoying him and his wife and he got tired of it. His most recent venture into history was when a bookseller in Sligo wanted to re-publish a history of Co. Sligo and Des put up the capital. He left the table to fetch it, and gave it to me to look through while he took the Americans to the boat.

Later, in bright, hot sunshine, we joined the others at the silage-making. In two large fields the grass had been cut and put into rows, and at the side of one of the fields was the silage clamp or 'bench' — a low, sloping, squared-off mound of grass almost surrounded by a barbed-wire fence to keep cattle away. The fields were on a height with a view across part of the lake towards the Bricklieve mountains on the far side. Des told me that was where Carrowkeel ·was, a cemetery of ancient stone cairns covering passage tombs. I could see a cairn like a pimple on a rock promontory. In one of the fields the pick-up, operated by the contractor, was collecting the grass, slicing it somewhat, transporting it to the silage bench, and depositing it on it. Two men raked it roughly flat, and the contractor's assistant, attaching a levelling machine to a tractor, levelled and rolled it. Then a boy walked over it, dousing it with molasses to help fermentation and to give the grass a good taste.

When I asked Des what sort of a town was Boyle, he looked in its direction, scowled and said, 'That was the garrison town, and although the garrison's gone — not only the soldiers but their hangers-on who lorded it over everyone — you still find the old mentality there in the few that's left of them. I went to one of them the other day who has a shop. I was asking him to bend the rules a bit. And there was the old stony face, no smile, and when I asked him to make very clear was he actually saying no, he said, "Yes, I'm saying no".' It was not promising but I set out for the town, stopping on the way in Ballyrush to buy a mass card for Madeleine Stuart and to get the curate to sign it. The church reminded me of Des's musical activities. He had played the church harmonium for a while, but stopped 'because the people didn't appreciate it'. Then he had taken young people from the parish to a great musician called Armstrong in Carrick, who had taught them music and harmony, and the upshot of it was that the parish now had *four* céilí bands, all of them going to compete in this year's National Fleá in Listowel. The curate was in his shirt-sleeves behind his house, digging. I said, handing him the mass card, 'That's the wife of Francis Stuart', and then, noticing his questioning eyes, 'But perhaps you don't read novels'. 'Occasionally,' he said, 'but light stuff. I don't read that much these days. I'm an activist. It looks like rain' — and he pointed to a spire on a distant hill which could be seen very clearly. I posted the card to Francis in Castlebaldwin directly under the Bricklieve mountains.

I had decided to try out a farmhouse from those listed in the Bord Fáilte booklet *Farm Holidays in Ireland*. I chose one in Knockvicar, across Lough Key from Boyle, which offered all sorts of facilities for anglers and children. I was looking forward to a farmyard with chickens picking and cattle mooing and the woman of the house baking home-made bread. It was a Georgian house in a grassy demesne and there was no sign of a farmyard or of farming appurtenances. The girl who opened the door brought me downstairs to a stone-paved corridor in which an old woman told me her son and daughter-in-law were away, and asked me to sign a book. I was shown to my room, which was fine, but I was dismayed by the silence in the house and by learning that, although it was a big house, there was only one other guest. When I went out — it was late evening now — to get into my car to drive to Boyle, the girl came running after me to ask about breakfast next morning. Would I have orange juice? Well, yes, I supposed so. Corn flakes, rice crispies or porridge? That was more difficult, but I said rice crispies. Then making a great imaginative leap into the unknown territory of the following morning I said rapidly that I would also have tea and scrambled eggs.

The *Roscommon Herald*, quoting the County Development Plan, had prepared me for the physical aspect of Boyle. The authors of the plan found that the 'overriding impression is one of elegance which is derived from the extensive use of stone in boundary walls, the number of large stately buildings, and the fine stands of mature trees which provide shelter and colour. Closer examination, however, reveals the existence of an unduly large number of areas of blight. The river is a major feature of the town. . . . ' Yes, indeed it was, rushing brown and swollen under the old bridge; and the Royal Hotel beside it was also a major feature, and I liked both. The Royal Hotel was that kind of solid old country-town hotel which you feel has been receiving travellers, feeding them and sleeping them, since the days of O'Connell and the stagecoaches. Much of the Arts Festival seemed to be taking place in it. A poster in the hall said that the Attic Theatre Company from Sligo was that very minute performing Geraldine Aron's *The Galway Girl* upstairs, and would later be doing Brendan Behan's *Richard's Cork Leg*. The dining-room was closed, but the head-girl strongly recommended Roger's Fast Foods in the street around the corner. She was right: they were the best chips I had eaten on my journey, and the hamburger was excellent too. To put me in even better humour, I had been noticing since I arrived in the town — noticing for the first time since I began the journey — numbers of strikingly beautiful girls: 'West of Ireland' types, as I and the world understood that, with dark hair, sparkling eyes, mystery, beguilement. With a pang I remembered, on the boat to Holyhead back in the '50s, two farmers' daughters from Roscommon who were working as 'clippies' in Birmingham, and how I had travelled with them until they changed trains at Crewe, and how I had stolidly held my seat and continued to London, hating my cowardice.

In the lounge upstairs in the Royal, in the interval after *The Galway Girl*, about sixty people were sitting on red chairs chatting and drinking. I got a drink and sat among them,

104

The Airport: 'We touched down, turned, and taxied towards the terminal building. Under a large D there was a glass door and people standing behind it had their faces pressed to it.... It reminded me of arriving once at a small airport in Yugoslavia.'

Ballina: 'It is the biggest town in Mayo, with a population more than six times that of Swinford.... It had the bustle, and the multi-coloured look, of a real town.... The town had a telephone directory and a street-map, two signs, I always feel, of urban self-possession.'

Lough Cullin, Co. Mayo: 'The sunlight, falling from an unsettled sky, showed the water luminous and leaden, and a patch of hillside very green. Then the light moved over the hillside and a touch of blue appeared in the lake. It was like a shot being set up for some celestial camera. With that surprise which Irish people sometimes experience when they travel in Ireland, I understood why an Englishman or a German, coming here to fish, would think this paradise.'

Sligo: 'You can see girls in Sligo with that washed-out look which you find only in towns. The young man in the newspaper shop has a defensive, aggressive edge to his voice which implies that your custom is a purely formal matter, of complete indifference to him, and that he could just as easily be driving a Ferrari down the autostrada from Florence to Rome.'

'Lough Key Forest Park is one of the great showpieces of the Forest and Wild Life Service. ... At the quay, near the restaurant and car-park, where boats leave for tours of the lake and its islands, several cruising boats were anchored which had probably come from the Shannon. I asked a middle-aged woman hanging out washing on deck where she was from. She laughed, turned into the cabin and said to a boy, "Ich kann gar nicht antworten".'

The grave of Douglas Hyde: 'In the churchyard, which I found as indicated, there was a line of Hyde graves with simple Celtic crosses on the headstones. ... His own simple grave declared him to be First President of Ireland, in Gaelic and English. A small memorial plaque from the GAA lay on the gravel. I wondered at this grave – such a far cry from, say, the Washington Memorial: and why?'

Killary Harbour: 'I walked to the sea-wall and looked out over the calm fjord in which someone once said the entire British fleet could anchor.'

'Clifden is on high ground beside the sea, but, probably because its "sea" is extremely tidal and its harbour therefore not up to much, it faces inland. Partly because I have seen the town in all seasons. Clifden in summer has always struck me as a painted stage-set.... On that Sunday afternoon, its main street and adjoining streets were a riot of colour in bright sunlight. I say "riot" deliberately because it suggests unruliness: you could see there what "shocking" pink or green or yellow really means – and that they can be appropriate in a place of fantasy.'

'Roundstone is the demure summer sister of gaudy Clifden; a place where families, mostly Irish, like to holiday with their children. A white-grey-yellow village, with a discreet touch or two of light green and blue, it stretches out above its snug harbour.'

The Aran Islands: 'In Aran, stone comes truly into its own. If you want to see it at its best then turn aside when you see a signpost to one of the many antiquities, say, Teampall an Cheathrair Álainn. You come to well-wrought stiles, walk along trodden stone paths, mount sets of steps, and see all sorts of stone outhouses and walls.'

'The distinctive hills of the Burren are to the north and north east; to the south of these lies a high fissured plateau. Burren, from the Gaelic boireann, means rocky country or karst. It was over the plateau I was travelling now, in solitary stillness, meeting hardly anyone. This is where I find the magic of the Burren.'

'I would say that Galway is now the best city in Ireland to live in. During the past twenty-five years it has ceased to be what it was for so long: a romantic, stagnated city, dwelling in the memories of its great mercantile past and offering wistfulness to the tourist. . . . All Ireland meets and mingles there in a population sufficiently small – there are 40,000 inhabitants – to allow the immigrants to create a new milieu. It is a young people's city.'

'It was only fourteen miles further to Athlone. The road cut a swathe across the southern tip of Co. Roscommon. Athlone sprawled to meet me and drew me to the Shannon. Scores of cruise boats floated on the shimmering river. . . . On a boat moored a few yards away a woman in the cabin window was mixing salad. On the other bank, the eastern town, presenting what you might call its back view, climbed from the river towards its central street.'

waiting for *Richard's Cork Leg*. Behind me I heard a woman talking, and from what she was saying I gathered she was the Bernadette Foley who was giving an arts workshop in the festival week. I heard her telling a man she had asked this child from Carrick had they arts in his school, and the child said, 'Since they put down the carpet we don't have painting'. Carpets in schools? I assumed a national school. Was I that out of touch? I sat transfixed until I got the opportunity to ask her, 'Do they have carpets in schools now?' 'Oh yes', she said, 'all the new schools have carpets.' It said so much about the Republic of Ireland these last twenty-five years that it seemed too good to be true: 'Since they put down the carpet we don't have painting.' Des McDonagh would have loved it.

Next morning after breakfast, the owner of the farmhouse, Mr Burke, told me about his farming. He had cattle and sheep, but he believed that meat farming was going into a permanent decline. People weren't eating as much meat as before, and the US, with its huge meat surplus, was moving into Third World markets, such as Tunisia, Egypt and Iran, where we had been doing well. So he was looking for something more profitable, perhaps a forest nursery. That appeared promising because pension funds were increasingly being based on forest. The generous state aid was encouraging this — and I at last succeeded in getting a clear account of what this was. The state paid a private person 85 per cent of the cost for draining, planting and fencing a piece of land; for companies, it was 75 per cent.

I had decided to move into the Royal Hotel to be at the centre of things. On the way there, driving between Lough Key and Lough Arrow, I passed a thatched cottage which had a notice outside, 'Thatching Company' and stopped to talk to three men spreading gravel. 'Where do they do their thatching?' I asked. 'Are there thatched houses hereabouts?' They were Germans, I was told, and they did a special thatch — with reeds. But there weren't many thatched houses around. They looked at each other, searching their recollections, and one mentioned a house in one village, another a house elsewhere. 'There's any number of thatchers hereabouts, but they don't have work. You'd have to travel far to make a living of it.' I thought of the reed-thatched houses of Northern Germany, village after village of them, even the hotels and night clubs in holiday resorts, and saw these local Germans as missionaries of tradition in a land that had turned its back on it. I entered Boyle through the Curlew mountains, first ascending and then descending the steep and tortuous 'pass of the North', where, in 1599, Aodh Rua O Dónaill defeated Sir Conyers Clifford, governor of Connacht.

I stopped at magnificent Boyle Abbey, founded in 1161 by Cistercians from Mellifont. Battered in many wars, it was the nucleus from which the town grew. In the fully-restored gate-house I paid 50p and mounted a stair to an upper room where there was an excellent model of the abbey as it once was. The most impressive of the remains are the massive romanesque arches of the south nave. The arches of the north nave are in transitional gothic. At the tourist office not far away, buying a booklet on Roscommon, I was struck once again by the great and imaginative advance in what Bord Fáilte puts on display in the way of booklets, maps and posters. I picked up a delightful publication on the placenames of the *Táin*. It was written by Tom Kinsella, who had walked the entire route of the *Táin* from nearby Cruachain to the Cooley peninsula. At the Royal, the manager, Vincent Regan, gave me a room low down in the hotel, on the river side, so near to the rushing water that not alone was its sound a constant presence in the room, but you could reach your hand out the window and almost touch it.

The Boyle River issues from Lough Gara to the west of Boyle, flows through the town into Lough Key, and continues through a series of lakes to the Shannon at Carrick. Lough Key Forest Park is one of the great showpieces of the Forest and Wild Life Service. Essentially it is the old Rockingham estate, which passed from the King-Harman family to the Irish state in 1959; and the Rockingham lands had earlier formed the core of the MacDermot lordship of Moylurg. I cycled through the park past fine stands of beech, oak and sycamore, and giant cypresses. It was drizzling and there were not many tourists. At the quay, near the restaurant and car-park, where boats leave for tours of the lake and its islands, several cruising-boats were anchored which had probably come from the Shannon. I asked a middle-aged woman hanging out washing on deck where she was from.

She laughed, turned into the cabin and said to a boy, 'Ich kann gar nicht antworten'. Lush forest surrounded the lake and covered the islands. A short distance out stood the Rock, Carraig Locha Cé, where the MacDermots had their chief castle for centuries. The tiny wooded island, with its castle-like ruin topped by a slender turret, looked as romantic as anything on the Rhine; never mind that the guidebook said the building was a nineteenth-century folly. Úna Bhán MacDermot — she of the famous song — was confined there by her father, in the original castle, to prevent her meeting Tomás Láidir MacCostello. When she died of love-sickness, and was buried on Trinity island, Tomás kept swimming out to visit her grave until, poor man, he caught pneumonia. But MacDermot granted his dying wish to be buried with her, and so it was done. I left the quay and walked to the Bog Garden across the Fairy Bridge. Entering the garden by a log-bridge above a pool of water-plants, I found myself on a damp path, paved with oak slices, between high rhododendron hedges, and that path led to other similarly hedged paths. It was a sort of maze. I heard a boy's voice calling, 'I see you, you're running, you're trying to get away', and then a girl's choked giggle and running feet. It was so like a 'Thetis and Amaryllis sporting in the shade' act that I wondered for a moment were the voices recorded — like the moans of the sufferers in the dungeons at Westport House. But soon, as I continued my wanderings, I saw a girl of flesh and blood crouched behind a bush in a clearing, watching a path. I was disappointed that hardly anything was flowering — all that was offered to the eye was a variety of greens. It was a garden for early summer, when the rhododendrons and azaleas would be in bloom.

Back in the town I went to the Cé Arts exhibition — 'Cé' from the lake. I was puzzled as I entered the duskily lit room. In frames on the walls I made out groupings of what looked like lichen-covered sherds. A metal sculpture of geometric shapes stood on a pedestal. 'What's this about?' I asked a young man standing at the door, who turned out to be David Knight, a photographer. 'Would you like to see our slide show, "Tribal Landscape"?' he asked. 'Then all will be revealed.' I assented and he disappeared with a companion into a compartment behind a screen. The screen lit up with a picture of the sea and I heard a voice proclaiming the first lines of the druid Amergin's poem:

> I am wind on sea
> I am wave in storm
> I am sea sound
> and seven-horned stag...

Then there were pictures of black geometric solids in various groupings, and stones on a shore among sherds of green broken glass, all of this accompanied by an Indian kind of singing. Instrumental music followed, backing images of elemental things, and of elemental man, and occasionally a voice made profound statements or asked profound questions. When it was over, both of them came out and asked me did I like it. It had gone down well in the town, they said, though initially they were afraid they would be taken for loonies. Both of them were from Dublin. The Cé Arts group, I learned, was made up of people from various parts of Ireland and local people, and there had been a fruitful interaction between them. To a great extent, their inspiration came from Carrowkeel, the Stone Age cemetery in the Bricklieves. 'Have you seen that wonderful place?' David Knight asked. I said I had years ago, on a trip from Sligo. 'You can't imagine what's grown up around it, and the people who have come here because of it — faith-healers, spiritualists and so on. But for the artists around here — and there are about two hundred people round here writing or doing arts or crafts — it's very important too. Many of us believe those are not just graves, but that they were ritual buildings of people who worshipped light. A lot has been destroyed. That awful guy who wrote *The Way that I Went*, Lloyd Praeger, he and another guy *dynamited* several of the tombs, like they did later at Carrowmore. They found crystal pendulums, that had been used in the cult, and they were taken to the British Museum, though the Irish government has got some of them back. You must read Michael Poynder's poetry — he lives out there — you'll get his book in the crafts show, and see what he makes of it all. I don't really know about that side, the religious side, but I've photographed it from the air, and seen all sorts of alignments with other ancient places, Croagh Patrick and so on.' David Knight, I learned later, was chairman of the Arts Festival committee.

I visited the arts and crafts exhibition in the GAA Social Centre and was amazed. This was not, as one might expect in a town of 2,300 people, a display of work by enthusiastic amateurs 'who were putting their free time to good use'. Excellence and exquisiteness characterised the brassware and hand-painted mirrors, the pressed flowers on cards or framed as 'paintings', the candles embossed with flower designs, the pottery and hand-made notepaper, the screen-prints and children's clothes, even the toys made from clothes-pegs. At the end of the room a German gold-and-silver smith, fat, bearded and bespectacled, stood over his tray of wares, explaining his work to children with infinite good humour. I bought Michael Poynder's book of poems, printed by the *Leitrim Observer*. It was called *The Carrowkeel Crystal Poetry* and had a foreword by Sir George Trevelyan which predicted a great flowering of 'the Celtic soul, the real Folk Soul' in Ireland. Michael Poynder, I read, was a Londoner of Irish extraction, who had settled near Carrowkeel in 1961. His poem 'Ireland' began:

> This Island can become a jewel again,
> The centre of the earthly crown...

Readings by the women writers' group were to begin in a pub up the town at 8.15. At 9.30, when they got under way, about forty people were present, a quarter of them men. (More arrived later, most of them men.) Five women — Bernadette Foley of the night before was one of them — were listened to in silence as they read prose and verse, and each of them was applauded generously. During the interval, Mary Cryan, who had been introducing the readers, told me, 'We're not very experienced, but we're hoping to advance. We write as women, but for a wider audience.' The women writers' group in Ballinamore, Co. Leitrim, had helped to get the Boyle group going. Peg Sheehan, who had founded the Ballinamore group — though she lived most of the time in Brussels with her husband — was present as a sisterly delegate and guest of honour. I had forgotten that Boyle was the political headquarters of Seán Doherty, the politician, but was vividly reminded of it when the readings resumed and his wife, Maura, was introduced as one of the readers. She read a polished short story about Black and Tan times on Stongia, a wild moor on Arigna mountain near her home-place. 'Seán

109

thinks well of you, you spoke up for him when he had his troubles,' she said, when I was introduced to her later. I was gratified to find one article I had written, four years previously, so graciously remembered. When I talked to her about her writing, she said she had learned a lot from William Trevor and Molly Keane.

A feeling was growing in me that, from Ballintrillick and the Dromahair area southwards, I had been moving through a region that was sharing and evolving a common and distinctive consciousness. The town of Sligo was its northern pole, Boyle its southern one. Through the '70s and '80s, and through the interaction of immigrant and native elements, a surge of collective self-possession and self-confidence had been taking place. With little attention paid to the rest of Ireland, a distinctive 'style' of mind and feeling had been taking shape. And as always in such cases, there was an outward, assertive thrust, on various levels, against the established order of things and power. At one extreme, based on the Swedish excavations at Carrowmore, there was the challenge to the primacy of Newgrange in the Stone Age, and to the Dublin archaeological establishment which upheld it. At the other extreme, in the most contemporary of political terms, there had been the simultaneous ascent to ministerial power in Dublin of Ray MacSharry from Sligo and Seán Doherty from Boyle — and the violent backlash of the Dublin establishment and its media which had arraigned them and tried to destroy them. In yet another sense, Doris Manly and her *Ballintrillick Review* were part of it. In the Royal Hotel that night, on the way to my 'river room', and with céilí music sounding from the upstairs lounge, I had a literally eye-opening confirmation of my hunch. I ran into Vincent Regan in the hall, and when I told him of this impression I had been getting, he said, 'You might be interested in this' and handed me a handsome folder, covered with scenic photographs, which was entitled 'Lough Key Country'. Inside was an illustrated map, its back covered with printed notes on 'places of interest', and the map extended from Tulsk and Strokestown, ten miles south of Boyle, up through Co. Sligo to Lough Gill and Dromahair, and up through Carrick-on-Shannon and Drumshanbo to Lough Allen and the mountain forests of North Leitrim. It had been published, I noted, by

110

Lough Key Promotions Ltd of Boyle. 'Lough Key Country' — now there was percipient imperialism for you! But what struck me most about it was that there, mapped before my eyes — except for the extension southwards — was the very area whose distinctive unity I had been sensing.

I was aware that Frenchpark, Douglas Hyde's birthplace and home, and Cruachain, the ancient royal seat of Connacht, lay a few miles to the south; and both evoked debts of piety which I wished to pay. Passing through fat grazing country into the village of Frenchpark, I averted my eyes, incredulously, from a pub-sign, 'The Hyde-Out', and stopped at another pub to enquire. Hyde, I was told, was buried at a Church of Ireland church a mile and a half out the Ballaghadereen road, and the place where his house, Ratra House, had stood, was farther on, down a turn on the right. 'It isn't standing then?' 'The roof had fallen in, so they knocked it down.' In the churchyard, which I found as indicated, there was a line of Hyde graves with simple Celtic crosses on the headstones. Just beside his own was the grave of his wife, Lucy, *uxor dilectissima* and his daughter, *Nuala Eibhlín filia dilectissima*, who had died aged twenty-two in 1916. His own simple grave declared him to be First President of Ireland, in Gaelic and English. A small memorial plaque from the GAA lay on the gravel. I wondered at this grave — such a far cry from, say, the Washington Memorial; and why? But as yet I had hardly turned my mind to what I had heard of his house. Farther along the road I turned down a lane and came to crumbling gate-posts and a rusting gate. Grass stretched beyond them and there was a low mound with bushes around it. A man carrying a bucket emerged from a cottage to the left, and I asked him where the house had stood. He pointed to the low mound. 'Who knocked it down?' I asked. 'The Gaelic League', he said. 'It's a pity', I said. 'It's not the only one,' he said. 'Sure them are all gone now', and with a vigorous turn of his body he strode off across a field swinging the bucket.

Back in the village I looked up Dermot Allman in the post office. Maura Doherty, when I told her I was going to Frenchpark, had said he could tell me anything I might want to

111

know. He was a big Kerryman. Douglas Hyde, he said, had left Ratra House to the Gaelic League, and they had left it in the care of Fr Tom Lavin, a curate of the parish, who was an official of the League. In order that the League wouldn't have to pay rates on it, he had had the roof taken off. Later the League sold it to a farmer called Flynn. Then, when a contractor, J. V. O'Connor of Castlerea, was looking around for 'fill' for the foundations of the milk products factory in Ballaghadereen, he bought the stone of Hyde's house from Flynn — he also took the stone of Lord Freyne's house in Frenchpark. 'Under Shannon-side Milk Products, Ballaghadereen, that's where it is now. Sure for these people here, God is a bullock. They don't even support their own football team. Maybe in Kerry we build too many monuments. But we know who we are. These people have no sense of identity.'

Sitting in his living-room off the post-office, over coffee, I asked him about the Catholic Bible sects which bishops in those parts had been warning about a few years previously. It had all begun, he said, with Canice Clark, who was a teacher in the diocesan seminary in Ballaghadereen and a promoter of the charismatic movement. It was through him that Tom Mahon, a businessman with well-known republican sympathies and a member of Alcoholics Anonymous, became attracted to the movement and decided to form a group which would apply to it the 'twelve steps' of AA. He became 'its self-appointed high priest or archbishop and his wife the female equivalent'. They had baptismal ceremonies, by full immersion, in Lough Gara on Sunday afternoons. 'Which reminds me of a story. One Sunday a crowd of the lads were coming home from the pubs and they lurked in the bushes watching. Mahon's lot was about to baptise a young girl, who was totally in the nip, and he was just casting out the devils when there was a loud noise at her rear end. One of the fellows called out, "Jaykist, the divils are well out of her now.' Then there was another group started in Castlerea by a fellow, also an AA type, who was a college lecturer in Limerick, and there was a big row about a local woman teacher who became its chief apostle, so to speak. She lost her job there and later tried to get one here, but she didn't because the parents didn't want her and the Bishop of Elphin supported them. But if you want to know about their doctrines and methods, look up Mahon when you're passing through Ballaghadereen. He runs a guesthouse called the Western.'

As an informant Dermot Allman had come up trumps. I thanked him and set off on the Tulsk road to look for Cruachain. I knew from a learned article I had read that the entire site included many earthworks, some of them notable, covering an area of four square miles. Along with Tara, Emain Macha and Brú na Bóinne, it is one of the four principal sites of ancient Ireland. All I wanted, however, was to stand on the principal mound, Cruachain proper, so to speak. I will not go into the hide-and-seek details of my search for it. Suffice to say that the neglect and disrespect with which Cruachain has been treated by Roscommon County Council, the other authorities concerned, and the local people — either actively or by acquiescence — does none of them any credit. There were some signs on the road, true enough, but they were useless as signs. Eventually, following the directions of a local woman, I went in through an open gate; crossed a pathless, stone-strewn field within yards of a silage-pit; slid under an electric fence; and climbed onto the broad, circular mound where Ailill and Maebh had their pillow-talk that launched the armies of Ireland against Ulster. Freshly-baled hay lay around me. Miles of flat Connacht land stretched to the horizon. There was no naming or explanatory notice of any kind.

Setting out to return to Boyle, I gave a lift to a man who wanted to go to Elphin. Just after we had turned off the Tulsk-Boyle road, heading for that town, I saw a large IRA memorial. Raised on a lofty plinth were three giant figures of republican guerillas carrying rifles; two of them standing, the third on his knees. I recognised it as the work of my deceased friend, Garry Trimble. The inscription on the plinth, in Gaelic and English, read: 'In proud and loving memory of the Roscommon soldiers of the Irish Republican Army whose names are inscribed hereon, who made the supreme sacrifice in defence of the Republic proclaimed on Easter Monday 1916.' Underneath this: 'Ireland unfree shall never be at peace. P. H. Pearse' and about forty names in Gaelic. It reminded me of one Sam Cryan 'of Carrowrae, Carrick-on-Shannon, Co. Roscommon', whose trial I had been reading about in the papers a short time before. He had been jailed for having eighty-four Kalashnikov rifles in a shed near his house — arms destined for the IRA in the North, it seemed. I recalled at the time a man by the name of Cryan whom I had met once in Carrick after giving a lecture there. The road I was on was pointed towards Carrick, and I guessed from the 'Co. Roscommon' in the address that Carrowrae could not be far away. In Elphin I made enquiries and found I was only a few miles from the place.

The house was on the top of a hill on a back-road near lakes. The man standing beside a car in front of it said he was Dick Cryan. 'I'm calling because of Sam,' I said, 'to say I'm sorry for his trouble.' A boy of sixteen and a girl of about thirteen were with him. 'My niece and nephew,' he said. 'Come in for a cup of tea'. Dick, it turned out, was the brother who had lived with Sam. In the kitchen I met another brother, Pádraig, the father of the children, who had driven up from Carrick. He remembered me from the lecture fifteen years previously. Dick and the girl disappeared and Pádraig made me tea. He was obviously the head of the family. 'I was a butcher in Carrick', he said, 'until my eyesight gave. Since this happened to Sam, I come up here as much as I can to help with the farm.' He talked about the day Sam and Dick were taken to Carrick for questioning. 'Well,' he said, 'the people around knew for days before that something was going on, only Sam didn't seem to know. Two men were seen on the hill over there, looking through binoculars. They said they were hunting. Then people down the road saw this van marked 'Ordnance Survey' and two men working with an eye-level and acting as if they were measuring the road. And when a woman who lives there spoke to one of them, and he began to explain what they were doing, the other called him over and shut him up. And there were these cars with a man and a woman in each of them passing along the road. They had brought detectives down from Dublin, and on the day they took Sam and Dick in, there were about a hundred of them around the house. A man called Hegarty in Derry was the informer. He disappeared the same day to England, and later when he came back he was shot. Dick was let go but Sam was taken to Dublin for trial. But in the court they had no evidence. Sam said he knew nothing and you'll see for yourself there's a separate entrance to the shed where they found the stuff. But then at the end of the trial, the Sergeant handed a piece of paper to the judges and Sam was sentenced to seven years. Hegarty gave others away too — along the route, you might say. There was a man in Gurteen near Boyle and a man in Strandhill near Sligo. Besides, they *had* observed a van coming and going here and had followed it.'

We talked for a while about a four-province federal Ireland — the theme of my lecture — and how it would be a good thing and why it hadn't taken on. The boy had been listening all the time, and to bring him in I asked was he interested in politics. 'He knows the slogans, "Brits Out" and the like,' his father said, 'but his older brother has more of an intellectual grasp.' 'I must be going', I said. 'But you must have a drink,' said Pádraig. 'They'll be back any minute.' They came shortly after with whiskey, Dick and the girl, and Pádraig poured me a generous glass. 'It was the monument made me think of calling on you', I said. 'Yes,' said Dick, 'our own crowd put you in jail now for doing what those ones did. When they got power, they got corrupted.' 'But doesn't that always happen?' I said. 'It's easy to be pure in your ideals when you haven't power.' We thought and talked for a few minutes about power and its mysteries. Then Pádraig took me out and showed me the shed and its separate entrance. As we approached my car, the others were there before us and they moved towards us. 'So that's the famous shed', I said to Dick. 'Yes,' he said, 'and who knows but one day it really will be famous. Ours is a strange history.' He stood facing me. 'I'll tell Sam you called,' he said. 'He'll be very pleased.' 'It was the least I could do.' 'It was the most you could do.' I saw that he was almost crying. I looked towards the girl, who was looking at her uncle, and saw with a shock that, like all young girls, although she had said nothing, she had taken everything in, felt everything, knew everything, and she was trying not to cry. I shook hands abruptly with the men, got into the car, and drove off, waving to them; and I, too, staring blankly at the road, managed to hold the tears back.

That night again, there was music in the Royal Hotel. It began with traditional music of the first class. A young man in black trousers stood on the stage playing the bodhrán while another man, seated, played the accordion. I was sitting beside the bearded, bespectacled German goldsmith, whose name was Erwin, and his Swiss girlfriend, Vitta. I had got into conversation with them in German. Erwin told me he had been three

115

years in Ireland. He sold his work through a Swiss gallery and a jeweller's in Dublin. Deirdre Cunningham, the bodhrán-player's wife, who had been giving a music workshop during the festival, was in charge of the evening. After the traditional music she gave us some French songs. Later when I met her, and asked her, because of her accent, was she from Dublin, she said she had picked it up living for five years among Dubliners in Holland. A family played traditional music. Then a woman played the piano with a man on a guitar and a youth on a fiddle. 'You know, the musical talent in Ireland is incredible,' said Erwin. 'Just listen to them, and they've never played together before.' I met the young Englishwoman, Annette Preston, who had done the exquisite pressed flowers, and told her next time I came there, when I wasn't on a long journey and watching expenses, I'd buy up her whole stock. Now the music was country and western and, a little later, old-time waltzes, and the floor was full of dancers. When it changed to rock, and finally to Irish dancing, there was never any lack of takers. I asked a couple of women out and another woman asked me. It was the best night-club I had been in for a long time. I remembered that the philosopher, Michael Tobin and his Dutch companion, Caroline Kujper had been living near Boyle and sending me their newsletters about the New Age. Then a rich American woman bought them a large house in Donegal. Vitta said she had known him, Erwin was doubtful. 'He believed', I said, 'that the Irish Folk Soul would be the salvation of the world.' 'Oh well, that's true', said Erwin, as of something obvious. A man had sat down on the other side of me, and I had judged by his accent that he was a Westerner. He turned out to be a German engineer who had thrown up his career and settled near Boyle only six months previously; and the plump little woman beside him, who bought us all a drink, was his wife. She told me he was writing science fiction and had some very good ideas. I think they finished by playing the National Anthem. That was my last night in Boyle.

5.
BOYLE
TO LEENANE

AROUND noon, taking the Frenchpark road, I set off for
Cleggan in Connemara. A few miles out I turned west onto the
potholed road that crosses between the two parts of Lough Gara.
I stopped and talked to a man who told me that, when the lake
was drained in the early '50s, they uncovered three hundred
crannógs or lake-dwellings 'where people had lived maybe
hundreds of thousands of years ago', and many boats hollowed
out of trees. 'It hasn't been as good for fishing since, but there's
still a good deal of pike and roach and bream and perch. Lots of
English will be coming to fish it soon.' Northwards over the lake
I could see Knocknarea near Sligo. The village of Monasteraden
was spruce and pretty. A woman in a shop said some lads did a
lot of work on it under a 'Manpower scheme'. Near the church,
for the first time on the journey, I saw the clustered yellow
flowers of St John's wort. The road to Ballaghadereen ran past a
large bog and a long stretch of low wet-looking country. As I
approached the town, I saw at some distance the large high
buildings of what I took to be Shannonside Co-op, under which
Douglas Hyde's house lies buried. A graceful neo-gothic spire
held sway over wide streets. I enquired for Tom Mahon's guesthouse and was directed to a side-street.

A girl, who turned out to be his daughter, said he was looking
after his furniture shop in Swinford, and her mother was away
on holidays. I said, 'I wanted to talk to him about his — sect or
cult', and knew I had blundered. 'It's not a sect or cult,' she said.
'They're just Christians.' 'Are you a member?' 'No.' 'Why
haven't you joined them?' 'It's not a question of joining them. I
go to some of their meetings.' She didn't know whether they had
any literature, I'd need to ask him. I said I was sorry to miss both
her parents. I admired her for her loyalty and wished I could

117

have shown her better that I had no 'attitude', and only wanted information. I sat in the car for a few minutes listening to a radio discussion on current affairs from Dublin. The political correspondent of a newspaper was pontificating on 'rural Ireland' — meaning, as Dublin journalists do, the entire Republic outside Dublin. Then I had some lunch and left for Ballyhaunis.

After a couple of miles the road became incredibly bad. Much of it was a succession of parallel cracks; the whole thing seemed about to disintegrate into the surrounding marsh. On both sides was the most desolate country I had seen since North Mayo, with farms on low hills in the distance. A green sign at the entrance to the town said 'Halal Meat Packers Ltd. Turn left on square'. I did and came to a long street with walls and buildings extending along its left side as far as the eye could see, and a wide gate some distance down. Refrigerated container trucks, Irish and foreign, were coming and going or standing parked in the yard inside the gate. The Halal containers had green cabs and bore the word 'Irlande'. As I parked in a large car-park to the right, I saw, across an open space where machines were levelling the soil, a new white two-storey mansion. The bottom storey had four broad arches pointed discreetly in Muslim style. A man in the street told me it had thirty-six rooms, and that Mr Rafique wasn't living in it yet. All the Pakistanis, he said, about thirty of them, had been living 'in that low building behind the wall over there'. Yes, Mr Rafique was married, 'but he has only one wife. In his religion they have only one, but in parts of his country the men have five or six wives.' Halal employed about 350 people.

The girl at the reception window said Mr Rafique was away, but Mr Khalid would see me. As I passed through the general office on the way to the waiting-room, I noticed among the men in white coats several with brown skin. After ten minutes or so, the stoutest of these came to talk to me, but almost immediately he had to take a phone call beside me. 'John', he said, 'I want you and Liam McDonnell to go to Limerick for me. Do you think you could manage? Liam isn't tied up? There are three tons of fillet there I want examined.' Turning to me then, with an open, intelligent face, and speaking softly, he went back to the beginning. There were six Pakistanis there permanently, with their families. They had been in England first — from the way he used the word 'we' I took him to be speaking of an extended family — and had come to Ireland in 1973 looking for a meat plant to buy. This one, in Ballyhaunis, had been closed down and was the only one available, so they took it, brought it up to EEC standards, and opened it in 1974. They began by exporting lamb to Libya. 'Halal' meant the Muslim method of slaughtering — slit the throat, let all the blood out. Yes, the green on their road-signs and trucks was the Islamic green, though happily, he smiled, it coincided with the Irish green. Gradually they had expanded and were now exporting all over North Africa, the Middle East and Western Europe. They had two other plants in Connacht — in Sligo and Ballaghadereen — three in other parts of Ireland, and two in Britain. Their Paris office looked after their trading on the continent. They were now the biggest lamb processors in Europe, but only the second biggest beef company in Ireland, Anglo-Irish being the biggest. In Ballyhaunis they had a slaughtering capacity of 2,500 cattle a week. When I said I had been told they had a take-it-or-leave-it attitude to the farmers, he said, 'There's about thirty meat plants in this country, they don't have to come here. We treat everyone exactly equal, whether they have a thousand cattle or ten. Our pricing manager works with a girl on a computer. The price is agreed beforehand on the phone.' Would I like to look around? He phoned Seán Byrne, the general manager, and handed me over to him.

As Seán, a young, soft-spoken Mayoman, took me through the general office to get me a white coat and helmet, a lad said something to him, pointed towards the office, and, raising his two hands, bowed his head twice. Seán told him what to do. Glancing back to the office, I saw that all the Pakistanis were absent. 'He was saying they were gone to pray?' I remarked to Seán. 'Yes', he said, 'they have a prayer-room in their house. One of their prayer-times is during office-hours.' First he showed me a chamber of carcasses 'for an English supermarket', then pointed to a truck 'for a customer in France'. They could dispatch 140 trucks a day, each carrying twenty tons, but normally dispatched about seventy. In a room where meat was being packed into boxes, he had one of them opened, showed me a large piece of meat wrapped in a transparent envelope, pointed out how lean it was, and then noticed that the envelope did not fit the shape of the meat exactly — he could grip a piece of the plastic material in his fingers. Calling over the man who had opened it, he said, 'Get that fitting tightly and check through that pile.' I noticed that everyone who approached him called him Seán. He showed me a chamber kept at twenty degrees below zero, where meat was frozen for export by ship to Iran, Iraq and Egypt. I entered it briefly, shuddered, and withdrew. I asked him what, in his experience, was the real difference between Halal slaughtering and how it is normally done in Ireland. 'The principal thing is that there's a mullah to say a prayer and cut the throat. We have three mullahs here, one for lamb, one for beef, and one in reserve. Also great care is taken to treat the beast humanely, not to cause stress of any kind in the moment before slaughter. We have special equipment for that. That's in accordance with their religion, but it also makes for better meat.' We passed the sheep and cattle lairages and crossed through the empty slaughter-room. We ended our tour in the new canning plant where they had begun to can burgers and corned beef. Seán said that Halal was now by far the biggest buyer of meat in Connacht, and had been a great benefit to Western farmers. 'You remember how they used have to sell the young cattle to the Midlands and Meath and leave the finishing to be done there.' 'Yes', I said, 'I've been hearing of cattle being finished here, and I was taught at school that Connacht simply didn't have the land to do that and *had* to sell east. *Can* it be finished properly here?' 'Well', said Seán, 'not in Connemara maybe, but in parts of Mayo and Sligo, and in Roscommon, and in South Galway and around Tuam, you can finish it as well as anywhere.'

From Ballyhaunis it is only six and a half miles to Knock. As I approached it I saw with excitement the slender tall spire of the Basilica above trees. Passing bungalows with fine flower-gardens and B and B signs, and the Basilica off to the left beyond a lawn and young trees, I turned into the long main street which is also the Galway-Sligo high road. About two hundred cars were parked along it. It reminded me of Charlestown with its assembly of eating and lodging houses. I parked and took a walk.

The fifty or so booths specialising in the pilgrim trade are in a special area off the street, and are truly amazing. One wonders what unknown factories supply all these wares. One woman-

120

vendor estimated to me that she carried about 200 lines, and her booth was typical. There were all sizes and colours of rosaries, rosary rings, Knock pen-knives and tea spoons, plastic holy-water containers, Padre Pio and Sacred Heart wall-plates, toy cameras, Knock rock, all sorts of souvenir biros, Virgins, and Infants of Prague, crucifixes in all sizes, every kind of holy medal, miniature beer glasses marked 'The Greatest Dad' or 'With Love to Grandma', little trays with a standing picture of Monsignor Horan holding the Pope's Golden Rose and, in front of it, a tiny statue of the Virgin. 'Has that been made since he died?' I asked. 'No,' said the girl, 'we had them before but no one seemed to bother with them.' But the stock in the booths was as nothing to that carried by the half-dozen large pilgrims' shops, with elegant striped awnings, near the Church of the Apparition on the main street.

At the gable of this church, the original village church, a glass structure enclosed large white marble statues of the Blessed Virgin, St Joseph and St John — depicting the apparition. On benches within, people sat praying and chatting. From inside the church, over loudspeakers, came the voice of a priest giving out the rosary. Circling the church and the open-air stations of the cross behind it, several hundred people, moving in procession, responded to him. They were led by a group of stewards, royal-blue sashes over their suits, carrying a statue of the Virgin surrounded by flowers. Immediately behind them came about twenty invalids in wheelchairs pushed by handmaids in head-veils. Echoing across the great piazza, between the decades of the rosary, the priest's voice spoke prayers and meditations: 'Comfort me when I am sick or lonely or depressed.' 'All life is sacred, in the womb, in the streets, in the hospital bed.'

From the old church and the stations of the cross the piazza slopes downwards parallel with the street, past beds of roses, to a line of evergreen trees and the entrance from the South Bus Park. Beyond the trees, grass rises steeply to flower-beds, a line of conifers and the sky-line. To the east of the piazza, beyond a forty-foot Celtic cross, stands the circular, concrete Basilica, designed expressly to serve its functions. Inside its fifty-six glazed doors, a wide corridor, running around its circumference, allows the sick to attend services on stretchers and in wheelchairs. Five chapels, each internally divided so as to form in effect ten,

121

converge on the central sanctuary. According to the amount of seating used, the Basilica can hold from 7,500 to 20,000 people. On the open ground behind it, on the site chosen by himself, I visited James Horan's flower-covered grave. Beyond it to the south east stretched the quiet lawns and flower-beds of Our Lady's Domain, and beyond that again, in gently rising fields, lines of young conifers pricked the skyline. The beauty of Knock is growing, literally, year by year. Horan, the romantic, has left romance after him.

'Baile Glan, Baile Álainn', said a notice at the entrance to Claremorris, and this multi-coloured town lived up to it. As the road took a generally western slant, Croaghpatrick stood ahead of me far off; to the south of it, the Partry Mountains, and those of North Connemara, all limned wraith-like against an amber break in the sky. At Hollymount I turned off the main road to visit George Moore's place on Lough Carra. The lake was dead calm in a landscape of rushes and scrub. Driving along it I came to a sign 'Moore Park. Forest and Wildlife Service', standing in front of a forest. A narrow road between the trees and the lake brought me past an anglers' club into a large car-park, at the far end of which a single red car was parked. I parked near it and got out. A young man in a white pullover was bent into the boot of the car and I got a shadowy impression of a girl in the passenger-seat. Looking around, I could see only trees, no sign of Moore Hall. Did the house — I knew it had been burned — stand in this open space, and had they done a Ratra on it? I asked the young man was he from these parts, and he answered in an English accent that he wasn't, was I looking for something? 'A house', I said. I drove back to a bungalow near the 'Moore Hall' sign, and the woman who came to the door said yes, the Hall, or rather the skeleton of it, was still standing. I must drive to the end of the car-park and there was a wooden stile there leading to it. At this time of the year it was probably hidden by foliage. Returning to the car-park, I stopped again near the red car. Through the misted window of the passenger seat I saw what I took to be the man's white pullover suddenly heaving into a great commotion and a man's bare bottom presented itself at the glass. Averting my eyes, I stepped out, headed into the trees, found and crossed the stile, followed a path through spruce, then birch, and saw the big house with its two chimney-stacks, Georgian door and three storeys of gaping windows. Gazing at it I thought I heard voices in its rooms. When I regained the car-park the red car was gone, but a potted plant in a plastic bag stood where it had been standing.

Driving between long stone walls, in desultory rain, I reached Ballinrobe. It had some stone buildings; otherwise its 'country' colours (mainly grey) were broken only by a few discreet touches of green. In Neale about fifty parked cars outside the church suggested Saturday-evening mass. Skirting the wall of Ashford Castle I entered the picturesque village of Cong, with its twisting, humped streets, and on a bridge over a lovely pond, disturbed by bubblings and eddyings, entered Co. Galway. I was making for Leenane, eighteen miles away. A large pearl-coloured break in the darkening western sky disappeared from view as I passed through long tree tunnels into the Joyce Country, glimpsing the first of its dark-blue mountains. Then, around a turn, there was the spread of Lough Corrib, vast and splendid with its islands. The road twisted and turned above it; it was a regal road. Hedges heavy with red and purple fuchsia blossoms completed the unmistakable Connemara *mélange*. The road left the lake, passed through Cornamona, and climbed into the mountains. Suddenly down ahead, at the foot of massed, black mountains, what seemed to be another lake — a long, narrow lake — took me by surprise, until I realised it was an arm of Lough Corrib. Seeing a red glow ahead over one of the black mountains, I muttered 'Goodbye sun'. After Maum only the grass near me was still green, and then a shower made that black too, and green showed only under the headlights. The road was narrow and winding but well-surfaced, and I maintained speed by practising the skill, learnt in South Connemara years before, of hugging the left margin. Through a gap in the mountains I saw a V of blue and amber light. Would it last until I reached Killary Harbour? There were lights in houses on the valley sides. Sheep ambled along the road or lay down on it nonchalantly. The V disappeared from view and I was grateful for the little reflectors on sticks placed along the sides of the road. As I began to descend a steep defile, Leenane announced itself in a line of houses on the side of the road, some with B and B signs. Emerging from the defile, I saw the last of the light on a full Killary and parked outside Gaynor's, Select Bar and Family

Grocer. I walked to the sea-wall and looked out over the calm fjord in which someone once said the entire British fleet could anchor. Seeing the faintest last light in the gap between the mountains seawards, I felt thankful for the light, thankful that we know it will come again. And feeling I deserved a pint, I walked back into Gaynor's.

6.
KYLEMORE VIA ARAN TO KINVARA

I WOKE to see strong sunlight through the window, pink wall-paper, a shower and lavatory *en suite*. I recalled that this was Kylemore House, that it cost £13, and that, in an attempt to reach Cleggan from Leenane, I had been lured by the lit-up house perched just above the road. But I had no idea of the sight that would meet my eyes when I stepped out on the front porch: almost at the end of the lawn, it seemed — the intervening road was hidden from view — a sunlit lake backed by steep mountains and fringed, on the near side, by fuchsia.

At breakfast I heard Raidío na Gaeltachta from the kitchen and the first *sean-nós* song of my journey. That, too, I had for-gotten it, was an ingredient of the Connemara *mélange*. But I was a little surprised — though there could be various explana-tions — to hear Raidío na Gaeltachta, for I knew that Gaelic wasn't spoken in those parts. When I asked the woman of the house, Mrs Naughton, about it, she said that neither she nor her husband were Gaelic-speakers — though he, who was from South Mayo, knew some — but that they simply liked the music and the *sean-nós* singing. Visitors to North Connemara, which is where most of the tourists come, are often surprised for an opposite kind of reason; there was one such woman in Kylemore House that day. They expect, because they are in Connemara, to hear people talking Gaelic, and are surprised when they don't. In fact most of Connemara is English-speaking, and you are about as likely to hear Gaelic there as you are in Dublin; which means, of course, that you may, occasionally. The only part where Gaelic is the everyday language is along the coast, and some distance inland, from Bertraghboy Bay or Cárna almost to Barna on the edge of Galway; that is to say, in a large part of South Connemara; the part that, along with the Aran

Islands, we 're-named' Iarchonnacht in the civil rights days of the early '70s. Iarchonnacht was the old name of the entire area west of Lough Corrib and the southern half of Lough Mask that is now called, loosely, Connemara; that name was restricted to the land and coast around the Twelve Bens.

As we left for mass in Kylemore Abbey I noticed on the wall of the porch a large framed sheet illustrating sixty-two fishing flies. There was a short text on each, and a long historical piece about the family firm, Rogan of Donegal, established in Ballyshannon in 1830 — all in *Swedish*. 'You who long for the estuaries of Norr-land, or let your dreams dance over Lappland's silvery streams, you have heard the name... Rogan of Donegal.' At the bottom was an address in Stockholm. Once again, as on so many occasions, I thought how little I knew about Ireland.

After mass in the Abbey, I looked at the lake — another one — the crowding mountains, the castellated Abbey set against the wooded mountain, and knew that no amount of picture postcards could make it banal. I set off for Cleggan between hedges of rhododendron and fuchsia which were so luxuriant and well-tended that it was not until I saw people saving hay, and ordinary cottages and road-signs, that I was sure I was not still in the Abbey grounds. On my entire long journey, the creamy meadow-sweet had accompanied me — the wet summer suited it — and by now I had developed an affection for it as for a travelling companion through thick and thin. Occasionally, seeing it combined with purple loosestrife, I could ask for no more. Now, on the road to Cleggan, that com-bination ran rampant. In the last couple of miles, the red and yellow mombretia, a runaway from gardens, appeared, first in patches, then continuously along the road.

Cleggan had improved its looks compared with, say, the early '70s when I first visited it. Then it still had the Cleggan Disaster written all over its sad, desolate face. The Disaster was the loss at sea in one night in 1927 of forty fishermen, mostly from Cleggan and Inishbofin. The pubs and shops along its street had put on fresh paint and a look of prosperity. There were fishing-boats again in the harbour. That, and its being the point of departure for beautiful and popular Inishbofin, had helped. But the harbour, even granted that it was a work-place, was still ugly. The Pier Bar, though agreeable inside, had a bleak exterior.

And the approach to the harbour was past a wasteland of nettles and rusty corrugated iron, and a patch of weed-filled grass in which park seats and children's swings stood abandoned. You saw straight away that no Manpower or youth employment scheme had been at work in the recent past, and that the place had no Tidy Towns Committee or community council. It was what I had seen in Ceathrú Thaidhg all over again: co-operation paralysed; private splendour, public squalor.

Coyne's big pub was filled with handsome men and women with large well-shaped bodies and intense dramatic faces, expressing themselves in forceful speech. The men — no pot-bellies here — wore grey or navy trousers and white or blue shirts. The women, whether in leather skirt and long-sleeved satin blouse, or in green corduroy pants, or yellow skirt and grey, white and yellow short-sleeved top, wore their clothes with what they call in Connemara 'shtyle'. It was the afternoon of the Meath-Kerry football final and the television was blaring, but no one was watching it, for it was the Minors' match that always precedes the big match. A woman, turning her head towards it, asked her neighbour, 'Who's playing in the Minors?' Poor Minors.

In Cleggan the simplest way of introducing myself is as 'Cilian's father', for my son, Cilian, graduated in fishing here under the tutelage of Pat Walsh (pronounced Welsh). But Pat had retired from fishing to become a fish-buyer and to open a fish-shop just above the harbour. When I visited him there, in his house beside the shop, he told me he had just bought the fine red-sandstone house across from him which the poet Richard Murphy built when he lived here. I asked him to recommend a B and B 'with a view', and he sent me to Feeny's a mile up the road beside the sheltered Salerna beach where the two survivors from the Cleggan Disaster struggled ashore. Pat told me that much, but later I discovered that Michael Feeny's father, Festy, had been one of those survivors — Michael is also a fisherman; and his wife, Marion, showed me a newspaper article about her father-in-law. Their house, called 'Ocean Wave', had the view I wanted — out over open sea to Inishbofin, Inishturk, and the smaller islands between them and the mainland. Because Cleggan is far up a bay you need to go some distance out from it to see the open sea.

I cycled to Clifden, about eight miles away, the St Tropez of Connemara. I was struck, as I had been from Kylemore onwards, by the increase, since I was there last, in the number of guesthouses, restaurants and the like with Gaelic names. On the northern edge of Clifden there is a well-known hotel which used to be called simply the Abbeyglen, but which has now added 'Castle'. Tommy Fitzherbert, manager of the Belleek Castle in Ballina, had told me that his friend, Paul Hughes, who managed the Clifden hotel had been adding 'battlements and things'. I turned in to see it and immediately noticed the castle-like protrusion in the front which had been added quite skilfully — though it did have a certain *papier-maché* quality — to the dignified original building. As it happened, an American, accompanied by his Chinese-looking daughter, was examining the front closely, and pointing out to her where the new joined the old that he had known during his visit there eight years previously. I wandered inside and upstairs, noticing some feudal additions to the furniture and a notice on a lounge-door indicating that it was the office of a film company.

Clifden is on high ground beside the sea, but, probably because its 'sea' is extremely tidal and its harbour therefore not up to much, it faces inland. Partly because I have seen the town in all seasons, Clifden in summer has always struck me as a painted stage-set. But even in summer you can get this impression if you view it from the back, so to speak; from the harbour or seaside. For then there is hardly a sign of the brightly-painted facades, and you see in the grey and brown and uncared-for backs what the town 'really is', or would be without the tourists. On that Sunday afternoon, its main street and adjoining streets were a riot of colour in bright sunlight. I say 'riot' deliberately because it suggests unruliness: you could see there what 'shocking' pink or green or yellow really means — and that they can be appropriate in a place of fantasy. Expensive cars were parked or cruising among the hotels and bars, the restaurants and coffee-shops, the shops selling crystal and tweed. People from several European nations and the USA strolled about in holiday clothes. Fresh fruit and vegetables were being sold on the square. Among the new restaurants, I noticed particularly one called O'Grady's that was painted white and stood beside a narrow white lane. Enticed down this lane by a sign saying 'Wine Bar', I tried the door and found it wasn't open. Continuing past the office of a Danish travel agency, I emerged in another lane running at right-angles and saw men working on a wooden structure which they were covering with a plastic substance to make it look like old stone work. My heart sank as I surmised that this was an extension to the restaurant, but one of the men told me they were making a set for a film about a boy who left Ireland for America during the Famine. It struck me that the sight of this actual stage-set being tacked onto a town that was itself a stage-set was an appropriate culmination to my walk around Clifden.

It was dark when I reached Feenys' house, and I could see lights on Inishbofin, though not so many as I would have expected; it has 250 inhabitants. Marie and Peter, the two older children, were sitting watching television. Marie gave me a cup of coffee. She had just finished primary school at Claddaghduff. Yes, she said, it was a good school, 'and we've become cleaner since the new curate arrived. He's brilliant. He pays you for every paper you pick up and gives you two pounds for cleaning the school grounds'. She was going on to the Community School in Clifden. (For the past twenty years or so, all the schools in Connemara have been co-ed.) Her hobby used to be collecting stamps, now it was coins. When her father went out with another man lifting lobsters, she rowed the boat for them. Talking of her brothers and sisters, she said 'The one Mammy's going to have is her seventh. There's the two of us, and two younger ones in bed. And there was one who was handicapped and died after a year and a half. And one she had for one and and a half months and had to get out.' She was referring, I gathered, to a miscarriage.

Next morning there was a total reversal of the weather: it was raining, cold and windy. Mrs Feeny gave me a booklet-guide to Cleggan-Claddaghduff. It was very well done, with all the information a visitor would require, and in view of the uncared-for impression that the Cleggan harbour area had made on me — and the deductions I had drawn from it — I was surprised to see that it was published by 'Cleggan-Claddaghduff Community Council'.

Pat Walsh had told me that the fishermen from Inishturk came into the harbour every evening about eight with fish, so I had planned to take the regular ferry to Inishbofin in the morning, come back about five or six, and then hitch a lift to Inishturk. But when Paddy O'Halloran finally arrived with the ferry from Inishbofin around midday, the weather had become so bad that there were no day-trippers to take in. He said there was no one on the island wanting to Cleggan either, so he would not be returning in the evening. Up in Coyne's they said Kevin Heaney would be coming in from 'Turk to bring three ESB men to the island to install a generator. So I settled down at the bar to wait for Kevin Heaney and the ESB men. But when I got talking to Tony O'Toole from 'Turk, he said it was by no means certain Kevin would be coming, and if I wanted to be sure, then to go down to his boat in the harbour and ask Kevin by radio; it was set on the right wavelength. 'Just take down the microphone. The boat's the red one out from the end of the pier. There's a young lad on board, but he may be asleep.'

I went down, climbed over a couple of boats to the red one, entered the wheelhouse, heard voices speaking on the radio, took down the microphone, said something, and the voices stopped. I kept calling 'Hello Inishturk' and then pressing a button on the mouthpiece. No response, nothing. I gave up, went down into the cabin, saw a figure wrapped in blankets, and spoke softly to it. A blond boy of about fourteen with pink and white skin, fine-featured, like an angel in a school play, sighed himself awake. 'Your skipper said I could speak to Kevin Heaney on the mike, but I can't get it to work.' 'I'll have a try,' he said. 'You just press the button and speak, then release it.' 'Oh', I said, 'I was doing it the other way around.' It transpired he was Tony O'Toole's son. They had come in the night before, and he had been to a disco in Claddaghduff and arrived back at the boat about three. After a few minutes he came up, took the mike and said 'Réalt na Maidne' a few times. Then, 'Marita Marie. That's a cousin of mine.' 'No', he said, 'he isn't coming or he'd hear me. There's none of them out. I'll try later and come up and tell you if there's word.'

I returned to Coyne's and sat at a window making notes and occasionally looking out at the rain falling on the harbour and on the pile of gas cylinders standing on the quay. At a table near me Tony O'Toole was sitting with two men and two girls who were talking about a night they had spent on 'Bofin. One of the girls, whom I gathered was from 'Turk but working in Castlebar, was telling how hard it had been to waken the two men when she knocked on the doors of their rooms. The man with her was from Castlebar. They started comparing 'Bofin and 'Turk people. 'You'd be drinking with 'Bofin people half the night', said the other man, 'and in the morning you'd meet them and they wouldn't speak to you.' 'On 'Turk,' said the Castlebar man, 'if you were stranded, people would ask you if you wanted to spend the night. On 'Bofin they wouldn't bother with you.' It struck me that, since 'Bofin was well-provided with hotels and guesthouses, and 'Turk, from what I'd heard, had only one guesthouse — 'Delia's', beside the harbour — that was not really remarkable.

I asked them could I join them and they made room for me. The other girl was from Ballaghadereen, and the man with her was working there but came from Roscommon. When I told them I had spent a couple of days in Boyle, the Ballaghadereen girl said — with the Roscommon man nodding assent — 'We find the Boyle people very stand-offish, they're interested only in themselves.' 'Where are you from?' the Castlebar man asked me. When I said Dublin, he said he wouldn't have thought so from my accent, it must be a posh Dublin accent. I said that my Belfast background had cancelled out the Dublin accent and produced a hybrid. He asked me had I heard about the Castlebar International Song Contest, and I said indeed I had, and about its International Walking Race too. 'It's the capital of Mayo', he said. 'You've probably heard about Davitt House where they brought several hundred people from — what do you call that thing in Dublin?' 'The civil service', I ventured. 'Yes', he said, 'the civil service.' 'Back', I said, 'at the beginning of the '70s, what with those competitions, and your new airport and the fine new roads into the town, Castlebar was getting itself talked about, but you've been very quiet for some time.' 'Well,' he said, 'Monsignor Horan stole a march on us with *his* airport.' 'Here's Kevin anyhow,' said Tony O'Toole, and we all followed his gaze and saw the top of a mast moving along the harbour wall towards the end of the pier. 'You know everyone on 'Turk is called O'Toole', said the Castlebar man. He mentioned a few people I should speak to when I was there, including his girl-friend's father. 'But don't tell him you saw *me* here', she said. He laughed. 'Tell him you met both of us in Cleggan, and he'll say what the fucking business was *he* doing there with my daughter?' 'I'm sure', she said, referring to me, 'he doesn't appreciate that language.' 'Sorry,' said the Castlebar man, 'slip of the tongue. But it's useful' — he said to me — 'for you to know who to talk to, for they won't know you. They don't read books or newspapers or pay any attention to what's going on in Ireland.' Tony, returning from the bar, overheard this and said, 'Oh I don't know about that now.' 'But you're one of the elite, Tony', said the Castlebar man. 'Is there an elite?' said the 'Turk girl. 'I suppose there is.'

Kevin Heaney arrived with his two brothers and they looked like older versions of Tony's son whom I had seen on the boat. Kevin said he would be going when the ESB men came. They were supposed to arrive at two-thirty, and since that time was approaching I went across the road to the Harbour View restaurant run by Oliver Coyne's sister, Ann. I had a well-cooked three-course meal with coffee for £4; fresh mackerel for the main course. The restaurant looked well, with pine-wood, house plants and tweed. Ann said her sister, Marion, had married a man on Omey Island — which is connected to the mainland when the tide is out — and he had done most of the work for her. In the summer, she said, Marion moved into Cleggan with her three children and helped her in the restaurant. Ann had never been to 'Turk, but she had spent a year in Munich, first as an *au pair,* then working in a hotel. We talked about the many nationalities, and the beauties and excitements, of that city. I told her I thought 'Turk people were very handsome, and she said, 'Yes, the old people are very nice'. 'But what about the young ones, the young men, don't you think they're handsome?' Avoiding the question, she said 'I don't know. When they've been off to school in Westport and Louisburgh, they're not so friendly as the older people.'

I went back to the pub. The ESB men showed up about four-thirty. They had been doing a job on Inis Oírr, the smallest of the Aran Islands. On Inishturk the people had electricity from their own generators, one for every few houses. Now they were to be brought into the ESB system. The poles had been erected and the house for a diesel-fuelled generator built; all that remained to do was to install it. Then the people would have a more abundant supply of electricity and be able to use power tools and more domestic appliances. It later transpired that the men were not strictly ESB employees, but a sub-contracting team from Clare working for a contractor to the ESB in Westport.

Finally, about five-thirty, when they had loaded all their equipment aboard Kevin Heaney's boat, we put out from the pier. It was a 38-foot trawler made by Tyrrell's of Arklow. It was raining still and the sea was rough. When we emerged from the relative calm of Cleggan bay, the boat gave some jumps which made my belly jump with it. I climbed out of the cabin and joined Kevin in the wheelhouse with one of the 'ESB' men who didn't much like sea journeys. We were heading north. The wind was from the north east and the boat was managing to head more or less into the waves. The sky was dark grey. Every few waves we would hit one hard and the sea would wash up against the window of the wheelhouse, erasing all visibility for some seconds. Sometimes this occurred twice in rapid succession. I asked Kevin how he would describe this kind of sea. 'The sea's smooth enough', he said, 'but the wind's strong.' We saw the shape of 'Bofin dimly to our left and 'Shark behind it; there were headlands to the right. Somewhat later Kevin spoke by radio to a cousin in his house on 'Turk and repeated that the sea was smooth, the wind about force seven. 'Turk became visible to the left ahead, somewhat like a seal on the surface of the water; then Caher, with a semi-circle of cliffs rising like a fortress out of the sea. Further ahead, beyond Caher, lofty Clare Island rose like a mountain-peak, and beyond that again there was a dim suggestion of one of the mountains of Achill. This was the island world I had been looking forward to re-visiting, though I would have wished myself a better day to see it. I say 'island world', correcting in my mind our usual way today of looking at these islands, singly or in pairs, off the coast, thinking instead of the ruined churches or forts on most of them, and of how, in the centuries when those were built, and when travel in these parts was usually by sea rather than land, all these islands formed a north-south archipelago, an interlocking system, emanating from the great metropolis of Aran to the south. Now we were parallel with 'Turk and, as we turned west towards it, the sea began thudding regularly against us from the right, or should I say, to starboard, so that we kept lurching low to port, and righting ourselves and lurching again. Ahead of us 'Turk was now a woman's spread thighs, with the harbour and a cluster of houses where they joined, and we were heading into that cleft. Entering the harbour, we swung right around the end of the pier into a snug haven. Two wide-beamed boats were tied up at the quay and six or seven upturned currachs lay on the sand across from us. They looked light, like Aran currachs, not like the wooden Connemara ones. Later I discovered they were wooden frames covered with canvas and calico, a sort of compromise.

Someone pointed out to me the lighted windows of Delia's just beside the harbour, and I headed there, followed by the 'ESB' men. On the way I passed a JCB, several tractors and a Volkswagen, and wondered how they had got there. Delia, a neat, smiling, youthful-looking woman met us at the door. Later I was to discover with surprise that she was the mother of two boys in their late teens, and of a teenage girl and a younger boy whom I saw moving around the house. In my mind I was still so present on the stormy sea that the sight of the teenage girl nonchalantly carrying a laden tray from one room to another — so much at home in a domestic, dry-land world — amazed me. Delia showed us to our rooms and set about preparing food. My bedroom was pink and looked out on the harbour. There were pictures of a dog, two puppies, two apples, and the Sacred Heart. The dining-room was bright with potted geraniums and vases of wild roses and purple loosestrife. In the corner there were bottles of wine and brandy on a table, the remains, I learned, of a recent visit by some politicians.

At table I was beside a fair-haired boy of ten who was sitting opposite a handsome, bearded man. The man spoke very clearly and deliberately to him, chatting about the boy's fishing. Once the man spoke a couple of sentences in German. Later when we moved into the sitting-room, where a big turf fire had been lit, I discovered that he was Peter Jankowsky from the Goethe Institute in Dublin whom I had met once, without the beard, and who is well known both as an inspiring teacher of German and for his readings and presentations of German literature. He told me that he and his painter wife had, for some years past, been dividing their summer holidays between Clare Island and

'Turk. His first visit to 'Turk was in the company of Fr Pat O'Brien, then the curate on Clare, and more recently, one of two priests in the Tuam archdiocese who had spoken out in favour of divorce during the referendum and been silenced by the bishop. As it happened, only a few days before, Peter had met my friend Bob Quinn on Clare filming the bawdy, best-selling novel, *Súil le Breith* by the other of the two priests, Pádraic Standúin. Both Bob and he live in South Connemara, in An Cheathrú Rua.

Peter said that what he and his wife had seen and observed on Clare and 'Turk over the years had enabled them to understand many things about the experience of humanity today in distant places; for instance, when they saw films of Africa. The change-over to the 'modern' style of living was going on everywhere, with the same effects and tensions, gains and losses. He was using his holidays partly to prepare a new one-man show for the Institute in the following year, 1987, which was the 750th anniversary of Berlin. The Ambassador, a Berliner like himself, had intimated that he would like it to be suitably celebrated. Delving into Berlin literature — and re-discovering his attachment to his native city — Peter had come upon Glasbrenner, a neglected writer of the 1840s, who had created a character called Nante Eckensteher, a typical Berlin wit; and he was going to base his presentation on him. Everyone, he said, knew about the 1920s in Berlin, but Berlin had a longer literary tradition than that and he wanted to show some of it.

The nine o'clock television news came on and it was all about gales and floods, and how the tail-end of Hurricane Charlie from the US had been hitting Ireland, but especially the East. Delia's husband, John, an older-looking man in peaked cap, with a craggy, Western face, sat in for a while to hear the news. When I talked to Peter about my fascination with this 'island world', he remarked that it was odd there were no church remains on this island, but there was a collection of *dún* names near an inlet on the south side, indicating ancient habitation there. I learned that there were about a hundred inhabitants, most of them living around the harbour, and that the population was increasing. We looked at a framed Ordnance Survey map of the island that was hanging on the wall, and I noticed that there were a lot of placenames beginning with Oogh. When Peter said that nearly always indicated a narrow inlet, it

135

occurred to me that it was *uaigh,* which normally means a 'grave'. Delia pronounced the local placenames in impeccable Gaelic, quite unlike the crude anglicised renderings on the map. But she didn't understand any of them and couldn't remember when Gaelic was spoken on the island. 'I learned it at school, out of books,' she said, 'but that meant nothing to me.' Peter started playing 'I spy with my little eye' with Delia and the children. When one of the children went to bed, Delia called after him, 'Don't put on any lights, now, when they're not needed. We only have the small generator on.'

I went out to the island's only pub. One of the sons guided me to it three hundred yards away. I heard the generator humming against the noise of wind and sea. There were four or five men standing around the counter. One of them told me they had known for days that an east wind was coming. Before it did, the sea always made a strange echoing sound in certain rocks. When I told him that Kevin Heaney had called it a 'smooth sea' today, he said that Kevin had been comforting the passengers when he called *that* a smooth sea.

When I rejoined them in Delia's we played charades for a while with the names of songs and TV programmes. Later, as I sat reading in bed, I noticed on the mirror a clown's head sticker which I hadn't seen before. Then the light went out and there was no more humming sound.

In the morning the wind had died and the water in the harbour was scarcely rippling. Out at sea it was still choppy but settling. At breakfast, looking through the window, I saw two trawlers getting ready to put out. On the radio there were reports of floods and devastation in the East and of serious farm flooding in Munster. As the morning went on, the sky blued and the sun came out.

Behind Delia's house the land rose steeply. Unable to discern a road that led to the summit of the island, I started climbing through the fields, encountering dry stone walls with wire fencing on top; searching for crossing places and often finding them in the corners of fields; negotiating the walls carefully while wondering as always at their solidity; remembering the stone walls of 3500 BC in Belderrig and reflecting that there had been enough time to learn the art; meeting cattle and sheep and once a Connemara pony with its tiny foal; walking over grass and rock and moss past clumps of wild iris not in flower. As I searched for suitable places to take pictures, I kept looking down at the harbour and the white houses scattered around it. Caher was sunlit and seemed close at hand, less formidable than yesterday. The two fishing-boats were moving back and forth in the sea between it and the harbour. A tractor scurried along a road, the Volkswagen along another. A tractor with a large shovel affixed in front came out of the water onto the harbour beach like a huge insect surfacing. I photographed from Clare Island down to the Twelve Bens. Then, climbing higher until I was on one of the summits of the island, I looked north to Achill in the teeth of a biting north wind and saw the white houses of Keel clearly. I wanted to photograph the whole fabled coastline from Achill and Croaghpatrick to Connemara, but decided that it would be in vain; the camera would not show what I saw. I wanted to take it into me and hold it forever. On the way down I passed an abandoned house and joined a road, and one of the Heaney brothers scuttled past me on a tractor. When I reached Delia's she said that Jack Heaney, a cousin of Kevin's, who was in one of the boats at sea, had radioed that he would be going to Cleggan at five and would take me. I said thanks, I'd go with him, and she sent her daughter to the Heaney house to tell them.

At five o'clock, following instructions, I clambered down to the rocky shore and joined Jack Heaney's boat which was taking a load of skate, plaice, brill and crab to Cleggan. The sea was lively under a bright sun. South of 'Bofin, we had a good view of High Island, a cliff-ringed plateau. This time, in the clear weather, I could see Salerna beach and Feenys' house above it.

I set off via Clifden for Roundstone, taking the longer road that passes directly under the Twelve Bens and traverses the medley of forest and lake which begins at Ballynahinch Forest. In the foothills of the mountains I was glad to see new, growing plantations adding to the mature forest. Roundstone is the demure summer sister of gaudy Clifden; a place where families, mostly Irish, like to holiday with their children. A white-grey-yellow village, with a discreet touch or two of light green and blue, it stretches out above its snug harbour. I was there to visit Tim Robinson, the Englishman who had settled some years

137

before in the Aran Islands and had lately moved to Roundstone. I first became aware of him when he published the best map ever of the Aran Islands, with their full panoply of place-names — even to cliffs, strands and townlands — in meticulously correct Gaelic. Later he published a map of the Burren. When the IDA set up an estate for crafts and small industries in Roundstone, he moved in with his own map-making enterprise, Folding Landscapes. For the last couple of years he had been walking South Connemara to make a map of it, and writing a weekly column on his researches in a Galway newspaper, the *Connacht Tribune*. Shortly before, in Dublin, I had been at the launching of a book of his about Aran; a book which dealt in three hundred pages with a walk around the periphery of the large island, Inis Mór. What I liked about him and his work was that he was bringing to these Gaelic western places that more than enthusiastic, more than romantic, *seriousness* which foreigners seem more able to bring than Irishmen. I mean that sort of humanistic seriousness which values these places and their culture primarily as a particular revelation of man.

I found the estate at the end of the village in the grounds of an old Franciscan friary. It was a live-in industrial estate, with rows of houses and gardens alongside workshops making musical instruments and pottery, and a factory making electronic gadgets. Tim Robinson and his wife Máiréad were entertaining an English couple who had been coming to Connemara for twenty years. The two men had met when they were invited to give lectures in the new audio-visual centre that had been opened in Connemara National Park. Mr Hawkins' contribution was a presentation about Connemara done with two slide-projectors. Tim had missed the public event and Mr Hawkins had come to give the show again privately. When it got going, we saw pictures of landscapes and natural objects dissolving into each other, and heard, interspersed with these on tape, a commentary, Irish music, two poems about Connemara by Cecil Day Lewis, excerpts from the Finlandia Overture and Tchaikowsky's First Piano Concerto. By the time it was finished, one was left in no doubt that Connemara was a very beautiful place.

When the Hawkins were gone we got to talking about Tim's recent work in Connemara. He said his intention had been to make and record a sacred journey. 'Sacred?' I queried. 'Well, not in any supernatural sense, but in the sense of a very important journey in which I tried to imprint the image of the landscape's being on my own being.' He spoke, too, of the sacred relationship he conceived to exist between the people living in these parts and the Beanna Beola or Twelve Bens: 'sacred, not in any mystical sense, but because the Beanna Beola form a massive geometric being, visible to the people who live around, and creating with them, willy-nilly, a relationship'. He spoke of the conflicts between, on the one hand, the economic and living interests of the people, and, on the other, aesthetic and ecological considerations. Local farmers were resentful of the National Park because it excluded tracts of land from farming, giving only limited access for sheep. ACOT policy was to have the Beanna declared a 'mountain region' by the EEC, thereby qualifying it for more cash for sheep-farm development. Already there were grants to farmers to cover fencing and the use of a helicopter to spray the mountainside with fertiliser and anti-bracken and anti-reed chemicals. Fencing was being carried right up to the summits, and the numbers of sheep were increasing. But Tim agreed with those who said that the increase in grass fertility would be temporary, and the end result a waste-land. There was also the matter of the forests. Tim was not happy about the forests invading the Beanna Beola. He resented, too, forest cutting across one of his favourite stretches of wilderness in Rosmuc parish. I knew what he was referring to: a stretch of country I called the Connemara 'high plateau', covering most of the interior of South Connemara. 'Emptiness, wilderness, are necessary for man,' he said, 'and they are going to become a very scarce commodity.'

We compared our own two different relationships to Connemara. I suggested that mine — during the years I had spent in the Gaeltacht part, and still — had a predominantly social content, and that his was to a large degree non-social, personal and aesthetic. Much of what he told me reminded me of conflicts I had myself witnessed between modernisers and 'naturists' or traditionalists. Conflicts about planning permissions, and about whether the Gaeltacht should not be left as it was, with all its 'traditional values' intact, instead of being launched, as we activists wanted, into the twenty-first century;

the point being that, in our view, it could survive only if that were done.* Apart from that there was my predilection for seeing the marks of man on Irish landscape; my feeling that we had had, in our history, enough of wilderness. Tim said his own work did have a social dimension. For example, in his recent lecture in the audio-visual centre he had tried to re-create something of the consciousness of place that had existed for the people there in the nineteenth century. He had used local poetry and stories and placename lore, 'trying to add to the indigenous mental stock what it lacks, namely, general concepts'. I took this point, though I had previously appreciated it rather differently. It seemed to me that — in his book on Aran, for example — he was trying to restore to people's perception of their place, dimensions that had been lost when, in the transition from poverty to modern economics and technology, their relationship to their environment became narrowly utilitarian and exploitative.

The following afternoon I drove through the straggling village of Cashel and around Bertraghboy Bay into South Connemara. In Cashel there is a hotel in which General de Gaulle stayed and another in which a German President stayed. When I was living in Maoinis, some miles to the south west, Cashel was always for us the beginning of North Connemara, the first feel of it. Those are loose terms, but significant ones, North and South Connemara. Essentially, the North is the classic tourist country, extending northwards from Cashel to Killary and Inishbofin, though the part around Clifden and Roundstone sometimes describes itself as 'West'. But the road south to Oughterard, and the village itself, also belong with the North. The North has the more dramatic scenery, especially because of its mountains. South Connemara is essentially the Gaelic-speaking district extending from Bertraghboy Bay south and south east almost to Barna. Whereas the South, in keeping with its flatter terrain, has a democratic culture and few hotels, North Connemara has a big-house culture that has been transmuted into a hotel culture,

*A point worth making is that 'modernisation' is anti-traditional only when — as has often been the case — it despises the present and the past. When it respects them, it saves the traditional by providing forms for its transformation and continuance.

with descendants of tenants and labourers transformed into servants of tourism. (I am speaking very generally, of course; North Connemara also has sheep-farmers.) The North, basically because it speaks English, but also, I think, because it has for long played host to 'people of quality' in its big houses or hotels, has a tradition of looking down on the South, and of regarding southerners as backward and wild; and the southerners reciprocated by feeling inferior. But this relationship was thrown into disarray during the '60s and '70s. The South became much more industrialised than the North, with young people being sent to Italy and Sweden for industrial training. The Gaelic-speaking Aran Islands acquired one of the biggest and most modern fishing fleets in the country. The South, in electing parish councils and establishing a couple of successful co-operatives, showed itself better at organising itself than the North. The revival of interest in Irish traditional music drew attention to the rich musical resources of the South, especially in *sean-nós* singing. The various campaigns under the auspices of the Gaeltacht Civil Rights Movement — including that which led to the setting up of Raidió na Gaeltachta — thrust the South into national prominence.* It was difficult for the Northerners to readjust to this new situation, and it was sometimes comic to see them trying to reconcile their inherited feeling of superiority with their envy of the South's advances in technology, industrial employment, wealth and general *savoir faire*. All of Connemara remained, comparatively speaking, demoralised and beset by the 'dole mentality'; but within Connemara, when one passed from South to North — specifically when one visited Cashel — one seemed to be passing from a buoyant society to a depressed one. However, to round out the picture, I should add that from the mid '70s onwards, a considerable shift from Gaelic to English began on the fringes of the South Connemara Gaeltacht, and, patchily, throughout its entire extent.

As I entered Cárna village I noticed that the building which had once housed the famous Mongan's Hotel, and which Meaic Mylotte, when he inherited it, had made into a bar with a room

*I have written at length on these matters, and on South Connemara generally, in my book *Beyond Nationalism*, and, generally speaking, will not repeat myself here but simply continue with the story of my journey.

for dances, had a sign outside it saying 'Carna Hostel'. On the way across the bridges into Maoinis island, I saw polythene tunnels, like those in the Leitrim tree-nursery, outside the shell-fish research laboratory that is run by University College, Galway and known locally as 'the lab' or, in Gaelic, *an leab*. All the new houses dated from the housing boom of the '70s that had ended before I left — there were no newer ones. Eighteen years before, when I was looking for a house, Mícheál Ó Móráin of Cárna had driven me out to Maoinis on a bright sunny day, and continued down the lane that faces you as you enter the island, to emerge on An Trá Mhór, where the blue waves were dashing themselves onto a yellow beach. Now, bowing to nostalgia, I took the same route to the beach. The waves were not dashing; the blue-green water, striped with ultramarine, was lapping quietly against the cinnamon rocks. Beyond the water, on a height, was the graveyard, and beyond it stood Tigh Finnell, full of memories, now in other hands. I was sure that it was still known as Tigh Finnell, if for no other reason than that its high situation, and its high roof, had made it into a 'sea-mark' for local fishermen. Over the whole scene, out to the rocks called Na Scéirdí, rose that 'great dome of sky' which I waxed so lyrical about in *Beyond Nationalism*.

Driving back down the lane, I was just parking outside Máirín Brown's shop when her husband, Duncan arrived home from the lab. She joined us from the shop and gave us tea, and we engaged in a great outpouring of talk. Meaic Mylotte, I heard, had rented the bar downstairs in the old hotel to people from the North of Ireland, and his son Séimí was running the upstairs as a hostel, with self-catering. Yes, John Mercer, director of the lab, was still moaning about lack of funds and forecasting imminent closure. Irina, the Russian woman, who had the cosmetics factory in Cárna, and who had amazed us all with her face shampoos made from mud taken from the Shannon, had up and disappeared one morning. Was Máirín Casey doing B and B this year? Yes, said Máirín, hadn't I seen her B and B sign just outside? Her husband, Pádraig Casey, who came from a well-known Maoinis boat-building family, had been fishing in the '70s and had built himself the biggest house on the island with eight bedrooms. Then he left the fishing to work for the lab as the skipper of its research boat.

142

I arrived at the Casey's house as Pádraig was returning to it. A broad smile lit up his fisherman's face. Máirín was in the kitchen, as radiant as ever. They had four children now, the youngest a very pretty girl. They brought me up to date on Meaic's scheme for raising coral from the bottom of Cill Chiaráin Bay. The steamer, the 'Julia T', which he had bought in Wexford for the purpose, was lying rusting with a hole in her. Another boat he had got from Tralee had run aground and was also prone. But he had just got an extension on his licence for extracting the coral. Two or three divers with a couple of girl-friends were staying in the Casey's house. I wasn't clear whether they were there in connection with Meaic's coral or with the local salmon-farming company, Bradáin Mhara, which P.J. Carroll, the tobacco manufacturers, had just bought. But Máirín had a room for me. When I mentioned to her that I saw no new houses, she said things weren't buzzing in Cárna. She had been recently to An Cheathrú Rua, some thirty miles by road to the south, and, noticing the many big new houses, thought what a difference having some industry made.

When I met Meaic in the pub that night, I found him by no means cast down by his troubles. He is one of the greatest and most persistent dreamers I know. He was jubilant about having got his licence extended to fifteen years, and said he had at last — he had been disappointed on several previous occasions — found the right people to back him. He was about to make the big breakthrough. John Mercer, the lab's resourceful and devoted director, explained the polythene tunnels I had seen outside it. He said the lab's main practical achievement in its first years had been to spawn and rear native and Pacific oysters, and clams, in lab conditions. The next step was to develop a cheap and simple method of doing that which could be used by local communities. Hence the polythene tunnels, each of which contained a simple 'heat machine' made from loops of ordinary black water-pipe. By these means water could be heated and kept at the temperature necessary for the oyster and clam spat. Apart from the tunnels, John was particularly happy that they had been able to persuade the fishermen around Cill Chiaráin and Beirtreach Buí bays to form an effective co-operative, Sliogéisc Chonamara Teo, for the cultivation and harvesting of oysters, scallops and clams. In the lab itself, they had been working on the ormer, the world's most expensive shellfish, for which the Channel Islands had previously been the northernmost limit. Now they were supplying the Channel Islands with young ones.

Late at night Séimí Mylotte came down from the hostel upstairs. When I had last been in Cárna he was behind the bar. He was glad not to be there any more, he said. 'Now I've joined the people,' he said laughing. 'When I was behind the bar I used to be a person of authority. I used to help them with filling out forms because "I knew better". I regarded them as demoralised, or at least I listened to those who said they were. Now I admire their way of life, their system of living. With their few cattle, and the seaweed, and maybe a bit of fishing or whatever else they can turn their hands to, and whatever they can get from the government, they manage to have a good life. The people who come here value this life, in which *you* may have a Mercedes and the man next door a bicycle — and that happens — but the man with the bicycle doesn't feel he has to have a Mercedes. All in good time.' He had found, he said, that with the hostel as a facility he could make this culture available to those outsiders who valued it. Recently he had run a course for fifty people of Irish origin from London who were interested in the language and music and everything local. 'I enjoyed organising it, I put on a damn good show for them.' He said he encouraged people to come to him 'with any request no matter how far-fetched — a seminar on psychology, a religious retreat, a study-in of business executives. My attitude is "Give me a few days to think about that." I've found I can come up with what they want, even with something that amazes them. I've found I can draw on an amazing repertoire of resources, human resources and natural ones.' 'You know,' I said, 'Séimí, it's seldom people find in one man a combination of innkeeper and philosopher.'

Next morning I crossed the bridges out from Maoinis, turned south in Cárna, and followed the coast road to Cill Chiaráin, noting as I entered it the large, well-painted houses which serve as its pubs, shops and hotels. Down below it, near the harbour, smoke rose from the factory where three hundred men deliver seaweed. When dried and transformed into powder, it is collected by a boat from Scotland. For lack of a bridge to Leitir Mhóir, which would take me to Ros a' Mhíl in twenty minutes, the road continued in a great detour around Cill Chiaráin Bay; first under the gleaming rock wall of Cnoc Mhordáin, then, in Rosmuc parish, past the Pearse Cottage and the cluster of notices advertising the delights and services of the Rosmuc peninsula. This was flat, rock-strewn, watery country, with low mountains to the east towards Oughterard. At that stolid sentinel of the bogs, Scriob power station, the stocks of turf were low. On the road through Camas I encountered the first ticket-booths of the two competing boats for Aran, 'Dún Aengus' and 'Queen of Aran', which make the crossing from Ros a' Mhíl. A few miles further on, just before Doire Né, I passed a large, red-brick industrial estate, where the number of cars and their distribution indicated that several of the factories were in operation.

Doire Né is the great crossroads of South Connemara, where the road down from the north meets the east-west road running from Galway to An Cheathrú Rua. That latter road is also the artery of what you might call the South Connemara industrial belt, which comprises a score or more of factories and workshops from Na Forbacha westwards. At Doire Né, to the east across a flat rock desert, lies Ros a' Mhíl; to the west, in the immediate vicinity, the courthouse, the humming hostelry of Tigh Chit, the space for street markets, a big car-service station, Raidió na Gaeltachta, and then a continuous line of houses leading to the 'metropolitan' sprawl of An Cheathrú Rua. What is town here, and what country? The categories are overthrown, and that re-commingling of the urban and rural is achieved which Thompson, Marx, AE and Mao, and de Valera, dreamed of.

As I drove towards Ros a' Mhíl, the Aran Islands came into sight and I noted from the ticket-booths I passed that the boats departed at 12.30 and 1.30. The building of the new fishing harbour at Ros a' Mhíl has become a textbook example of the inefficacy of the Irish administrative machinery in carrying out government policy — which in this case was to provide proper harbour facilities for the expanding fishing fleet in the Galway Bay area. Planned in the 1960s, and begun in 1968, the construction of the harbour and the provision of shore facilities were drawn out over more than twelve years owing to the number and the lack of co-ordination of the government services that were involved, and the lack of a local authority to co-ordinate them. Then, no sooner was the work finished than it was found that the harbour was too small and that an extension — in fact another harbour — would be needed. As I approached the port, I could see, beyond the cluster of industrial buildings around it, a remarkable new one, tall and rectangular, in cream and blue, with pillars along its side which made it like a Greek temple. I knew this must be the building which Tim Robinson said he had dealt with in his article for that week in the *Connacht Tribune* — glad that at last he could praise a new building in Connemara. Turning away from the harbour, I arrived at the Breizon factory where my Breton friends, the Trahans, prepared fish for export. After years in the fish business in Lorient, Bernard Trahan sold out, came to Connemara, and started again from scratch. At a long table women were filleting, cutting and packing fish, and in the middle of the floor my son, Oisín stood, in yellow apron, talking one minute Gaelic to the women at the table or the girl from the office, the next minute French to one of the Trahan sons, as he passed through, and then again, English, to a man who came to the door with a spare part for a lorry.

After a while, when he could make himself free, Oisín joined me and we went back towards the harbour for a drink. He said their Spanish market was expanding and would soon be as big as their French one. There was a lot of money around in Ros a' Mhíl, but how so much of it came to be around was a sort of a mystery — and that despite the fact that it had been a very good season for lobster, with fishermen some of the time making £2,000 a week. The biggest factory in Ros a' Mhíl, which used to tin crab for Denmark, had been rebuilt to deal with barrels of salted herring. The man who owned it, Gerry Joyce, had gone into partnership with a Norwegian to build the new temple-like factory, which would process vast quantities of fish offal, and unmarketable fish, into concentrates for feeding to fish or animals. I learned that the 'pillars' along the sides were silos.

At 1.25 Oisín drove me to the quay — I had asked him to take my car to Galway for collecting later. The boat, punctual to the minute, was beginning to move. 'Are you going?' called a girl on the quay. 'Yes', I said, running to the boot of the car to extract

146

the bike. The gangplank, almost pulled aboard, was put down again. 'Have you a ticket?' asked the girl. 'No.' 'He can get one aboard', said someone aboard. I trotted across the gangplank with the bike and went below deck. As we passed the 'temple', standing on a small headland, I saw that the front of it contained a large aperture, like a maw into which the fish would be poured to satisfy the god. As we left the bay, the three Aran Islands and the Clare coast stretched out ahead of us.

I had been told that boat services now connected Inis Mór with the other islands, and the most easterly of them, Inis Oírr, with Doolin on the Clare coast. So I wanted to make the round journey, not least because it would enable me to experience the islands and the Burren — the northern part of Clare — as the single unit which they are, both geologically and as an area of ancient civilisation. Both of those features go together, the first of them, the limestone, seeming to have been the principal cause of the second. The limestone, covered originally with a thin layer of soil, yielded rich grass: even today Aran cattle are fatter than those of Connemara, where the south is granite and the north quartz and schist. Not surprisingly, the Aran islands belonged for most of their history to Munster; for centuries, until they were seized by the O'Flaherties of Connemara in Tudor times, they were part of the O'Brien dominion. The large number of stone forts, churches, monasteries and castles in the Burren and on the islands, and the size of the forts, particularly on Aran, testify to affluence from early times, and contrast with the absence of anything comparable in Connemara. Aran people, in my experience, consider themselves one of God's great gifts to mankind, but in such a relaxed and indisputable way that they would respond only with a raised eyebrow to any questioning of the proposition. Like the people of Gaoth Dobhair in Donegal, they are that rare thing in modern times — a Gaelic-speaking community with a superiority complex.

It was a delightful crossing on a lively sea in bright sunlight. A man from Dungannon talked to me about Northern politics and asked me why I had stopped saying — that is, writing in the papers — that there would be no progress or peace in the North until Britain recognised and respected the national identity of the Irish there. 'I got tired saying it', I replied. 'I thought for a time I was being heeded when they made this Anglo-Irish Agreement,

147

but I was wrong — they weren't serious.' 'But it must be said nevertheless, again and again,' he said. ARAN BICYCLE HIRE in large letters on a wall was the first message which Aran sent towards us. The crossing cost £7. When we docked at the end of Cill Rónáin pier, beside the big 'Galway Bay' from Galway, two minibuses awaited us offering tours of the island. As I cycled towards the exit from the pier, passing anchored trawlers, I came up against three large notices headed RABIES, LA RAGE, TOLLWUT, dealing with the importation of animals. Near them were half a dozen ponies and traps, one of them already loading visitors. I felt sure that the relegation of these traditional Aran tourist vehicles to the back of the quay by the minibus men represented the outcome of an island power struggle.

The village, as we entered it, was an unbeautiful cluster of restaurants, derelict houses, pubs, patches of weeds, cycle-hire sheds and guesthouses, around a Celtic cross 'erected by the islanders and a few friends in memory of the Rev. Michael O'Donoghue, for eleven years the beloved priest and benefactor of Aran. 1893. RIP'. The cluster was dominated by a large yellow house, in one side of which was The American Bar. From inside the bar came a man's voice singing 'The Galtee Mountain Boy', and then an accordion playing jigs. Looking down towards the harbour I could see to the right a long row of slated cottages stretching towards Cill Éinne, the airstrip, sand dunes, and beyond them, Inis Meáin with its houses.

As the village progressed up its rising, winding street, it improved. The people I spoke to were friendly and — especially the older ones — very articulate. In to the right was a shop, 'Powell, Siopa Ginearálta', with notices in Gaelic in the window for a *céilí discó* and a *rás snámh*. Inside, beside piles of *Ireland's Own,* the *Sacred Heart Messenger,* Dublin papers and the *Connacht Tribune,* were some books for adults and children in Gaelic. Continuing up the road I came to a single-storeyed white building with the sign 'Deochlann Joe Watty' on it, some wooden tables and benches on the grass in front, a gaping hole in half of the roof as if there had been an explosion, and a faded notice on the door, 'Please feed the cats'. Beside it, pointing down a lane, was a sign, 'Traditional Irish Cottage. Handcrafts, Books, Knitwear'.

I decided, though I had done it a couple of times, and it was a corny idea, and what every day-tripper to the island does, to visit Dún Aonghasa — simply because it is a world's wonder. A cold north westerly wind was blowing and the road was steep. A couple of miles out I noticed to the left, a short distance before a chapel, towering stone walls beside what looked like a ruined lighthouse. I decided it must be Dún Eochla, which on previous visits I had passed without seeing. Leaving the road, and following a trodden path to the *dún,* I passed through the outer circle to the inner one whose wall, about fourteen feet high, had a terrace running around its inner side. Somewhat off-centre in the circle stood a large rectangular pile of stones with steps up onto it. The sight convinced me, thinking of Dún Aonghasa with its terraced interior wall and the altar-like stone at the cliff-edge, that the inner circles of these forts were used for rituals, with people standing on the terraces, looking inwards. Tim Robinson, moreover, had remarked to me that none of the Aran forts had a well inside. The explanatory notice inside Dún Eochla had been torn away. I climbed up onto the wall and, in the teeth of the gusty cold wind, surveyed the scene from Inishbofin down the Connemara coast to the turn into Galway Bay. There, after the houses of An Cheathrú Rua, the gap of Casla Bay, and Ros a' Mhíl, there was a piece of empty coast, and then, from Indreabhán eastwards, a line of white houses and other buildings stretching on and on until it disappeared from view towards Galway. Behind this coastal belt extended the vastly empty plateau of South Connemara which I mentioned earlier. Looking south east I could see Black Head, the bleak hills of the Burren, the line of cliffs along the Clare coast. Nearer at hand, on the island itself, great expanses of limestone wilderness, chequered with stone walls, extending towards cliffs and towards Cill Éinne. I got down again, grateful for the shelter, borrowed a stone from the 'altar' pile, sat on the ground poring over Tim's map and its meticulous notes, and smoked my pipe. I noticed that he called the big island, in Gaelic, Árainn, as the people in all three islands do. I am convinced that Inishmore — and much worse, Inis Mór, which I have written above because it is frequently used — is a bastard form, originating from the Ordnance Survey maps, that has crept into contemporary Gaelic. Carefully replacing the stone, I returned to the road, went to the chapel and said a prayer. In the porch there was a notice in Gaelic giving mass and confession times, and a poster about a pilgrimage to Mám Éan in Connemara.

Discouraged by the cold wind, and feeling that Dún Eochla had satisfied my *dún* needs, I decided to continue only until I would see Cill Mhuirbhigh Bay. A few of the houses and outbuildings along the road were thatched, but most of the houses were slated and two-storey and stood grouped in villages. I came to Fearann an Choirce and saw Gort na gCapall across an expanse of fissured limestone to the left. Then, on one side, Cill Mhuirbhigh came into view above its strand, and, on the other, Dún Aonghasa stood guard on its cliff. I turned back. The wind and the sun were behind me now, and the sun was illuminating the stones ahead, mellowly. In Aran, stone comes truly into its own. If you want to see it at its best, then turn aside when you see a signpost to one of the many antiquities, say, Teampall an Cheathrair Álainn. You come to well-wrought stiles, walk along trodden stone paths, mount sets of steps, and see all sorts of stone outhouses and walls. Nearer to Cill Rónáin I passed roadside stone pillars commemorating, in English, persons who died in the nineteenth century. This is Aran's Via Appia.

Meaic Mylotte had told me to visit Fr Waters. After a meal in Cill Rónáin I went to the curate's house, but he wasn't in. As I stood near it looking at the sea, an old man joined me smoking his pipe. He had spent forty years in England, he said, and come back a few years previously. 'I couldn't believe my eyes,' he said, 'so much had changed. When I left, there were no electricity poles or buses or aeroplanes.'

I decided to look for a place to stay in Cill Éinne. From Éinne's — Saint Enda's — time until the Congested Districts Board built the pier at Cill Rónáin, Cill Éinne was the capital of Aran. On the way I visited Teaghlach Éinne — 'Enda's Household' — a lovely little eighth-century church at the back of a cemetery. Standing in it I felt in touch with Éinne, the man from whom the aura of Aran came, gentle like this sand-duned part of the island. We know where his monastery stood but there is nothing of it left. Its stones were used, I think, by the Cromwellians to build a barracks when they stationed troops here. On a height inland there was a large white house with big letters on its wall which at first I took to be spelling Arts Centre. But then, having come on no bed-and-breakfast house, I looked again and read Ard Éinne, and as I approached, it turned out to be what I was looking for. The woman of the house, bright and bespectacled, spoke halting Gaelic. She told me her name was Enda — yes, though it was unusual for a woman — and that she came from Drogheda, which was where the saint had come from more or less, and was married to an Aran man, who was head of the vocational school, and was called Caomhán, the local form of Caoimhín or Kevin. And that was a remarkable coincidence, and a re-enactment of the past, for St Kevin had come to stay with St Enda in Aran. But after a while they fell out, and Kevin went off to found his own monastery, in Glendalough, and it outlived Enda's by several centuries. When she had gone into the B and B business a few years previously, she had discovered that, by a tacit island decree, Cill Éinne was a 'closed area' for B and Bs, and her venture was not seen well by the Cill Rónáin people. But she had done well by conducting her own vigorous marketing in Galway and Dublin papers, offering weeks and fortnights at special rates.

I was glad to be spending the night in Cill Éinne rather than Cill Rónáin. Before I went to bed I stepped outside and saw the other village shining brightly across the bay. Beyond it, across a gap of darkness, the north coast of Galway Bay was marked by a string of lights extending far to the east — ending in a vague glow in the sky which I took to be Galway.

The less said the better about my attempt the following morning to find the puffing holes. Enda had given me clear instructions, but I made the mistake of thinking I could cut corners — or rather, could cut straight across the network of stone-walled fields at random. All the walls have their convenient crossing-points, but the outsider, with his untrained eye, will often not be able to find them. In short, I got desperately lost, and just about managed to make it back to Ard Éinne in time to jump on my bike, race to Cill Rónáin, buy a £6 ticket to Inis Oírr from a booth near the quay, and take my place on the boat three minutes before it departed on the dot of noon. It was a small broad boat partly covered by an awning, and there were about ten passengers, mostly tourists. The crossing took about thirty-five minutes. As we drew near to Inis Meáin we coasted along a

151

sandy, rocky shore to the side farthest from Árainn, where the
pier was. Most of the passengers disembarked, while a man and
boy joined us. A JCB waiting at the end of the pier was driven
forward until the big wheels were just at the edge of the concrete
wall above us. It appeared that we were carrying a generator
which had been sent to the mainland for repairs and was now to
be lifted ashore by the JCB. The JCB lowered its scoop, and a
boy attached the generator to it by a single blue rope. I was
reminded of the precision work, so often photographed, of
loading cattle from currachs onto the 'Naomh Éanna'. 'If this
breaks, I hope you're all prepared to swim,' said our skipper.
The JCB tightened the rope, pulled on it; it tautened, quivered,
slackened again. This happened several times as we watched.
'He can't lift it,' we thought. Then it tautened again and the
heavy generator rose into the air. As it rose there was a loud
metallic clatter from something on the pier and the big
Aranman beside me jumped. Then, with our boat drawn clear,
and the generator swaying in the air, the JCB withdrew from the
edge of the wall. We were already under way and twenty
minutes later were at the Inis Oírr quay.

There was an Oifig Fáilte in a caravan and a local girl in it.
She confirmed, when I asked her, that the 'Naomh Éanna' still
came out from Galway and the cattle were hoisted from
currachs onto it. The last captain used come into the quay, she
said, but the present one didn't. A boat would leave for Doolin
at three. The island sloped upwards to a height from the quay.
The houses and other buildings, mostly white but with an
occasional yellow, were scattered in all directions as far as the
eye could see. On the brow of the hill stood an old ruined castle
and a windmill. The sight was comely and prosperous. I was
glad there was no semi-urban imitation as at Cill Rónáin. As I
cycled off I noticed that the houses were connected by a network
of roads and lanes running between stone walls. I passed a
modern, one-storey Óstán Inis Oírr and above it a very large
complex of residence, pub and shop which belonged — large
letters said so — to Ruairí Ó Conghaile. Some distance to the
left from this was a new building which appeared to be a community centre. Against the skyline in the other direction I could
see two slender white and black structures which seemed each to
have two pillars or a portico in front. I asked a young man what

the buildings 'like two chapels' were, and he said they were advance factories built by the Údarás, but still to be filled. Looking out to sea I could see the gentle, shaved hills of the Burren, grey and green, and a single currach fishing. I turned back and followed a sign to a restaurant, stopping on the way at a shop selling tweed and other souvenir articles, and a series of Connemara and Aran Island cards that I hadn't seen before. One of the series featured a leprechaun as a figure of fun. While eating my meal I re-read the note about the Aran Islands on the back of my Ireland West map: 'Ireland's true traditional lifestyle may be experienced by taking a trip by air or sea to the Aran Islands...'In other tourist literature I had seen worse, but I wondered why the people responsible continued to write this sort of drivel, raising false expectations, and misrepresenting both Aran and Ireland. In no way that a tourist's eye could see is the lifestyle on the islands today 'traditional' (meaning 'old-fashioned'); and never, even when it was 'traditional', was the Aran lifestyle Ireland's lifestyle — it was always, for obvious reasons, untypical. But anyone wanting to hear Gaelic spoken will not be disappointed on Aran; all of the people, of all ages, speak it among themselves. After a period of hesitation, and encouraged by their new pre-eminence in fishing, they seem to have opted for it, decisively, as the 'Aran' language, quite regardless of Ireland.

As three o'clock approached I returned to the quay. Two wide boats were waiting, with people on both of them. Three boys and a girl, all in jeans, were in charge of the nearer boat, which I boarded. The ticket to Doolin cost £6. The other boat left at two minutes to three, ours on the dot of three. A short distance out, two Aran-type currachs passed us, leaping through the water on outboard engines, two or three men in oilskins in each of them. I was surprised by the outboard engines, which I had seen used in Connemara with wooden currachs, but I thought these were of tarred canvas. When I asked one of the boys with us, he said their hulls were of fibre-glass. As Inis Oírr became distant, and the Clare coast drew near, we passed about half a mile from the cliffs of Moher. The Burren hills came down to the water's edge as terraced limestone. After the Aran islands the houses on the green slopes behind the quay looked small, and the fields big.

153

I cycled towards the village which is some distance from the quay. My intention was to make for Kinvara, just over the Galway border, through the heart of the Burren, past the old stone fort of Caherconnell and through Carron. I passed big fields covered with ragwort; even this poor, persecuted weed can look well *en masse* set against green grass. I arrived at O'Connor's pub, fabled from Sweden to Brittany. The sound of traditional music came from within. When I entered I saw that three young men were playing, seated in a corner beneath a wall covered with photos and a variety of emblems from all over Europe. They were playing flute, banjo and fiddle. Their faces were serious, attending to the music, except when some happy event or variation in their playing, some concord or discord, caused them to smile with pleasure. Two girls sitting near them, contemplating them, completed the circle of stillness in which the music sounded. One of the girls, blonde and slight, her back to the rest of us, was smoking a cigarette, her hand rising and falling. During a pause, the elderly publican behind the bar, who I gathered was Mr O'Connor, passed the musicians pints of stout. Around the counter were young men and women of several nations, a couple of the men with beards, one of them in a black sleeveless waistcoat, the other wearing a broad-brimmed black hat. Even in the intervals between pieces of music the visitors spoke in hushed tones. The rich voices of four Aranmen, seated against the wall, could be heard in animated conversation — Gaelic taking its place again among the languages of Europe, on its own ground. A couple of Welshmen came to the bar, displaying their T-shirts to Mrs O'Connor. The shirts bore a design and the words 'Doolin 1986', and the men said they had bought them in Wales. Presently a girl behind the bar held up a tee-shirt for a customer with 'O'Connor's Pub, Doolin' on it. The young men at the counter spoke to the O'Connors respectfully, as if they regarded them as administrators of a shrine and themselves as privileged to be there.

Along the first stretch of road between Doolin and Lisdoonvarna there were batteries of signs indicating a developed tourism. I recalled what a young Lisdoonvarna woman had told me when I visited there in the mid '70s. When she was growing up in Lisdoonvarna, people used regard Doolin as a 'rough place', a fishermen's place, where a nice girl wasn't supposed to go. No one had any respect for the music that was played there. Then, as she put it, 'the German students discovered Miko Russell and took him off to play in their universities'. Gradually, as the interest in traditional music grew, in Ireland and elsewhere, and the music was sought out where it could be heard, Doolin became a centre of the universe, and Lisdoonvarna, famous spa that it was, often a mere stop on the way to it. In Lisdoonvarna I asked a shop-owner and two hoteliers for the road to Caherconnell, but none of them had heard of it, though it was marked on my Michelin map and is one of the better-known Burren antiquities, only a few hundred yards from the Poulnabrone dolmen, the most famous of Irish dolmens. Pretty Lisdoonvarna seems still to be, in its own mind, a genteel Victorian resort town, relating, true enough, to the traditional 'tourist sight' of the cliffs of Moher, but otherwise mentally isolated from its wild environment.

Following my map and my sense of direction, I got onto the narrow, tertiary road west of the town that I had been looking for. At first there were some potholes, but later it was reasonably surfaced. The distinctive hills of the Burren are to the north and north east; to the south of these lies a high fissured plateau. Burren, from the Gaelic *boireann,* means rocky country or karst. It was over the plateau I was travelling now, in solitary stillness, meeting hardly anyone. This is where I find the magic of the Burren. There were large fields of rough pasture with stone walls, the grass yellow-tinged, and occasional outcrops of limestone. Gradually the terrain became harsher. Then suddenly, passing through masses of hazel bushes, I found myself entering a lovely valley. A fine bungalow with a flowering garden marked the entrance. It was a green, narrow valley, walled magnificently by limestone cliffs. In the middle of it I came on the old ruined church of Kilcorney in a cemetery. I was using Tim Robinson's map. A couple of miles further on I passed Caherconnell on the left — small by comparison with the Aran mammoths — and emerged on the main Ballyvaughan-Kilfenora road. Continuing across it up a narrow road which a signpost said led to Carron, two miles away, I suddenly saw the road ahead of me mounting a hill of such steepness that I couldn't believe my eyes, and the road directly in front about to plunge into a precipitous descent. Braking desperately all the

155

way down, I lost the benefit of it, and then mounted a hill which I was not only unable to cycle up, but unable to walk up continuously. The pannier bag, which was far from heavy, exerted a leaden drag, so that I had to stop every twenty feet or so. Eventually, reaching the top, I saw beneath me a post-office and a few houses, and a large lake which I didn't remember from my last visit to Carron, so that I was in doubt whether this was indeed it. Freewheeling down, I found myself faced with a pub called *Croí na Boirne* (The Heart of the Burren), which both confirmed that it was Carron and put me in excellent spirits. What a well-named pub! I entered it in celebratory mood and ordered a large whiskey. I told the young man behind the counter I was drinking it to the name of the pub and to recover from the hill. He said he used to be in training for cycling, and would do seventy miles on a Sunday afternoon around Ballyvaughan, Black Head, and down to Liscannor, and force himself at the end to finish with that hill just when he was longing to lie down or to have a drink. He told me the lake was a *polje,* which he said was a Russian word (I found out later it is Serbo-Croat). The Castletown river, which was there in all seasons, had treacherous ground to either side — though it looked normal, there was soft mud underneath — and occasionally, in wet winter weather, it became the lake I saw. I suggested that that was what we call in Ireland a turlough, but he said, 'Did you ever hear of a turlough that high up?'

Heading north east for Cappaghmore and Kinvara, I took the road that descends from Carron past the UCG research station and the perfumery. This was Burren 'bush' country, covered with hazel, whitethorn, and other stunted trees I didn't recognise, and occasional heather. At Coskeam I entered another lovely valley, structured like the one at Kilcorney. At first I doubted it was Coskeam because there was a group of five or six houses not marked on the map. But a bearded young man, at the door of one of them, confirmed it. The 'cottages', he said, had been constructed recently by Shannon Development. When I said I was heading for Cappaghmore, he said, 'Don't expect to find much there. I was looking for a pub there the other day and couldn't find one. Anyhow you've just one more hill and then it's downhill.' I met the 'one more hill' and then it *was* downhill, a long way. As I descended from the plateau onto flat ground between the northern Burren hills — into the fabled valley of Saint Mac Duach and King Guaire — I came face to face with two classic Burren hillsides: terrace after terrace of rock descending. That, it occurred to me, is what they were thinking of, and imitating, when they built the tiered interior walls in the old forts. In the fading light I joined the straight road north east, passed for miles between two dense walls of hazel, and emerged in Cappaghmore, Co. Galway, three and a half miles by the signpost from Kinvara.

Now the country was 'normal' again; as normal, indeed, as the Central Plain, of which, via East Galway, it was a remote outrunner. Suddenly ahead of me, as I mounted a rise, were the lights of Galway city, extending several miles along the other side of the bay, startlingly clear and bright, though about twelve miles away as the crow flies; two lights among them so bright that they looked like fires. I reached Kinvara at nine-thirty and circled its streets for food; but the last café open had closed at eight. Then I bethought myself of Winkles' Hotel and the Moylans. Contemplative Ciarán greeted me with a nod as if we had last met the day before. Mrs Moylan made me three very tasty large sandwiches. Yes, of course, she said, they had a room for me.

I sat at the bar counter drinking whiskey, remembering the day, years previously, when I had sat there watching 'Bracken' on television with the sheep-farmers around me hushed and mesmerised — it was a drama of sheep-farming in Wicklow. Ciarán told me about that year's *Cruinniú na mBád,* Kinvara's annual festival, which his son Tony had inaugurated in the '70s and in which he was still, his father said, very active. It begins each year with a re-enactment, in sportive form, of the annual 'gathering of the boats' in the old days, when an armada of hookers and *gleoiteogs,* laden with Kinvara's turf for the winter, used sail from An Cheathrú Rua and race up the bay. This year was the best yet, Ciarán said: there were six hookers and fifteen *gleoiteogs.* As the pub filled I found myself beside Seán McMahon, who had spent sixteen years as a teacher in Carron and who was now head of Kinvara primary school and had a grocery shop in the town. Several others standing near were from the Burren. With Seán as the leading commentator, and the others occasionally chiming in, I went back over every step

157

and wheel-turn of my journey — the turns in the road, the ruins of church and castle, this house, that house, and that hill — and all was explained and annotated.

Later, in bed, it occurred to me that Kinvara might well have been spelt, and called *Ken*vara, and that the fact that it wasn't, suggested that, in the nineteenth century or earlier, the place hadn't come to the attention of educated, middle-class townspeople. Let me explain. In the vernacular English of the West of Ireland, the syllable *en* of standard English has traditionally been pronounced *in*: pen, penny and Fennell became *pin, pinny* and *Finnell*. (On more than one occasion, as I dictated my name clearly in a shop or office in Galway, I have actually seen it being written down F-i-nn...) Consequently, when educated townspeople encountered names of towns, summer resorts or natural features that contained the syllable *in*, they assumed, wrongly, that this was 'dialect' for *en*, and transformed it, for their own use, into what they imagined was the 'correct' version! Thus, for example, such genuinely correct names as Innis, Innistymon, Inniscrone, Rinvyle and Rinmore became Ennis, Ennistymon, Enniscrone, Renvyle and Renmore.

I fell into this trap once myself when I was out with a party on Meaic Mylotte's steamer, the *Julia T,* watching the St Macdara Day regatta at Cárna. I asked Meaic, in English, when he would be using the boat to carry cargo, and he answered, 'As soon as we get a winch on board'. Moving to the other side of the deck, I was chatting, with some visitors from Dublin, when one of them asked, referring to the boat, 'Isn't he going to use it to carry cargo?' 'Yes', I said, 'as soon as he gets a wench on board' — not realising what I had said, until they stared at me and burst out laughing, because I had automatically, and quite unconsciously, made the 'correction to standard English'.

7.
KINVARA VIA GALWAY AND TUAM TO ATHLONE

WHEN I went out in the morning to buy a paper, Kinvara looked like a cared-for place. I noticed the public seats, the pleasing colours of the buildings, and the good shop-fronts. At the harbour, where the tide was in — in Kinvara, as in many seaside towns, it makes a big difference — sections of hooped railing on the quayside were painted bright red. Seeing one of them against a green boat on the blue water, I thought 'that's how pretty ports are made'. There was an old stone house which had not been pulled down, as it might have been, but restored for the use of a 'unisex hairdresser' and sculptor. When I remarked on these agreeable sights to Ciarán, he told me they had an engineer in town 'who's on the County Council and takes a great interest in environmental matters'. And he added: 'Is mór an cúnamh cara sa gcúirt'. I thought of Cill Rónáin's loveless materialism. Kinvara had got beyond that to a materialism that *loved* the materials of things. But that, too, was for money? Only partly, and even if so, then better so, for it is good for people to live among and look at good material forms.

There were few buses to Galway from Kinvara, but they were plentiful from Gort about nine miles away; and cycling to Gort would bring me through Kiltartan and past Coole Park. I set off eastwards accompanied along the road by blue cornflowers that seemed to have broken loose from some garden and had their seeds driven along the road by the prevailing wind. Big fields of root crops — sugar-beet and potatoes — were a new sight. Clumps of very cultivated-looking purple flowers — like marjoram but unusually deep-hued — joined the cornflowers. Great herds of cattle and sheep made scenes from Constable under old trees. Reaching a north-south road, I turned south towards Gort and came to a Catholic church in a hollow

159

opposite a graveyard. An inscription in the porch mentioned Kiltartan. Beyond it, where the road joined the main Gort to Galway road, there were a few houses and a school. *Could* this be Kiltartan village? Amazingly, no sign said so. I asked a young lad driving a cow was this Kiltartan, and how far to Coole Park, and he answered in a flat London accent. Not what Lady Gregory found here. A short distance further, exactly as he had indicated, my old friend the Forest and Wildlife Service announced 'Coole Park'.

A boreen brought me to a parking space where signs pointed to Picnic Site and Autograph Tree. A box offered an explanatory leaflet for 15p. Entering a formal garden, with solid wooden picnic tables, I saw and heard two Dublin women, who were seated at one of the tables, discussing the in and outs of friends and relations. Continuing their conversation, which resounded in the silence, they rose and walked towards the white marble bust of Maecenas at the far end of the garden. I followed them. Maecenas could have been standing there talking to me, so powerfully did this sculpted face defy two thousand years. I walked to the Autograph Tree. A railing around it prevents the *hoi polloi* from adding any further initials — as many had already done — to those of the great ones: the founding figures of the literary revival and some other writers, such as Bernard Shaw, from the beginning of the century. Numbers painted on the bark beside a dozen or so incisions enabled one, with the leaflet's help, to decipher AE, Yeats, An Craoibhín Aoibhinn and so on. I was surprised that Edward Martyn was missing.

Returning through the car park, I took the path to the wood and lake, but stopped at the site of the demolished house. The leaflet made apologies for the demolition of the house 'in its then decaying condition, by the predecessors of the Service which now issues this leaflet'. It said the old walls had been re-built to a three-foot level to show the original outline, and it contained a sketch of the exterior of the house along with some explanatory remarks about the layout of the downstairs rooms. But wandering among the low brick walls I could not relate them to the sketch or to the explanation. When some trouble had been taken to make amends, what a pity that the rooms were not simply signposted. But how eerie to walk these interior spaces and think of the conversations that took place here! I wandered on through Coole Wood where AE saw visions and Yeats tried to compete. The lake is quite a substantial one, bigger than I had expected. Woods surround it. I sat on a tree stump, lit my pipe, and watched the swans.

It was only a mile or so further to Gort. Arriving at the Square, I stopped beside a man in a navy suit and open-necked shirt, with his hands in his pockets, who was standing outside the Bank of Ireland, contemplating the open space. In the middle of the square stood a market scales and a large statue of Christ the King. Sullivan's Royal Hotel was to the right. 'Where do the buses stop?' I asked him. He said if they were going to Limerick they stopped across from us, near the statue, where some cars were parked, but if going to Galway, they stopped outside the Hotel. I propped my bike against the bank and started to unstrap the pannier bag. 'How's Gort these days?' I asked him.

'Fine, it's doin' fine.'

'Apart from shops and pubs, what do people do here?'

'I wouldn't know that.' Silence.

'What do you think they do?'

'I don't live here, so I don't know.'

'Is there any industry?'

'No, nothin'. There's a place out there on the edge of the town makes kitchen-tops. There's two or three factories up there' — pointing up the main street to the left — 'closed down.'

'Had you the *fleá* yet this year? I was at a *fleá* here once.'

'I don't think there's been a *fleá* for some years now. It started up, there was a lot of talk about it, and it came to nothin'. That's the way with a lot of things here. They come to nothin'.'

After a couple of minutes' silence he walked away. I took out my Provincial Bus Timetable and, with much turning of pages, found a bus to Galway departing at 14.42, and another, but only in the summer period, at 15.12. I wheeled my bike across to Sullivan's Hotel. A red carpet stretched from the pavement under the glass-panelled door. Inside, at the reception desk, I saw a hand-written timetable of bus departures pinned to the wall. The 15.12 bus was missing from it. A girl came through from the bar and I told her there was a bus in the printed timetable at three-twelve, but I didn't see it mentioned in her notice. 'There's never a bus at that time', she said. I asked her where the buses left from, and she said over near the statue,

161

where the cars were parked. 'All of them?' 'Yes', she said. I reflected that it would be a great help to the bus-using public — and might even increase that public — if CIE were to erect a 'Bus Stop' post in every town, with a timetable of arrivals and departures attached to it.

I went into the bar and had coffee and a sandwich. In the foyer previously, and now here in the bar, the people had a 'country' look about them. What, I asked myself, is a country look? The men, especially the older men, have soft eyes with a certain twinkle in them. Many wear caps and, if they don't, their hair is tousled. Men or women, they have a good colour, the men more tanned or weatherbeaten than the women; the women's skin clear. Their clothes are unpressed, hang easily on their bodies. They have an ambling gait, especially the women. The men have a somewhat formal and elaborate mode of address. I listened to a man beside me asking some people did they know where a certain woman in the town lived.

Suddenly, outside, there was a blaring of car-horns and through the window I saw cars, with streamers flying, converging on the hotel. The cars were beeping to the rhythm of the words 'Here Comes the Bride'. I went to the main door and saw the bride, a woman in her late thirties dressed in white, being helped from a car. She was joined by the middle-aged bridegroom. There were bridesmaids of mature years in pink and violet. The men, with red faces and tousled hair, wore navy suits and looked imprisoned in them. All of them walked up the red carpet past me.

I went to the bus-stop and the bus arrived. The driver was a young bearded man with a ready smile. With great good humour he got out of the bus and helped me put the bike in the luggage compartment. As I paid the fare, I asked him was there a bus at three-twelve. 'Yes, in the summer', he said. 'The girl in the hotel swears there isn't', I said. 'You should tell her sometime.' He smiled, and started the engine. 'By the time I'd get round to that, the summer'd be over', he said.

We had tuneful pop music from Radio Two. The sun was shining brightly on big fields as we drove along. Clarinbridge announced itself as 'oyster country' and there were posters advertising its coming oyster festival. Until a few years ago the Galway city oyster festival was celebrated principally in

162

Clarinbridge. Then the Galway people confined their festival to the city and Clarinbridge set up its own. At Oranmore, five miles from Galway, we turned west and, after a stretch of woodland, saw the Galway Crystal factory on the left towards the bay, and then a sign announcing Galway as, oh no, not again that silly label, 'The City of the Tribes'. We were on the Dublin Road. We passed a hospital and big hotels, and the ugly Regional Technical College, and another hospital. Behind a line of bed-and-breakfast bungalows, the streets of Renmore housing estate marched down to the sea. We passed the rugby club, and signs pointing inland to industrial estates, and a sign proclaiming Galway twinned with Lorient in Brittany. Turning left through a patch of weedy wasteland, we glimpsed petrol tanks at the docks, then climbed towards the city-centre past the old houses and gardens of College Road. On the right, in front of a new, cream-coloured, two-storeyed building, gardeners, with rows of plants beside them, were filling flower-beds. A sign in Gaelic said it was the Corporation offices. Finally we entered a grey area. Beyond the big, grey car-park stood the low, grey railway-station, and, to the right, towering above it — its face to Eyre Square — the Great Southern Hotel showed its grey, ramshackle back to us.

I would say that Galway is now the best city in Ireland to live in. During the past twenty-five years it has ceased to be what it was for so long: a romantic, stagnated city, dwelling in the memories of its great mercantile past and offering wistfulness to the tourist. I suppose that the planned industrialisation, beginning in the '60s, the growth of the University, and the opening of the Regional Technical College, have been the three chief factors in making it the city it is today. For years during the '70s it was the fastest-growing city in Ireland and had the dearest houses, and I believe the latter still applies. All Ireland meets and mingles there in a population sufficiently small — there are 40,000 inhabitants — to allow the immigrants to create a new milieu. It is a young people's city. I have walked on a Saturday afternoon, when the colleges were in session, down the main shopping street — which has three successive names, but which I call by one of them, Shop Street — and wondered what youth congress

163

was going on in the city, only to realise — when it happened me a second time — that those crowds of young people were simply 'the population'. Theatre, film, music, restaurants, shops of all kinds, are available in sufficient quantity and quality for most people's needs. In the arts, it is a women's city: Garry Hynes leads in theatre, Jane O'Leary in classical music, Audrey Corbett in choral music, Mary Coughlan — well, Mary has left Galway behind her. Within the city limits, Salthill supplies by day the sports of the sea, and by night the razzmatazz of night life. And on the doorstep, so to speak, are Connemara and the Burren.

All of this would matter little if, as in so many instances today, the commercial renewal had led to the destruction or defacement of the city-centre. But in fact it has led to its embellishment. Those decayed streets were only romantic — not really good to look at. The revival has seen colour, purpose and chic spread along Shop Street and out from it, laterally, into the side-streets, and over the bridges into Dominick Street and the West End, as the city, year by year, repossessed itself. Many old semi-ruins have come to life again, though many still remain. Eyre Square was certainly botched when its old-world railings were removed and this splendid space cluttered with bric-à-brac. But I was glad to see, as I cycled from the station to collect my car, that the worst of the vulgarity had been removed during the city's quincentennial year. I liked the new centrepiece sculpture of bronze hooker sails, though I was to hear later that it is also a fountain which — of course and as usual — for some unknown reason was not working. What is it? What devious, subconscious refusal to celebrate our condition prevents us from ever having a fountain *working* in this land of water?

In the city's artistic activities it was the moment of pause between summer and autumn. The Druid and the Taibhdhearc had just finished their summer seasons and were taking a break. The Druid had been doing Geraldine Aron's *Same Old Moon,* the Taibhdhearc a Gaelic variety show. Hearing that Audrey Corbett's Galway Baroque Singers would be holding their first practice of the autumn in Taylor's Hill convent school, I stole in and listened for a while to Audrey taking about fifty men and women through parts of Bach's 'Magnificat' and Vivaldi's 'Gloria'. When I had last been in Galway, her choir was the

Corrib Singers, and I wasn't clear about the significance of the name change, if such it was. Slipping her a note that I would visit her the following day, I joined Brian Arkins in The Quays on Quay Street. He teaches Classics in UCG and is writing a book on the Graeco-Roman background to Yeats.

The Quays had been considerably enlarged since I was last there. Together with Tigh Neachtain, almost directly opposite it across the narrow street, it has become the social centre both of Galway's artists, drifters, and alienated intellectuals generally, and of the arty-crafty quarter which has developed thereabouts, between the Fishmarket and High Street. They are the kind of pubs to which respectable people like to bring visitors, occasionally, to do some entertaining slumming.

Teaching Greek and Latin in the late twentieth century, Brian has every reason to feel alienated; but he has another reason too. He is a member of an Arts Faculty which feels itself oppressed by the ascendancy of Science and Engineering in UCG. The basis of that ascendancy has been money: investment and expansion on the one hand, retrenchment and stagnation on the other, though Arts has more than a third of the under-graduate students. Or rather, that's what the Arts people think is the basis of it. On the way to the bar to order another round, I received a revelation on the matter which made me say to Brian that I now knew the full story. I had just heard a girl sitting with two others say 'But Jenny, you must admit that all the good-looking fellows are in Science, they're certainly not in Arts'. But that was to joke about what I knew was a serious matter. I had sat in a boat in Cill Chiaráin harbour late at night and heard Colm Ó hEocha, the President of UCG — and he was at that time also a member of the National Science Council — utter his vision of the future of Connacht. He said that in a rational, scientific use of the land of Ireland, the West should be given over to recreation, and to scientific institutes benefiting from the unspoilt nature, the unpolluted air and land and sea. All its people not employed in servicing those activities should be made to emigrate to a great industrial belt stretching from Dublin along the coast to Cork. Remembering the chill which I had felt at the time — all the more because he was a Gaeltacht man saying that in Gaelic in the Gaeltacht — I believed that everything Brian said was true.

165

Next morning I called on Michael Keaney in the city planning office on the Fishmarket beside the Corrib mouth. In the old days, when this square was *really* the fishmarket, the Claddagh women used bring their fish here to sell to the townsfolk. It was diffident, persistent, gaunt Michael Keaney, who, with his great love of materials and buildings and streets, steered, nudged and badgered Galway city-centre through the still booming years of the early '80s. Now, I found, he was no longer planning officer, and his days on the Fishmarket were numbered. He was in charge of sanitary services and environment, and the office would soon be joining the other Corporation offices in the new City Hall, as he called it, which I had noticed on College Road. Of his current work, 'environment' seemed to interest him more, and he showed me a photograph album of parks and flower-beds. He was particularly proud of Barna wood, Coill Bhearna, on the western outskirts, which he had turned into an 'amenity area'. 'Galway's a bit short on parks, isn't it?' I said. 'It has its waterways instead', he said. I reminded him of his dream of creating continuous walks along the river branches and the canal and asked him had it come to anything. 'Not really', he said. I was worried that he had been taken off the planning and wondered why. I remembered a walk he had taken me on through the streets, and how it brought the city alive to me in a detailed way I could never have imagined. I suggested we take a walk and he agreed. 'A street plan unchanged since 1651, and water — not just the waterways, but the sea too — those are the basic advantages you start out with in planning Galway.' He said that as we went down the stairs.

Outside he drew my attention to a house at the bottom of Quay Street which I had already noticed on the way to visit him. It had drawn my attention because it stood apart from the end of the street, and had been stripped of its plaster so that you could see the stone. 'I had quite a time', he said, 'convincing the woman who owns that house to leave it like that. She wanted to plaster it again. I said don't, leave it like that, and if you can't afford to get it pointed now, put up with the cold for a few years until you can. She ended by compromising — plaster on some parts of it which you don't see. But it looks fine, doesn't it?' He drew me up Kirwan's Lane. I had never been up it before. To the left were very old stone buildings with the windows and doors blocked up, but Michael helped me to imagine them unblocked, and the buildings restored as they used to look. Then we came to a plaque which said that at the end of the eighteenth century the city's only theatre used stand here and that Wolfe Tone had taken part in a play in it with the wife of Humanity Dick Martin, for whom he had felt a strong attraction. The story came back to me, I had read it in a life of Tone. He was staying with the Martins at the time, and Martin had built the theatre for his wife. I was astonished to realise that this old theatre and the Wolfe Tone association never figured in the tourist literature about Galway. Tigh Neachtain, a couple of hundred yards away, does get mentioned as Humanity Dick's town house. So that was where Wolfe Tone stayed. And the bridge down there at the Fishmarket was called Wolfe Tone Bridge. Had that happened by coincidence, or on account of these local associations — at some time when Galway's anti-republican ethos was temporarily in abeyance? On the right-hand side of the lane there was a potter's. Michael put his head in and I looked with him. A man and woman were at work. As we left Kirwan's Lane I felt I had walked through the city of two hundred years ago.

We admired High Street which has become the prettiest street in Galway. Michael commented approvingly or disapprovingly on a door here, pilasters there, window-sashes in another building. We stood in Shop Street opposite the 'space-age' shop-front of what had been Divilly's butcher's shop but was now a clothes shop. Michael told me he had hesitated about approving that at the time, it was so way out. What finally decided him was that Shop Street had no particular style which it could be said to sin against, but was a collection of individualistic and not very handsome buildings. So why not another odd building, which was attractive enough? Perhaps it might lead a style. Unfortunately it hadn't and he thought his decision had been a mistake. We walked down Middle Street past the barred-up Taibhdhearc and Kenny's new painting gallery, went in the back entrance of an arcade and climbed steps and came out on a patio with a number of houses around it. 'That, I've always thought', he said, 'is the way I'd like to have the city-centre, people living in among the shops and restaurants.'

167

Pádraig Ó Céidigh, professor of zoology at UCG, founded the shellfish laboratory at Cárna and I knew him from those days. I went to see him in his office in the College. The old quadrangle of nineteenth-century buildings has been joined by an extensive campus of modern buildings set in grass stretching along the Corrib. If Michael Keaney is lean and gaunt, Paddy Keady — as he is also known — has the physical appearance of the *bon viveur*. He loves the Continent; was just back from Venice where he often visits a marine biology centre; knows the restaurants of Paris; has fought and won a long struggle to breach the habit of having only British extern examiners (he has one from Padua, one from Dinard). When we had brought each other up to date on things, I said, to get him going: 'I hear this is a great Science university, and that the Arts are oppressed'.

'I suppose that's true to some extent,' he said, 'but if the Arts Faculty had had more fighters they might have done better.'

'But isn't there more to it than that? Hasn't it been a help to have a President from the Science side?'

'It has, but if you mean Ó hEocha coming from Biochemistry, that wasn't the start of it. The College had some eminent scientists as presidents in the nineteenth century, and I suppose the modern development of Science here began when Pádraig de Brún was president, back in the '50s. He was a scientist and he believed in the development of science in the college.

'You mean Monsignor de Brún, Gaelic poet, translator of Dante and so on? Was he a scientist?'

'A mathematician, he had been professor in Maynooth. And after him you had Newell, another mathematician. But while you've had a big development of Science generally, there has also been a special development in the marine sciences, which is where my own interest lies, so that the College has acquired a certain standing in that respect in Ireland and internationally. You could say it began with Máirín de Valera and her work on the botany of seaweed, and Tom Dillon and Vincent Barry on the chemistry side of it. When I became the first professor of zoology, my interests were already on the marine side, so we have specialised in marine zoology, but also in freshwater zoology — we have a boat on the Corrib. Then there's the Department of Oceanography, the only one in the country. And various other departments have a marine emphasis. In Botany,

Dr Michael Guiry has continued the work on seaweed. The Department of Geophysics does marine work. In Experimental Physics, there's Aodhagán Roddy's work on marine meteorology, and in Microbiology they've done a lot on fish diseases. We founded a School of Marine Sciences to link the marine work in all departments, but that hasn't worked out as well as I hoped. There isn't a degree in Marine Sciences yet. I think there should be. And of course, if you want the complete picture of marine studies in Galway, there's the course in the Regional Tech which deals with marine and fresh-water fish-farming.'

Seán Ó Cinnéide, professor of inorganic chemistry, looked in, and Paddy spoke to him in Gaelic and drew him into the conversation. 'That's the man you should be talking to about the development of Science in the College, for it all began in Chemistry really.' Prof. Ó Cinnéide smiled and looked bewildered. When Paddy had made him *au fait* with what he had been saying and with my line of questioning, he agreed that, yes, it had all begun in Chemistry, which was in a sense the mother of Science in the College. 'Back with Tom Dillon, who was appointed professor in 1919, and Vincent Barry who came in as a lecturer some years later. Then Frank Coll, who succeeded Dillon, divided the subject into the three departments, organic, inorganic and physical.'

Ó Cinnéide came from the Kerry Gaeltacht, from Corca Dhuibhne, and had spent sixteen years in Harwell working on nuclear fuels. He agreed that both from within the College and from external sources Science had been well funded in recent decades. There was a big increase in the number of science students after the first sputnik went up, in the late '50s. Their proportion rose to 22 per cent. But it had fallen again and now averaged about 17.

I knew that he had written a large two-volume textbook of Chemistry, *Ceimic Bhunúsach,* and I asked him about teaching in Irish; were there many students following courses through the medium? Uniquely among the colleges of the National University, Galway is obliged by statute to provide courses through Irish. He said there had been a great falling off, owing to the fall in the number of students doing their post-primary studies through Irish, and the general fall in the standards of

169

Irish-teaching. He had corrected the Matriculation papers last year, he said, and no one north of a line from Limerick to Dundalk had applied for papers in Irish. Of the eighty who had, most of them were from Dublin and Munster. In the previous year in College, of six hundred students doing Chemistry in their first year, only twelve had done it through Irish and most of those because they had scholarships which bound them to that. Paddy put in to say that he remembered when most of his students took the course in Irish. 'But of course', he added, 'there was always the question of staff. The government laid the obligation on the College, and no complaint about that, but it involved a double teaching load, and after the initial period there was no corresponding government support with regard to staff.' I felt that this matter was a great cause of sadness to them, and especially to Ó Cinnéide who had invested so much intellectual effort in it.

Paddy made signs of having work to do, and in a sort of concluding way he said, 'Of course, while it's true that Science has made great advances in the College, where the really heavy investment has gone is into Engineering. You should talk to them.' I said I'd heard about a department of hydrology which had established quite a name for itself. 'Professor Nash', said Paddy. 'That's not where I meant the heavy investment had gone — they get a lot of external funding — I meant Electronics, Industrial and Chemical Engineering. But if you'd like to talk to Nash I'll give him a ring.' He did and was told I could come over straight away; so I drove to the hydrology department on Nun's Island, between two branches of the Corrib.

Prof. J. E. Nash was waiting for me on the second floor and introduced me straightaway to a young woman, Jacinta Barrins, whom he described as his 'general panjandrum and poo-bah'. Her eyes, behind spectacles, were solicitous and shrewd. I later heard that she had come to the department as a lab technician after specialising in water engineering at the Regional Technical College in Sligo. Eventually, because, as Prof. Nash put it, 'she was the only one around with a sense of order', she became the department's administrator. The department belongs to the Engineering Faculty, but I got the impression from the first that it operates very much as an independent republic.

170

They brought me into a room with a view, offered me a drink, and presented me with a number of brochures and typewritten documents. These had to do with the postgraduate course, leading to an M.Sc., which the department provides, mainly to Third World students. Usually the confession of ignorance makes a good start, so I said, 'I have the impression that hydrology deals with irrigation'. It dealt, said Prof. Nash, 'with the movement of water under natural conditions, and in pipes and channels'. But I soon discovered that it dealt also with the non-movement of water, for he said the department had a special interest in forecasting floods and droughts, and in the frequency of these events. Before entering academic life, he had been a hydrologist with the ESB and the Board of Works, had spent some time in Britain — where he became first director of the Institute of Hydrology — and worked for the Ministry of Water in Nigeria.

They took me to lunch in their Land Rover. We drove to the large, salmon-pink Corrib Hotel on the Dublin Road and got a table with a view across the bay to the hills of the Burren. Prof. Nash said the department acquired its present overseas role in 1979 when the Department of Foreign Affairs asked it, as part of the government's foreign aid programme, to provide a post-graduate course for Third World students. The government supplied funds and fifteen fellowships. Other funding came from the World Meteorological Organisation and UNESCO. So far students from over forty countries had attended. They included, right at the start, the first two students to come to Ireland from Communist China. Prof. Nash has long-standing good relations with the University of Nanjing, the centre for hydrological research in East China; he is an honorary professor there. Miss Barrins plays mother to the foreign students, shepherding them through their cultural and climatic traumas. 'All of them', she said, 'experience some degree of culture shock, and many of them are very cold the first winter.' Staff from the department have lectured and given courses in many places in Africa and Asia. Since 1981 they had been attempting to get an M.Sc. course going at the University of Dar-es-Salaam, with the intention, ultimately, of transferring the Galway course there; but I got the impression that this hadn't worked out, and that the transfer will not take place. In 1985 a forecasting workshop

171

for experienced hydrologists was held in UCG. Three came from China, and one each from India, Pakistan and Malaysia. They brought data from the Yangtze, the Indus, a tributary of the Ganges, and a Malaysian river, and spent several months analysing this material with the Galway people. Prof. Nash said the second session of this workshop would be taking place in Nanjing soon. He spoke very warmly of Prof. Dooge of UCD, who is a consultant to the UCG course, and who also has a high reputation internationally. 'We hydrologists are a small club,' he said, 'and Dooge and I came into it at the right time, when maths was coming to the fore in it, and we both had maths. Hydrology in the British Isles is very much an Irish thing. You find our graduates in many of the top jobs in Britain.'

We drove back to Nun's Island. When we entered one of the rooms in the department, a squat, Mongolian-looking man was sitting there. Prof. Nash introduced me to him, mentioning his name. 'Is it Inner or Outer Mongolia?' he asked. 'I always get them mixed up.' 'Inner,' said the smiling Mongolian gentleman. Thanking them for opening the world of hydrology to me, I went to my car and drove back towards the Dublin Road to call on Brian Arkins' wife, Josephine, who works as a nurse in the health centre of the computer firm, Digital. Thinking over all I had heard that day about the sciences of water — salty, fresh and pluvial — it seemed to me that, whatever about the dry fountain on Eyre Square, Galway, in science, did justice to its aqueous destiny.

Digital is in the Mervue Industrial Estate which lies between the roughly parallel Tuam and Monivea roads. With nearly 1,200 employees, it is the biggest industrial employer in Galway. I took the Monivea Road and, following Jo's instructions, passed the Digital sign in the 'upper' estate. That was where Digital began in Ireland nearly twenty years ago, and they still retain the original small building there for their European Software Distribution Centre. I passed firms manufacturing telephones and fraction HP motors, forklifts, refrigeration units and injection moulds, and turned into the lower estate. How civilised industry is today compared with the days of the smoky chimneys! Low buildings in brick and concrete, linked by smooth tarmacadamed roads, were set among wide green lawns, young trees, and beds of shrubs and flowers with heather much

172

in evidence. Under a hot sun, and a pale blue sky with luminous clouds, pylons marched across the landscape. Directly in front of the Digital plant was a bright green football field.

While I was waiting for Jo to appear, I noticed on the reception desk a pile of posters advertising special trains to Dublin for the All-Ireland hurling final the following weekend, in which Galway would be playing Cork. I picked up a brochure and read that 'Digital Equipment Ireland is a wholly-owned subsidiary of Digital Equipment Corporation, Maynard, Massachusetts'. The Corporation, it said, employed 89,000 people in forty-eight countries. 'The Galway plant is the most complex of Digital's manufacturing facilities worldwide, using totally integrated processes from component module level through to end customer order configuration.' Apart from Galway, there were Digital units in Clonmel, Dublin and Belfast, employing over four hundred people. Jo arrived, bright-eyed and smiling in her white uniform, and asked me would I like to look around. I said, 'Yes, a look around, nothing too complicated'. She disappeared to fetch someone, and came back laughing, followed by Harry Ruane, whom I had last seen in Ballina when he took me down the bay to see Rosserk Friary. 'Of course, of course,' I said, laughing too. 'I had forgotten, you said you worked here!'

Harry, relaxed and happy-go-lucky, made a very good shower-around; not insisting I pay detailed attention to things I didn't understand and couldn't hope to. We began in the stores area, where 'automatic guided vehicles' — Harry told me the name — were moving on their own around the floor with a worrying appearance of self-will. Last year, he said, Digital supplied Galway Corporation with 40 per cent of its revenue. It struck me that it would be very difficult for the Corporation to cross such a rate-payer. We moved on to a large area where women were sitting in cubicles making circuit boards. Five different kinds of circuit boards progressed from stage to stage in five parallel streams. Most of the staff, Harry said, were with the firm between ten and fifteen years. All the exports went via Dublin. There was a regular shuttle plane to the plant in Scotland and the European headquarters in Geneva. The plane had to be kept in Shannon because Galway's little airport was too small. No, they would not be using Connacht Airport for their exports because the product was too bulky for air. When the circuit boards had been tested, they passed to men who inserted them into cabinets of various sizes. It all seemed very simple, if one didn't delve deeper. Harry walked back with me to the foyer and pointed out, across from the main building, a smaller one which, he said, housed a new Research and Development unit. 'We were glad to see that,' he said. 'It gives permanence to this operation, and it has a big graduate intake.' We parted, joking about how it would not be the last time; what would he be showing me around next?

I drove further up the Monivea Road to the rear entrance to Ballybrit racecourse. A medieval tower-house stood to the right of the entrance; to the left was a gapped stone circle with a national monument sign. It was the last day of the last meet of the racing season. Across on the other side of the track the two stands stood empty — it was between races — beside hundreds of parked cars. From the height I had now reached, I could see the Burren again to the south, and to the west the hills beyond Lough Corrib. Memories of the Pope's visit came flooding back to me; that was the last time I had been here. It was here he said to the thousands of young people, 'Young people of Ireland, I love you!' and set them dancing and singing for twenty minutes 'He's got the whole world in his hands'. A plane passed overhead headed for Cill Éinne. The white-coated stewards closed the gates on both sides of the track. Ten horses approached and galloped past, the jockeys standing in their stirrups, two of them close together, laughing. As I left I could see the horses circling in the stalls before the last race; behind them a forest of electricity poles and pylons stretching back towards Digital.

Farther up the road I turned left past the new, Parkmore industrial estate, which had more young trees than young factories, and reached the Tuam Road directly opposite a large wall-daubing, IRA — NO EXTRADITION. I re-entered the city proper between a long line of travellers' caravans and the ghostly-coloured, hill-climbing houses of the Tirellan housing estates. Galway may have managed to keep a fine city-centre, but its new housing estates are another matter.

On my last day in Galway I rang Nollaig Ó Gadhra at the Regional Tech, hoping he would invite me to have lunch in the staff restaurant, which is one of the best and least expensive in

Galway. It has this distinction because a CERT course in hotel management and catering is given in the college. But Nollaig said it wasn't open again after the summer holidays, so we agreed to meet for lunch in town. However, on the way to meet him I ran into Caoimhghin Mac Cathmhaoil on Shop Street, carrying plastic bags of food, and he invited us both to join him in his office for lunch. So we did that. We went to the courtyard off Dominick Street where Caoimhghin has his solicitor's office and, climbing the stairs, found him there, looking healthy and prosperous in his three-piece suit — I had known him in other days. I told him what I thought of the Anglo-Irish Agreement and he gave me a copy of a report on British media coverage of the North. Nollaig told us that his book on the Gillespie sisters, who had been imprisoned for years in England, had sold out its first printing and been translated into German, and he was to discuss a Russian translation with someone from the Soviet Embassy. Bob Quinn arrived and said he had finished his film which he was calling *Budawanny,* but had had his van, full of equipment, stolen in Dublin. He was excited to hear about Wolfe Tone's theatre on Kirwan's Lane and said he would go to see it immediately. Nollaig told me once again that my attitude to the Gaeltacht and the Irish language was negative and defeatist. 'There's more people today than ever can speak Irish, and are sympathetic to it. The only thing is they have no motive to speak it.' 'You mean the question-mark over "Ireland"?' I said. Yes, he said. Meanwhile Caoimhghin was plying us with tea and sandwiches.

We went our various ways. I picked up an *Advertiser* in O'Gorman's bookshop. It is one of Galway's two giveaway newspapers, and the oldest paper of the kind in Ireland. The city has two other weekly newspapers, the *Sentinel* and the *City Tribune.* About an hour later I called into The Quays. In the doorway to the backroom a group of people were gathered around a man at a piano. There was a television camera and Jim Fahy of RTE was there. So was Bob Quinn. I tapped him on the shoulder and he looked around and said, 'Make one of the crowd, get on TV.' With Jim Fahy co-ordinating things, the man at the piano started playing and then a group behind him chanted something with a very energetic rhythm. They did it again. I realised it was for the Hurling Final.

I drove to Barna, stopping at the lovely modern church in the village where I had attended more than one Midnight Mass on Christmas Eve. Barna was for many years the eastern limit of the South Connemara Gaeltacht. 'Ó Chárna go Bearna', people said, and meant 'within our local world'. Now it is a well-to-do bungalow suburb of Galway. I turned into the short street of old houses leading to the pier and stopped at Audrey Corbett's house. I remarked to her that Ty Ar Mor, the restaurant two doors away, looked very spruce and newly-painted. 'Well, you know Hervé's back', she said. No, I said, I didn't know that. So the Waterford adventure was ended? Years before, Hervé had come to Ireland as a lecturer in Breton in UCG. Then he gave up that job, bought the delapidated house on the pier, and, with his own hands, refurbished it and turned it into a first-class restaurant. But a couple of years after he had married a Breton girl, he leased it to his chef and went to live near Rinn, Co. Waterford, with the intention of devoting the rest of his life to fishing bass. Yes, Audrey said, he was back with Sophie and the children, and engaged on major expansions. He had added another storey to the flat upstairs, and wanted to extend backwards into the garden space. But that, she said, would block her view of the sea from her back balcony, and that view was essential to her periods of quiet meditation. She took me out the back and showed me what she meant.

We sat down and talked about her musical activities. After studying music in UCD, and founding the St Stephen's Singers in Dublin, she came to Galway in the '70s with her husband, a Galwayman, who plays and teaches the violin. Gradually she got into choirs, beginning with the Corrib Singers. Yes, she said, they still existed, but some years previously there had been a falling off in male participation, so she had made them an all-female choir which performed only in spring and summer. They had been to Cork, Dublin and Zurich. Galway Baroque Singers dated from 1983, when some people had come to her with the idea of staging Handel's 'Messiah'. She put together a mixed choir which performed 'Messiah' at the end of that year, as a sort of curtain-raiser for the city's quincentennial, and again, a year later, to bring the celebrations to a close. Since then they had been specialising in major choral works with orchestra. They took a break, annually, during the summer, so they were only resuming again now. Audrey said that the work with the Baroque Singers had meant her having to learn orchestral conducting, and here Geoffrey Spratt had been of great assistance. A young Englishman, who came to Cork as a lecturer in UCC, he had formed two choirs of his own in Cork and was an experienced orchestral conductor. He conducted the Galway performances of the 'Messiah', and Audrey attended a couple of courses he gave. With the Baroque Singers she had done, among other things, Haydn's 'Maria Theresia Mass', Mozart's 'Requiem', and Shaun Davey's 'The Pilgrim'. For each concert she assembled an orchestra drawn from the RTE Symphony and Concert Orchestras and other sources. Lately some people had approached her to start a choir of boy sopranos and — incredibly to me — she felt tempted. When she let me use her telephone to make a call, I saw in a list of 'things to do' beside the phone an image of her busy life. The 'things' were listed under 'Home', 'Children', 'Choirs'. We had to break off our chat for her to drive to Galway to fetch a son from school. I went to visit Hervé and Sophie.

The call I made from Audrey's house was to Lady Molly Cusack-Smith in Tuam. I wanted to see something of the hunting and horsey scene in the countryside east of Galway. I had been at the Galway Blazers' Christmas ball in Galway, and at Lady Molly's ball in Tuam for the Bermingham and North Galway Hunt; but no closer than that to hounds or horses. When I phoned Molly from Galway, she said that, at that time of year, all that was afoot anywhere was 'cubbing', but that it hadn't started yet in Tuam because the farmers had too much corn standing. Cubbing, she explained, meant a few riders going out in the morning to train the young hounds. But later, when I phoned Dónal Raftery, who has a well-known pub in Craughwell, the Blazers' headquarters, he told me they were cubbing there, and he got permission from Bertie Grattan-Bellew, a joint master of the hunt, for me to join them at a quarter to seven the following morning.

Craughwell is a village fifteen miles south east of Galway. As I approached it I noticed some unfinished and pretty massive construction work on the right-hand side of the road. It looked like retaining walls for shrubberies or flower-beds of considerable size. There was County Council equipment standing around, and I wondered why Craughwell was so privileged. In the village, following instructions, I took a side-road and drove up the drive to a large house. There were lights on in the top storey, but when I rang the doorbell no one came. I let myself in a small gate to the side of the house and entered a very large, square yard surrounded on three sides by black and white buildings, single-storeyed for the most part, but two-storeyed, and resembling dwellings, at the far end, where there was an arched entrance. There was another, uncovered entrance on the left-hand side. Approaching the arched gateway, I read above it 'County Galway Hunt, 1891'.

On the fourth side of the yard, nearest the big house, was a smaller house with a light on in the kitchen. I knocked and the door was opened by a fair-haired young woman in riding breeches, who seemed to be expecting me. Her name was Billy, and she spoke with an English or Anglo-Irish accent. I later learned she was the stud groom, who looked after the ten or so horses stabled in the yard. Two of these were reserved for the 'huntsman', who was in charge of the hounds and directed the hunt, and two for the 'whip', who assisted him. In the kitchen I met the huntsman and senior joint master, Michael Dempsey, who was sitting at the table having breakfast. Billy made me coffee. Then we went out into the yard where I met Bertie Grattan-Bellew, wearing a tweed riding-jacket. A member of an old Co. Galway family of Norman stock, he lives in London, and comes over six or seven times a year for the hunting. I asked him how many joint masters there were, and he said there were two others besides himself and Michael: an American businessman living in Ireland for some years, and an American woman. Somewhat like honorary consuls, joint masters are expected to put some money into the hunt, and so the ability and willingness to do this are important qualifications. Bertie's father-in-law and his daughter, Sophie, were there, like myself, as onlookers. The father-in-law was on a visit from South Africa where he had a stud farm. He had written some novels and was working on a book about thoroughbred horses. Bertie told me I could go with the terrier man, Gill Morrissey, in the Land Rover. He explained that the terrier man brings terriers along to ferret out the fox if he goes into a hole. He also gathers dead animals from the farmers, and the whip and he skin them and feed them to the hounds.

I approached a man standing beside the Land Rover in the middle of the yard and said, 'Are you Mr Morrissey?' 'I don't know about the "Mr",' he said, 'I'm called Gill.' Michael Dempsey, resplendent in red blazer, rode in through the archway from the kennels with a pack of hounds following him. A boy, also in red blazer, whom I took to be the whip, accompanied them. 'They're all bitches,' said Bertie's father-in-law. Bertie, who was now on horseback, asked Billy, on a horse beside him, 'How many couples?' 'Twenty-six and a half,' she said. That was fifty-three hounds; they're counted in couples. Bertie told me that was less than half the Blazers' pack. They hunted with bitches, dogs, or a mixed pack. Bitches were very intelligent and had much greater speed than dogs, but they tended to lose interest during a long hunt. Dogs were slower, but more persevering at working out the fox when the going got difficult. Sometimes a few bitches would be included in a pack of dogs to enliven it.

Gill started up the Land Rover and I climbed in. There were five yelping terriers in a cage behind us. We drove about a mile and a half and stopped at a gate beside a lodge and vegetable garden. I noticed a row of peas with their pods hanging — the first I had seen on my journey. A drive from the gate led to a wood. Gill said this was Moyode and told me to get down and open the iron gate, and another, wooden one nearer the wood, for the riders. He had to go and do something. Having opened the gates, and waited for some time, I saw the riders and hounds coming towards me along the road. A girl I hadn't met had joined them. Gill returned and Bertie told him a hound was lame and to take it back to the kennels. The father-in-law and Sophie drove up in a Mercedes, and we all proceeded through the gates into the wood and came to a halt in a clearing where four paths met. The trees near us were cypresses. The huntsman and whip went off down one of the paths to draw cover — to raise the foxes. A woman-rider and her two small sons on ponies joined us. We stood around, and Bertie chatted to me about the Blazers and hunting generally.

The Blazers were founded in 1839 and were originally the

only hunt in Co. Galway. They became known as the Blazers in the old days when most of them were rollicking country gentlemen; they burned down the hotel in Birr when they were on a visit there. Nowadays most of the riders in a Blazers hunt are local farmers for whom the hunting is free. Cubbing begins on 12 August, or when the corn is in, and hunting on 30 October. The purpose of cubbing is both to train the young hounds and to scatter the fox families out of deep cover, such as Moyode wood, around the countryside. They do it early in the morning because in the warmer weather it's cool at that time and the smell is near the ground. They hunt three times a week. On Thursday there might be thirty riders; on Tuesday and Saturday, seventy to ninety, sometimes more than a hundred. Some of these are visitors, who pay £50 a day and are an important source of revenue. Visitors may not bring their own horses but must hire them locally. People other than local farmers pay £200 a year to be members, and £5 a day field-money when they hunt. The hunt is ruled by a committee who raise funds, and by the joint masters who run the yard. Each body operates within its allotted sphere like an upper and lower house of parliament. The secretary of the committee was Monica McCarthy of Kilcolgan Castle — beside the bay a few miles away.

Bertie pointed out a fox ambling across a path some distance from us. A young hound who hadn't yet learned what she was there for wandered back to us. They shooed her in the direction in which the pack had left, and she, catching the scent there, dashed off. Bertie's ears picked up the huntsman, Michael, blowing his horn to rally the hounds around him, but to my unpractised ear it was difficult to distinguish from the continual lowing of cattle and the hooter of a passing train. Sophie remarked, ironically, on 'the peace and quiet of early morning in rural Ireland'. When the horn blew again, Bertie and the other riders went off through the trees in its general direction, and I was left with Sophie and the father-in-law. After a while we drove off in the Mercedes to try to find where the wood ended and perhaps see the others hunting. Driving in one direction, we saw the wood ending; driving in another, we spied Gill's Land Rover parked up a lane beside a house, but he was not with it. After waiting for a while, we saw him returning with his spade and his terriers. He said they had gone across the river after a fox. We all returned to the clearing, and, as we waited there, various riders returned singly, now from this path, now from that, and emerged in our clearing like actors coming on stage in a play. The wayward young hound, who didn't know what she was there for, kept returning to us, running around in circles, and then setting off furiously again to follow the scent where the pack had departed. Finally Michael returned at the head of the hounds, passed us to move down another path, and entered the wood again, the hounds following him. The father-in-law went home, and I went with Gill in the Land Rover in the direction he thought the hunt would be moving. The terriers behind me made an infernal din. Gill parked and took them out and I followed him up a lane to the beginning of a morass, but, not having wellingtons, went no further. Somewhere the horn was sounding — I could distinguish it now. Returning to the Land Rover, I waited for Gill there, and when he came we drove back to the yard. It was after ten. Bertie had asked me to stay to breakfast. I went to the kennels and looked at a crowd of hounds, mostly dogs, who looked up at me through the wire netting, expectantly, and with the utmost seriousness. In the kitchen of the small house, Billy was getting breakfast. She had come back, she said, because she needed to be getting on with the day's work.

When the other riders returned, I went with Bertie into his house and met his wife, an interior designer in London. He showed me a book about the history of the Blazers. During the Second World War, Molly Cusack had been in Craughwell, in charge of the hunt, and in recognition of her services the Blazers gave her a 'country' around Tuam to hunt. That was how the Bermingham and North Galway Hunt came into being; Bermingham is where Molly lives. At some earlier stage the East Galway Hunt had branched off. Bertie spoke with love and enthusiasm of the country stretching from Athenry towards Galway, which he said was classic hunting country. He spoke of its openness, and of the many stone walls and small fields. To be out in that country with a big Blazers hunt — that, I gathered, was heaven for him. 'Ireland', he said, 'is so much better than England for hunting. Here we don't have huge motorways cutting through the hunt. And we don't have huge crowds of followers and onlookers getting in the way.'

181

I thanked him, called on Michael and thanked him, and drove to Don Raftery's pub in the village. Don was brimming over with the good news. His pub had won first place, in the Western region, for pub and catering. Another year it had been declared the best pub, but now the catering was first as well. In the final, all-Ireland contest he would be against three other pubs. I congratulated him and told him about my morning's experiences. When I mentioned that I was going to Tuam to see Molly Cusack-Smith, he said he had heard the split in her hunt had ended, and her daughter, Oonagh Mary, was now accepted again as senior master by the dissidents. The trouble had begun when the hunt committee had challenged Molly's leadership of the hunt. She resigned, and Oonagh Mary replaced her as senior master, with a doctor from the town as joint master. Later a split occurred which had been represented, not quite accurately, as one between townies, or people new to hunting, and country people; the doctor headed a breakaway hunt. I asked Don about the construction work on the way into the village. He said it was a social employment scheme being carried out by the County Council. Some people in the village had the bright idea of using the scheme to construct flower-beds in the lay-by, and they got a chance to do so when the travellers who had been camping there moved away for the summer.

I returned to Galway and, in the late afternoon, set out for Tuam, twenty-one miles away. It was a fine road; a flat, wide surface, occasionally rising and falling gently, extended straight ahead. To either side lay a broad plain of large, stone-walled fields bearing hundreds of sheep and cattle. Now and then there was a field of sugar-beet or corn stubble, or a tractor reaping corn. Clumps of tall, old trees punctuated the scene. But there was a scarcity of wild flowers apart from briars on the road verges and, once, the brilliant yellow of ragwort filling a hollow. Alerted to horsey things, I noticed a sign pointing to a riding school a few miles out from Galway, and a couple of horse-boxes in the passing traffic. Then, as I approached Tuam, the network of fields grew denser, the land wetter, and to the left, just before the first houses, there was a whole field of meadow-sweet. I drove through the ancient town, which was capital of Ireland when the Normans came, and out the Clonbern road to Bermingham, named after a Norman family. I had last been there in January, for the hunt ball, Molly's fiftieth, and reputedly the last she was going to give. The house was being painted a new red: an empty paint can stood where the work had finished. The front windows were shuttered and there was no reply when I rang the bell. I went around into the yard, but there was no reply to my banging on the back door. Then I remembered that over a high wall abutting on the house was the garden, and in it a conservatory where Molly spent much of her time. Finding a foothold in the wall, I pulled myself up, jumped on one foot, and got a glimpse of her sitting in the conservatory with another woman. Just as I was picking up some chips of wood to throw at the glass, I noticed another back door, nearer the wall, which I hadn't tried. It opened into a passage, a left turn took me out into the garden, and Molly seeing me, smiled brightly, and beckoned me into the conservatory.

Her hair had a windblown look which went well with her roguish eyes and proud, fine features. She looked very much an O'Rourke, which was her maiden name, though she spelt it O'Rorke, for her family had made a point of distinguishing themselves from the Catholics of the species. She introduced me to the other woman, who looked after the garden for her, and poured me a gin sans anything, which was what they were drinking. She had been in Cong at a lunch given by the Dean of St Mary's, Tuam's old Protestant Cathedral. The Catholics were helping wonderfully to restore it, she said. 'Of course, it's nonsense, we should give it to them. There's no Protestants left in Tuam. I'm an agnostic, I never go to church.' I found that the news about the split in the hunt being healed was wrong; things were as bad as ever. But Molly didn't want to talk about it beyond remarking that the farmers around Bermingham were supporting Oonagh Mary, and that the other crowd had to go to Belclare, on the other side of Tuam, to get any farmers to tolerate them. She was making her house into a summer guest-house. Previously she had kept visitors only during the hunting season, and gone for a holiday in the summer, usually to Greece. We got talking about de Valera, whom she admired greatly as a republican who kept us in the Commonwealth, where we should be, 'and then there'd be none of this Northern trouble, would there?' She spoke of the O'Rourkes. 'We were always loyal to the O'Conors,' she said, 'and we came with them here to fight the Berminghams. Some of our lot were killed and buried where the gate to the avenue stands today.' She was reading an old book about Art MacMurrough Kavanagh who harried the English of the Pale. She loved those old books, she said, with their old-fashioned style of narrative.

Her friend left and we went into the town for dinner at her favourite restaurant, Cré na Cille, run by a local man, Cathal Reynolds. It was a very good restaurant, with a downstairs for snacks and bar and an upstairs for full meals. On previous visits to Tuam I had shied away from it because I am sensitive to the names of restaurants. Needless to say, I was well aware that Máirtín Ó Cadhain had written a famous *novel* called *Cré na Cille*, but that did not make me feel like eating in a place called 'Churchyard Clay'. But when I said this to Mr Reynolds, he told me all the good reasons he had for calling it that. Across the street from us, he said, was the old parish graveyard of Tuam, or rather, part of it, for it had once extended under this very house where we now were, and which was his old family home. Máirtín Ó Cadhain had been a friend of his father's and had often visited him here. And besides, the word Tuam itself, *Tuaim* in Gaelic, referred to a burial mound or tumulus which had been there in pagan times. In face of such many-layered erudition and piety, what could one say?

Around noon next day I went with Molly to see St Mary's Cathedral. On the way to the Square we passed the beautiful neo-gothic Catholic Cathedral, which I had seen floodlit the night before, and whose square tower can be seen for miles around in the flat countryside. Molly had to fetch the keys in a shop on the Square, and I took pleasure once again in this bustling, very urban space, not large by any means, where five streets converge. It is flanked by three fine buildings: the Town Hall in stone, with its clock tower; a handsome bank building marking the other extremity; and between them, the solidly traditional hotel facade of the Imperial Hotel. One street slopes down to a gracefully balustraded bridge. In the middle of the square stands the old Celtic market cross. A notice near it said 'Tuam Horse Show, September 14th'.

We went down High Street past Cré na Cille to St Mary's. A

notice at the gate said 'AnCO Community Youth Training Project'. It was a very large building, and a composite one. A fourteenth-century gothic church had a nineteenth-century neo-gothic church appended to it, end to end. The older church had been completely re-pointed and was looking new. Molly explained to me that it had been used as the Synod House. Our keys gained us access to the neo-gothic building. Once we were inside, and had walked to the juncture between the old and the new, I was surprised to find myself in a romanesque chancel with three romanesque east windows. Apparently the neo-gothic church had been built on the site of an earlier romanesque one. The chancel was the most beautiful example of hiberno-romanesque I had ever seen — better than the Clonfert doorway, which I had previously regarded as the best surviving masterpiece. And the windows were splendid too. Around the sides of the modern church stood glass cases with pictures and handwritten explanations which made it a sort of museum. There was a plaster cast of a stone cross from Dysert O'Dea belonging, like the town's market cross, to the twelfth century. Near it, from the same century, was a piece of a cross found in Tuam. It had a fine interlaced pattern on the front and back and bore the following inscription in Irish — St Jarlath is the patron and founder of Tuam:

> Pray for the successor of Jarlath, for Aed O hOisin, by whom this cross was made
> Pray for the King, for Turdelbuch O Chonchobair [Turlough O'Conor]
> Pray for the craftsman, for Gillu Crist O Thuathail

The words leapt out at me, conjuring up the beginnings here in Tuam of that Irish Christian medieval kingdom which was strangled at birth, in the reign of Turlough's successor, Rory. That other, normal European history which we might have had! A text in one of the glass cases told, symbolically, of the wrecking of it. It told how, in the nineteenth century, the market cross had been found in four separate pieces in various places — one piece stuck up a chimney.

We left and walked around the Synod House. Molly pointed out to me with anger where statues had been removed from niches on the wall by the Cromwellians. In the front, just beside the fourteenth-century door, they were building a small annexe with concrete blocks. Glancing inside, we saw it was a lavatory. Molly gave me the keys to take back to Mr Canney on the Square. Opposite Cré na Cille I saw a plaque in a high wall. 'Ancient burial ground of the Parish of Tuam containing the ruins of Temple Jarlath, the Parish Church, founded about 1360'. The cemetery was above street-level. I climbed some steps up to it and found myself among many grave slabs and headstones. There was a ruined church and some majestic yew trees. A few children were at play. The grass was uncut, and planted flowers were overgrown with weeds. It was desolate with neglect, and it could be a lovely place where children and adults would find room to dream. I called into the restaurant to greet Cathal and remarked on the state of the graveyard. He said an AnCO scheme had cleaned it up two years ago, but it had been let run wild again. When I reached Canney's and was giving the keys back, I asked Mr Canney did the Church of Ireland have any organised presence in Tuam. He said no, 'the Dean is in Cong, the Bishop in Crossmolina. They just have a keyman. I'm the keyman, though I'm a Roman Catholic myself'. I walked across to the market cross and tried to decipher what was left of the inscription on its base. I was moved when I was able to make out 'Do Thurdelbuch'.

Oonagh Mary Hyland (that's her married name) lives in a converted schoolhouse a couple of miles beyond her mother's house. I called on her in the afternoon. There were flower-tubs in front of the house and a well-stocked vegetable garden beside it. She was working in the yard at the back. She had just returned from Claremorris show where she had been jumping. In an enclosure just behind the vegetable-garden stood her yellow-brown jumper. She said she had ten other horses, including two ponies for each of her two children. She introduced me to them, a boy and a girl. Unlike her own mother, Oonagh Mary is a smallish, round-faced woman, and her fifteen-year-old daughter was taller than she. We went into the house, passing through the kitchen, where a man who was working for her was making tea. She hadn't jumped for many years, she said, but she had started again that year. She did it for fun, and so did many others, but there were professionals who did it for a living. They jumped horses belonging to other people. They would arrive at a show with five or six horses in a lorry, and jump them in their various categories, increasing their value when they performed well. The owners paid them for that, and paid them a commission when the horse was sold. In the season from May to October there was an average of a show a week. The season ended with Ballinasloe Horse Fair and Show on the first weekend in October. After that there were indoor shows, but people who hunted didn't go to them.

I asked her what was really causing the split in the hunt, and she said that it went back to when the committee tried to fire Henry Gordon, who had been huntsman for many years, and whose contract didn't expire until the following 30 April. When they told him to hand over the hounds, she and Henry took them to private kennels near Turloughmore, about fifteen miles away. Then the committee got another pack, went hunting on their own with Dr Tom Waldron as master, and applied to the Masters of Foxhounds Association for recognition as the North Galway Hunt. Last year they had got provisional recognition, but this year, she believed, the Association wasn't going to recognise either hunt. She didn't like the situation, but saw no way out of it while they insisted on getting rid of Henry.

The two children had gone off to practise on their ponies for the second day of the Claremorris Show. Oonagh Mary had to help her man put up hay, and later go to teach in a riding school on the Galway road. I left and set out for Athenry, intending to visit on the way a man called Peter Fox who kept riding-stables, and hired horses out for hunting. The Athenry road ran across a bog and poor grazing land. There were many sally bushes in the hedges and the moon daisies at last came into their own. I turned right towards Turloughmore and then left off the secondary road to climb by narrower roads to Peter Fox's upland farm. In front of his bungalow four children and a young woman, all in riding gear, were standing by the garden wall; beyond them stables and a barn. There was a warm sun and a sense of being high up in a tranquil place apart from the far-extending plain.

I found Mr Fox in one of the stables and he came out and walked about with me, showing me the one-mile jumping run he had laid out around his farm. At intervals there were jumps of various kinds — ditches, hedges, stone walls — such as a rider might encounter in the countryside. In each case there was a way around the jump so that the learners could do a round without actually jumping, and also a lower section in the middle so that the full jump needn't be taken at the start. Most of the pupils, he said, came from Galway city. Three daughters and a son did the teaching. I mentioned the riding schools on the Galway-Tuam road and asked him were they the same as this. 'Not at all,' he said, 'they're indoor. All the jumps are made of poles set at different heights, and the horses follow each other round like circus horses. People have a far better opportunity here for real training in jumping or hunting. We also take them hacking so they can learn to deal with traffic.' ('Hacking', I had discovered, was the horsey term for riding on a public road.) He had about twenty horses and, in the hunting season, he hired them out at £40 a day. I asked him about Willy Leahy, whom I had heard talked about as a big owner and hirer of horses near Loughrea. Someone had said he had three hundred horses. 'He has a lot of them certainly,' said Mr Fox. 'He hires them mostly to Americans and charges more than me. But in the summer now he's mostly in Connemara looking after his Connemara Way.' That's a week-long trek through Connemara, organised with half-day 'posting stations' where horses are available, so that you can join it at any point.

He took me into his kitchen where I met his wife. She gave me tea and something stronger and we chatted for a while. As I left, reluctantly, the pupils I had seen standing at the garden wall were setting off with one of his daughters to do some hacking. I had heard that Athenry was where the Galway hurling team were training, and I was reminded of this when I rejoined the Athenry road. A doll dressed in Galway's maroon and white colours sat on a gatepost, cradling a hurley. Another similar doll hung from a tree, and there were Galway flags in windows. I entered the sleepy old town — for such it was — through a Norman gateway, with considerable stretches of the old town walls on either side of it and a wall-tower off to the right. With its narrow medieval streets, its houses and shops in 'country' colours, its little market cross, its humble air, the town surprised me. I expected it to be bigger and more developed; it seemed to have stopped long ago. I had chicken and chips in a café. The chicken was tough and overcooked, the chips lifeless; they were accompanied by sad peas from a tin, and the lot cost £3.

At some distance from the North Gate by which I had entered, and outside the walls, there was a Bermingham castle with a yard. Beyond it stood the ruins of a Dominican priory, and between the two was a children's playground with some children playing. It contained, as one of the playthings, a 'stone circle' of medium-sized boulders, which gave me a frivolous notion about what those other, ancient stone circles were really for. Against the end wall of the priory church a handball-alley had been built. The lower part of a traceried window had been bricked up as part of the playing wall; a tarmacadamed road ran past the alley, and the tiered platform for spectators was on the other side of the road. Obviously some strong imperative had dictated that, despite the makeshift and the inconvenience, the ball-alley should be precisely there. I was surprised that other surviving sections of the town walls were so far from those I had seen; altogether the walls had enclosed a very large area, much greater than the surviving nucleus of the old town. I was also surprised at how frail they were, in military terms — nothing like the broad walls of Derry with the width of a road along the top — until I reflected that they had been built when there were no cannon and then apparently not added to after that. On the southern side of the town there was a huge cattle mart, and in the goods siding at the railway station — Athenry is a rail junction — a grain silo. Mart and silo fitted together with, made sense with, the Castle and the walls; they explained why the Normans had, so early on, made Athenry a stronghold. But until I left next morning not much else about the town made sense to me or cohered. Suburbs of new houses extended this way and that. At the tennis club a second court was being added and a clubhouse built.

The countryside to the south of the town looked ancient. The stone bridges were hump-backed. As I entered Craughwell I noticed a traveller's caravan parked in a small lay-by opposite the 'construction', on the other side of the road. The door was open. I stopped and walked towards it, and a man came out. 'Is this a scheme to stop you parking over there?' I asked, pointing towards the works. 'Yes,' he said, 'there were eight caravans there. But we've always been here, we belong here. I talked to the County Council and they said we won't be disturbed here.'

It had already occurred to me that 'social employment schemes' could be put to many uses. I drove through the village and out the other end, past the busts of Lady Gregory and the poet Raftery in their grass plots. The wide Dublin road and the plain of East Galway opened out before me. I passed through solid Loughrea, through its long central street which begins as suburb and ends as suburb — and I saw the biggest Galway flags yet, hanging from windows. The countryside was intensely green with the various greens of grass and trees. That of the grass roadside verges was broken only by buttercups. When the wetness of the land allowed it — but that was rare — there was a line or, in some fields, a clump, of meadow-sweet. The trees were big and old, oaks, chestnuts, sycamores. In a large encampment of travellers, among the caravans and cars, men, women and children went about their household chores and family life oblivious of the streaking traffic. A signpost said Aughrim to the left. Down an immensely wide road flanked by houses, I entered the spacious, almost grandiose town of Ballinasloe. Soon, alongside the road, there was the spread of the immemorial fairgreen where the famous horse fair on 5 October would end the summer show season and usher in the hunting. Towards the town-centre end of the green, on a jutting eminence, a Protestant church stood. Looking up as I passed below it, I glimpsed seats outside it in a high island of quiet. I stopped at Hayden's, that elegant and efficient hotel which never lets the traveller down, and sat for a while in its coffee-shop looking out at the garden.

It was only fourteen miles further to Athlone. The road cut a swathe across the southern tip of Co. Roscommon. Athlone sprawled to meet me and drew me to the Shannon. Scores of cruise-boats floated on the shimmering river. Not many travellers know that, at the bridge — as you approach it driving south along the Connacht bank — if you continue straight ahead instead of turning across it, you enter, past the Castle, a quiet 'old town' of narrow streets and small houses, complete with a Main Street. Across that street you see Seán's Bar with busts of Irish worthies in the window; and if, leaving your car, you walk down under the Castle to the river, and continue to the right along it, you see again a sign 'Seán's Bar'. Entering, you pass through the most genuine Mediterranean patio you have ever seen in Ireland, and at last you reach the bar.

When Seán had set the whiskey down, I said, 'I suppose you'll be cheering for Galway.'

'Well, really I'll be cheering for neither side,' he said. 'This is Westmeath here.'

'Surely we're in Roscommon,' I said. 'Isn't this the Connacht side of the town?'

'It's Connacht, but it's Westmeath,' he said. 'We pay our rates to Westmeath County Council.'

And so my journed ended, as it had begun, in ambiguity and semantic confusion. I returned through the patio to the quay. Four happy Germans, in black leather jackets and peaked naval caps, swaggered past towards the bridge. On a boat moored a few yards away a woman in the cabin window was mixing salad. On the other bank, the eastern town, presenting what you might call its back view, climbed from the river towards its central street. The water shimmered, no boat moved. I walked up the alley under the Castle, got into my car, drove back to the bridge and crossed the Shannon.